Bothered:

Helping teenagers talk about their feelings

MARGOT SUNDERLAND

ILLUSTRATED BY NICKY ARMSTRONG

Bothered:

Helping teenagers talk about their feelings

MARGOT SUNDERLAND

ILLUSTRATED BY NICKY ARMSTRONG

First published in 2012 by
Speechmark Publishing Ltd
2nd Floor, 5 Thomas More Square, London, E1W 1YW
www.speechmark.net

002-5785/Printed in the United Kingdom by CMP (UK) Ltd

British Library Cataloguing in Publication Data
A catalogue record for this book is available from the British Library.

ISBN: 978-0-86388-908-0

The exercises in this book have been used successfully with a number of clients. However, the author and publishers cannot take responsibility either for the choice of exercises by the professional or for the effect that any exercise might have on the individual client.

Contents

About the book

As the Institute for Public Policy Research (2006b) states, 'For too many children, the transition to adulthood is complex, messy and unsuccessful.' We also know that in the UK, 50 per cent of all mental ill-health shows up by the age of 14, leaving tax payers with a whopping £104bn bill (HM Government, 2011). Furthermore, of all the teenagers in the UK struggling with emotional and behavioural problems, a mere 30 per cent receive any sort of intervention or treatment. The other 70 per cent simply struggle through the pain and emotional turmoil, doing their best to make it to adulthood. Yet untreated depression in the teenage years can lead to depression in adulthood, antisocial behaviour and suicide. Shockingly, in the UK, every 22 minutes a teenager tries to kill themselves (Institute for Public Policy Research, 2006b). If far more people are empowered to have thoughtful, reflective conversations with teenagers about their life experiences, it really doesn't have to be this way. This book is a vital resource to support such conversations. It is full of tools for and techniques of what to say and how to be, underpinned by all the latest research, psychology and neuroscience relevant to adolescent development.

At this challenging developmental stage, when teenagers are finding things difficult, this book can really help. The tried and tested interventions are designed to help practitioners to connect with teenagers and support them to go on to enjoy a fulfilling adult life. Additionally, the psychological knowledge gained from the exercises in the book can empower teenagers to move from unhappiness, poor functioning or learning blocks, to a place of self-awareness, self-esteem and ability to thrive.

Part One: Why some teenagers mess up and how to help them not to

This part of the book offers a key assessment tool, namely, The teenager well-being profile (see page 3). This is designed for the practitioner easily to assess just how well the teenager is doing in their life cognitively, emotionally and relationally. After completion, it will clearly show the specific areas where the teenager needs support. The profile details the capacities that are key if the teenager is to 'do life well' now and in the future, and be able to navigate this challenging stage of human development skilfully. If the teenager is messing up in some area of their life, the profile will show clearly which life skill he or she has not yet mastered.

Part Two: The worksheets

About the worksheets: vital tools to start that essential and sometimes difficult conversation with the teenager

> *Even if the listening time with the adult is only for one hour a week [or over a short period of time], it is something [the teenager] can carry through the rest of their week, a little torch burning inside of them that reminds them that they are not alone in the world.*
> (Mears and Cooper, 2005)

The worksheets in this book address feelings and concerns that most teenagers grapple with at some time or other. Too many teenagers fail to get the help they need to address these issues well. So they make all sorts of mistakes, which can cost them dearly in terms of hurt and harm to self and others. Furthermore, adults often feel awkward at starting an important conversation with a teenager, particularly in light of the often monosyllabic or grunting responses to their very best efforts. Moreover, the pull for many adults is to talk at the teenager rather than to listen to the teenager and to find ways for them to talk. So these worksheets offer really easy-to-use structures that enable adults to be with the teenager in a confident, non-embarrassing and effective way so that the conversation flows rather than flounders. We have also provided up-to-date psychology pertinent to each issue, which teenagers usually find both fascinating and very useful.

If a teenager is to develop the capacity to reflect, quality conversation time is essential with a listening non-judgemental adult who can help them work through their life experiences in an insightful way. Through this process, the teenager will be able to clarify what they think and feel. In fact, it's really difficult to do this on one's own – for anyone of any age. It's true that, 'Often enough, we do not know our own mind. In the process of dialogue with another person, we are able to clarify what we think and feel' (Allen and Fonagy, 2006).

If not talked about, the teenager often discharges the emotional tension from painful feelings and difficult life events, in destructive or self-destructive behaviour.

One should never underestimate the power of such conversations with a teenager, when the practitioner is empathic, able to voice that empathy and validates the teenager's experience of events rather than lecture them or tell them what they should be feeling. Such adults often become hugely important to the teenager. They can call that adult to mind at any time as an encouraging presence, even when they are not there. In other words, the adult becomes a powerful inner advocate, a warm, benign presence in their head. At the bleakest moments of their lives, calling that adult to mind can pull them out of themselves into a warmer kinder world. The research shows that, for many teenagers, a sense of real connectedness with just one adult in their lives is enough to end their sense of aloneness, isolation, not belonging and not being understood, and prevent them messing up (Sroufe *et al*, 2009).

The worksheets have been tried and tested over years with teenagers and vetted by teenagers themselves. The underlying fascinating psychology tends to inspire their interest and curiosity in themselves and the human condition in general. They help teenagers to understand why they do what they do and why they feel what they feel, in a way that enables them to reflect on their life and get the support they need. They are very easy and interesting to do. In short, the worksheets demand very little from the teenager and offer a great deal.

Part One

Why some teenagers mess up and how to help them not to

The teenager well-being profile

Who should fill it in?

The profile should be filled in by any adult who knows the teenager well. You could ask the teenager's form teacher or relative if appropriate. It is good to have more than one person fill in the profile to avoid personal bias. You can then compare them.

What to do after completing the profile

After completing the profile, the practitioner can move straight on to the detailed information in Part one, which focuses on each life skill presented in the profile in turn. The practitioner can go directly to the life skills that the profile has shown the teenager to be struggling with. They will find a wealth of fascinating research, the psychology underpinning why the teenager is struggling in this particular area and, importantly, what to do to help them. A treatment plan can then be drawn up in terms of how the teenager can be empowered to master the life skills they don't yet have. Subsequently, a selection of relevant worksheets (*see* Part Two) can form an integral part of the important transformative conversational work with the teenager.

The teenager well-being profile

Name of teenager: _____   **Profile completed by:** _____

3 = Clear mastery of this capacity   **2 = Some mastery of this capacity**   **1 = Occasional evidence of this capacity**   **0 = No evidence of this capacity**

LIFE SKILL 1: CAPACITY TO GRIEVE AND PROCESS PAINFUL LIFE EXPERIENCE	3	2	1	0
Motivated to get help to process unresolved trauma or loss				
Acknowledges the impact of loss and trauma on their life				
Has a felt knowledge of the benefits of 'someone understanding you from the very depths of your personality' (Magagna, 2005)				
Able to process and grieve about painful life experiences with the help of another so that emotional baggage is not carried into adulthood				

LIFE SKILL 2: CAPACITY TO HANDLE STRESS WELL	3	2	1	0
The capacity to seek someone out for emotional regulation when stressed/distressed				
The capacity to use comfort well				
The capacity to manage stress well (not over-aroused or under-aroused inappropriately to the situation)				
The capacity to think well under stress instead of moving into impulsive action				

LIFE SKILL 3: CAPACITY TO REFLECT AND BE SELF-AWARE	3	2	1	0
Able to reflect on painful feelings, rather than moving into angry outbursts, anxiety or depression				
Able to reflect on the complexity of own and other's emotional states, considering underlying feeling (eg hurt)				
Able to speak about feeling hurt rather than defending against it or moving into an easier feeling (eg anger)				
An interest in how painful past experience can colour perception in the present				

LIFE SKILL 4: CAPACITY TO EXPLORE/BE CURIOUS/HAVE THE PASSION AND DRIVE TO MAKE GOOD THINGS HAPPEN	3	2	1	0
Motivated to explore, move towards, be spontaneous				
New experiences are welcomed as opportunities				
Able to play with new possibilities rather than moving into fixed or closed positions				
Has the passion, drive and will to move from the seed of an idea to making it a worthwhile reality				

LIFE SKILL 5: CAPACITY FOR CONFLICT RESOLUTION, DIPLOMACY AND NEGOTIATION	3	2	1	0
Capacity to negotiate, give and take				
Able to be diplomatic and navigate tricky interpersonal situations				
Capacity for resolution not blame				
Capacity to assert feelings in a non-blaming manner				

LIFE SKILL 6: CAPACITY FOR FULFILLING RELATIONSHIP	3	2	1	0
The capacity for enriching contact with others				
The capacity to develop, sustain and nourish relationships over time				
The capacity for mutually enjoyable playful engagement with others				
The capacity for genuine interest and curiosity in others				

LIFE SKILL 7: CAPACITY FOR EMPATHY AND COMPASSION	3	2	1	0
Able to be deeply moved by the distress of another				
Compassion for any human being in distress, not just those in their own social group, friends or family				
Appreciation rather than intolerance of difference				
Able to finds words to express empathy/compassion				

LIFE SKILL 8: CAPACITY TO SAVOUR THE PLEASURE/BEAUTY OF THE MOMENT	3	2	1	0
Able to just relax with another/others				
Able to be in the present moment				
Able to appreciate natural beauty, lovely relational moments, etc				
Able to be calm and still				
Able to experience a full range of positive affect states				

LIFE SKILL 9: CAPACITY TO BE ASSERTIVE	3	2	1	0
Felt knowledge of self as of real worth				
Self-confidence				
Felt knowledge of having a voice that should be both heard and respected				
Able to know what they want/don't want and to voice this, even if different from the group				

Why some teenagers mess up and how to help them not to

For too many children the transition to adulthood is complex, messy and unsuccessful.
(Institute for Public Policy Research, 2006)

As the teenager moves away from their parents to venture into a life of more independence, they often mess up, and sometimes very badly. This can be seen within the context of adolescence as a developmental stage of major changes: neurological, psychological, physical, hormonal, emotional, sociological and sexual. So turbulence is inevitable. The problem is that if the 'messing up' is not handled well, it can end up as a messed-up adulthood, as these statistics illustrate:

- Fifty per cent of lifetime mental illness, excluding dementia, starts by the age of 14, and 75 per cent by the time people are in their mid-20s (Centre for Social Justice, 2011).

- One in five girls aged 15–17 self-harm (Institute for Public Policy Research, 2006).

- In the UK, on average, a teenager tries to kill themselves every 22 minutes (Institute for Public Policy Research, 2006).

- Ninety per cent of young offenders have emotional and behavioural difficulties in childhood (Department of Health, 2004).

- Recent scientific data shows that mental health problems are increasing. Since the mid-1980s, depression and anxiety have risen for boys and girls aged 15 and 16, as have behavioural problems such as lying, stealing and disobedience (Centre for Social Justice, 2011).

The role of the brain in teenagers messing up
The teenage brain has a particular role to play in messing up. Neuroscientists often refer to adolescence as a time of the second brain growth spurt. (We used to think that there was really only one major brain growth spurt, which happens in the first three years of life.) This means that teenagers come to this stage in life with a brain 'still under construction'. As Jay Giedd (1999), chief of brain imaging at the child psychiatry branch of the National Institute of Mental Health, says, between the ages of 10 and 12, there is 'the most tumultuous time of brain development since coming out of the womb'. In fact, neuroimaging studies show us that the teenage brain continues to mature well into the 20s (Johnson *et al*, 2009). The parts of the teenage brain that are still immature include those to do with social sensitivity, the capacity to reflect instead of taking impulsive action, empathy and self-awareness. So it is, again, no surprise that so many teenagers mess up.

In colloquial language, one could say that the cement in the teenage brain is still setting. This means that the teenage years are a time of great potential but also a time of great vulnerability in terms of how that brain is used or misused. Moreover, the 'brain under construction', coupled with the major hormonal changes at this time, make teenagers particularly susceptible to emotional volatility, aggression, depression and anxiety.

Teenagers mess up because they lack vital life skills
In order to prevent so many teenagers messing up in ways that seriously blight their future, we need to look more closely at exactly *how* they mess up and the thought processes and feelings that go along with this. Basically, for any adult – let alone teenagers – to be able to do life well takes a lot of very sophisticated abilities and skills. Usually, these are the very skills that many teenagers simply don't have.

The life skills in the following table are needed for *anyone* to do life well. We will explore these and consider how teenagers can be helped to master each one. The longer version of the table, at the beginning of Part One, entitled *The teenager well-being profile*, can be used as a map for anyone working with teenagers. It can act as both an assessment tool for these essential life skills and as a focus for particular interventions. The table will empower professionals working with teenagers to be far more exacting in terms of where the teenager needs support in order to thrive instead of messing up.

Key life skills to be able to thrive in the teenage years and beyond

1 Capacity to grieve and process painful life experience
2 Capacity to handle stress well
3 Capacity to reflect and be self-aware
4 Capacity to explore/be curious/have the passion and drive to make good things happen
5 Capacity for conflict resolution, diplomacy and negotiation
6 Capacity for fulfilling relationship
7 Capacity for empathy and compassion
8 Capacity to savour the pleasure/beauty of the moment
9 Capacity to be assertive

Life skill 1: capacity to grieve and process painful life experience

About this life skill

This life skill is key if a teenager is to live life unencumbered by any painful experiences from their past. If we are unable to grieve for important losses in our life and process painful experiences, they will live on to haunt us in some form or other, spoiling health, happiness, relationships and capacity to function. This is something that has been recognised by great minds for many years:

'He who remains passive when overwhelmed with grief loses his best chance of recovering elasticity of mind' (Charles Darwin, 1872).

'A thing which has not been understood inevitably reappears; like an unlaid ghost it cannot rest until the mystery has been solved and the spell is broken' (Sigmund Freud, 1909, referring to painful life experience).

'The sorrow which has no vent in tears may make other organs weep' (Henry Maudsley, 1918).

Felitti (Dube *et al*, 2003) was a key author in the Adverse Childhood Experience (ACE) Study. This amazing study, involving three generations and 17,000 people, found that painful childhood experiences (that have not been properly mourned and processed) result in an increased risk in adulthood of:
- depression
- anxiety
- drug abuse
- teenage pregnancy
- difficulty controlling anger
- smoking
- alcoholism
- obesity
- sleep disorders
- promiscuity
- asthma
- heart disease, diabetes, stroke – sometimes leading to early death
- suicide.

The conclusion from this study has been that if we are able to address adverse childhood experiences, prevent them where possible and offer healing relational experiences to children, teenagers and adults where they cannot be prevented, the overall emotional health of society would improve dramatically. In light of this, Felitti (Dube *et al*, 2003) looked at population-attributable risk. Felitti estimated that if we could successfully prevent or successfully treat adverse childhood experiences, it could reduce societal ills by the following amounts:
- 50 per cent less drug abuse
- 65 per cent less alcoholism
- 54 per cent less depression
- 78 per cent less drug abuse
- 67 per cent fewer suicide attempts.

The ACE study provides sobering evidence that trying to just 'forget' about painful childhood experiences, or saying that 'the past is past', doesn't work. Furthermore, psychoneuroimmunology studies have also shown that suppression is bad for your physical and mental health (Salpolsky, 2004). And you can't just catch a mental illness. There are always childhood origins. So educating youth workers, child professionals, teachers, health care providers and parents about the evidence-based, long-term effects of childhood loss and trauma may bring home the importance of helping teenagers to speak about and work through their feelings.

Processing painful life experiences, as opposed to just trying to manage them, involves higher human capacities, namely the right and left frontal lobes working together in a beautifully coordinated way and in communication with the deeply feeling mammalian brain and body (Panksepp, 1998). This results in the integration of feeling, imagination and cognition. Processing feelings is most effective when done in the presence of someone who offers attuned empathic responses. It is this person's very presence that makes it safe enough to stay with the pain. This 'active listener' provides 100 per cent of their attention in terms of thinking and feeling about what it must feel like to be you and what you must have felt in terms of the painful life experience. Their in-depth empathy is then voiced.

The result of effective processing is that feelings about painful life experiences will be modified and assimilated, and so no longer cause such abject suffering. In effect, a teenager with this skill, when feeling emotional pain, will seek out an empathic adult for soothing and emotional regulation, rather than turning to drugs, drink, food, self-harm and so on, in an attempt to change their painful chemical state. If a teenager has mastered this skill they will recognise that shocks, traumas and losses *must* be talked about and grieved over. They will understand that if they don't, it will cost them too much in terms of the adverse effects that this will have on their relationships and on their physical and emotional health.

The particular suffering of teenagers who haven't mastered this life skill

Teenager: *'I just can't get over [my mother's death] at times ... when it's really hard, it's like losing part of yourself ... it's like learning to walk again ... Maybe the rest of them are just coping with it or looking as if they're coping with it but I'm not. There are times when I really don't cope at all.'*
(Centre for Social Justice, 2011)

Teenager: *'Life sucks. I just feel depressed all the time ... I feel anxious about everything ... I'm always getting into trouble because I have an anger problem – or so I am told!'* (Ribbens *et al*, 2005)

Teenagers who don't have this life skill are then left with only one option, which is to try to 'manage' their emotional pain. This usually entails one or more of the following:

- Developing a neurotic symptom (eg obsessions or phobias).
- Trying to change their painful brain chemical state by drinking, taking drugs, eating. Currently, too many teenagers turn to drink or drugs to deal with life's knocks – one in three men and one in five women drink over the weekly recommended limit (NHS, 2008).
- Self-harm – one in five girls aged 15–17 self-harm to 'manage' their feelings (Institute for Public Policy Research, 2006b).
- Discharging the pain through aggressive or violent behaviour.
- Ending it all – in the UK, every 22 minutes a teenager tries to kill themselves (Institute for Public Policy Research, 2006b).

Example
Milly (aged 14) was being badly bullied at school. She would come home and hit her mother. 'Revictimisation' is a common response to unprocessed trauma.

As we look at the statistics below, we can see the urgency for *all* teenagers to be helped to master this life skill.

Teenagers experiencing bereavement
Ninety-two per cent of teenagers in the UK will experience bereavement of a 'close' or 'significant' relationship (including pets) before the age of 16. Those who experience multiple bereavements, or bereavement alongside other difficulties, are statistically 'at risk' of experiencing negative outcomes, for example, learning difficulties, depression, self-esteem and risk-taking behaviour, in the teenage years or later in life (Harrison and Harrington, 2001).

Teenagers experiencing parental separation or divorce

More than one in four children will experience parental divorce by the age of 16 (Kiernan, 1997). One in two children will see parents split by the age of 16 (Centre for Social Justice, 2011).

After parental separation or divorce, children and teenagers will be:

- 75 per cent more likely to fail at school
- 70 per cent more likely to become a drug addict
- 50 per cent more likely to have alcohol problems.

In addition they will have:

- significantly more health problems, lower self-esteem, higher levels of smoking and drinking during adolescence and adulthood
- increased risk of behavioural problems (eg bedwetting, withdrawn behaviour, aggression, antisocial behaviour)
- increased likelihood of anxiety/depression, poor peer relationships, being admitted to hospital following accidents, leaving school and home when young, becoming sexually active/becoming pregnant/becoming a parent at an early age (Rodgers and Pryor, 1998; Centre for Social Justice, 2007, 2011).

The taxpayer is spending at least £20bn a year trying to repair the damage done by family breakdown (Centre for Social Justice, 2007).

Why teenagers in particular are hit so hard by the pain of trauma and loss

In childhood, defences against loss and trauma, for some, work pretty well. Children are often brilliant at deflection, at action as avoidance of feeling and thinking, at suppression with seemingly little adverse effect to health or happiness. But when they hit the teenage years, unprocessed trauma or loss from childhood can result in major meltdown. Robin Anderson (former head of the Adolescent Department at the Tavistock Clinic, London) states, 'Often in the teenage years, the personality cannot hold'. What he means is that with all the hormonal, neurological and physical changes, coupled with the pull to be more independent and move away from parental figures, defence mechanisms which were working well in childhood, no longer hold. As a result, the teenager is often flooded by what they have been managing to defend against – feeling! So they can find themselves in unbearable states of anger, depression or anxiety. Some become very emotionally unwell indeed, as in adolescent onset of psychosis.

What we can do to empower teenagers with this life skill

How can we teach a teenager to 'suffer well' with the inevitable shocks, let-downs, traumatic events and losses they will experience in life? It is vital that teenagers have access to an empathic adult to discuss their painful life experiences. So few troubled teenagers have any idea that the way they are behaving now, which is getting them into so much trouble, has anything to do with the fact that they have not worked through trauma and loss in their past. They often feel immense relief when they are helped to comprehend that their behaviour now is an understandable reaction to their particular trauma or loss and then are helped to grieve. It is often only then that they can start to put down the emotional baggage from their past and begin to live life unencumbered.

What parents can do

This listening other can be a parent, but obviously this is not appropriate where the parent too is suffering (eg from domestic violence, or a death that they have also not properly processed) or where a parent, due to their own childhood, lacks the capacity for empathy. Parents need to be aware of the psychology of trauma and traumatic loss, so that they can recognise the symptoms, in particular revictimisation (sometimes a sibling takes the brunt of this), depression, anxiety disorder or violence. They then need to refer on to a counsellor or therapist.

What schools can do

An obvious answer is to ensure that every secondary school has a sufficient number of trained counsellors available to every teenager in the school who has suffered trauma or loss. At the moment, there are trained professionals who see the most extreme cases of teenage anxiety, depression and aggression, but certainly not every teenager who has experienced a major loss in their life or the one in two teenagers who statistically will have experienced their parents separating or divorcing. Given the awful list of jeopardised life chances following family breakdown (*see* the box above), it is vital that schools offer help to *every* teenager who has suffered a traumatic loss. Adult-led, small-group time for all teenagers who have suffered family breakdown would be ideal.

Furthermore, schools must start to view bullying as a very significant trauma. Too many schools downplay it as 'boys will be boys' or the equivalent. All schools need to read the research (Teicher *et al*, 2010) showing that peer bullying causes actual brain damage. As Teicher says, 'Peer verbal abuse can result in anxiety, depression, anger-hostility, dissociation, "limbic irritability", drug use, and changes in actual brain structure – particularly the corpus callosum' (Teicher *et al*, 2010). These changes are due to cell death caused by the toxic levels of stress hormones resulting from being bullied. The Children Act 2004 states that 'the child's welfare is of paramount importance'. If it really was, we would put CCTV in school playgrounds to be 'read' during break times and lunchtimes by a psychologist. The playground would be sectioned, so that playground staff could quickly respond to instructions such as 'OK, bullying scene H2. Intervention needed now'. If we don't do this, we are actually condoning the brain damage in our schools of our children and teenagers.

Psychoeducation

While in schools we anxiously teach teenagers what they mustn't do (eg take drugs, get pregnant, smoke), we often fail to teach them vital skills for living life well or provide them with the research about how human beings thrive. In the light of this, I am advocating secondary schools adding psychoeducation to their curriculum. This will cover essential knowledge on the human condition, psychology and brain science. This way the teenager can make choices that are far more informed.

The following are the key facts about *Life skill 1: capacity to grieve and process painful life experience* that should be included in any psychoeducation curriculum about this subject:

- Grieving and 'suffering' well is an art, and is not possible on your own.
- Crying on your own in a way that really heals doesn't work. It's too lonely, too frightening and you stop yourself really doing the howling you need to bring about the physiological release of all the pain held in the body. As Bowlby (1978) said, 'It is not possible to grieve without the presence of another.'
- Research shows that unprocessed trauma or loss adversely affects parenting, however much you would like it not to. It is likely to leave your children vulnerable to problems with anxiety, depression and aggression at some time in their life.
- Research shows that emotional baggage carried into adulthood leaves you vulnerable to all sorts of physical and emotional illness and even early death (Dube *et al*, 2003).

When counselling or therapy is necessary

Some teenagers don't want to go to a parent to talk about painful experiences, as the relationship is too emotionally charged with its own difficult dynamics. Furthermore, with some trauma or loss it is far more appropriate to get a trained professional, as the intensity of feeling and distress needs specialist treatment. So teenagers who have suffered trauma or loss must have access to other empathic adults outside the family, ideally counsellors, psychologists or therapists. This is where we hit problems. For example, for one quarter of the country there is no emergency help for teenagers suffering from depression (NHS, 2006). Child and Adolescent Mental Health Services (CAMHS) waiting lists are often also extremely long. There are an estimated 30,000 children and young people on the CAMHS waiting lists (British Medical Association, 2006), most of whom will never get to see a trained psychologist.

> *As a teenager I was very violent and diagnosed as being mentally ill. I was completely traumatised by the repeated sexual abuse I had experienced as a child. The doctors knew that a talking therapy would help but I had to go on a waiting list for two years. By then they said I was too unstable to have therapy. They didn't want to take the risk. It's like they hold you in this awful state and there isn't the time or space to give you what they know you need.*
> (Harrison and Harrington, 2001)

The research shows that high numbers of bereaved teenagers never talk to anyone about their experiences.

Life skill 2: capacity to handle stress well

About this life skill
This life skill means that when you know you have triggered a primitive sense of threat (fear, anxiety, anger), which is adversely affecting your capacity to think well, you are able to find effective ways to regulate your emotions. With the accompanying physiological arousal, no one can *stop* themselves getting stressed. That's not the point. It's a survival instinct all mammals have. The point is that if someone has this life skill, they can effectively bring themselves down to a state of calm. The skill also involves knowing when you need someone to help you to do this. This means the ability to seek solace, advice and comfort from another person when bad things happen, rather than reaching for a cigarette, alcoholic drink, some food, going to bed, running away or fighting (verbally or physically) to stop the pain.

The particular suffering of teenagers who haven't mastered this life skill

> **Tim, aged 16:** 'When bad stuff happens, I usually go into my bedroom, lock the door and cut myself.'
>
> **Sally, aged 17:** 'When bad stuff happens, I tend to scream at Mum a lot, hit my sister, get drunk, or borrow Dad's car, play the radio at full volume and drive real fast.'
>
> **Elly, aged 14:** 'When bad stuff happens, I often do something that I regret afterwards.'

So many teenagers handle stress very badly. They act like toddlers when something doesn't go their way, particularly with parents. Then, just like toddlers, the angry unreasonable outburst is often quickly forgotten. For Mum, who has just been called 'fxxxing bitch' or something equivalent, it's not that easy just to establish normal life again. The teenager's meltdown has included a violent verbal attack and yet the teenager acts as if it was really nothing of any significance.

Example

Parent: 'Please put the rubbish out.'
Teenager: 'Later.'
Parent: 'I need you to do it now.'
Teenager [screaming]: 'I hate you. You selfish bitch. You are always nagging me to do something. You never say anything nice about me. It's like a boot camp here. I am leaving home. [Slams the door and marches down the street.]
(*Ten minutes later*)
Teenager: 'Hey Mum, what's for tea? Oh, and I need some more money for the cinema tonight.'
Parent [speechless – still reeling from the verbal abuse].

Teenagers respond to minor stressors as major emergencies. Like toddlers, they respond to the now as if it will last for ever. Furthermore, many teenagers get into a dangerous habit of using drugs or alcohol to handle stress. The problem is that these can become habit forming. Indeed, there is consistent evidence that higher alcohol consumption in late adolescence (15–19 years) continues into adulthood, often resulting in alcohol problems (McCambridge *et al*, 2011). The teenager can become a parent who misuses alcohol with huge knock-on problems for their own children. Up to 1.3m (one in 11) children in the UK live with parents who misuse alcohol (Cabinet Office, 2004). And so the cycle of emotional pain continues. We also know that glue-sniffing among 11- to 15-year-olds increased sevenfold between 1998 and 2005 (Department of Health, 2006).

Other teenagers handle stress by cutting off. For much of the time this is because they have not mastered *Life skill 1: capacity to grieve and process painful life experience*. But the cost of being emotionally under-aroused is that while they may not feel much emotional pain, they may not feel very much life either: passion, excitement, love! They may also suffer from lethargy, meaning they don't have the emotional energy and drive to make good things happen for themselves. Desire isn't strong enough. Rather they are left with simple pleasures such as eating, sleeping, passively watching television – little more than some simple mammals such as sheep or cows, which have far less brain capability than us. So teenagers without this skill can handle stress by being under-aroused or over-aroused inappropriate to the situation:

Toby, aged 13 (underly-aroused): 'I don't care. [*in other words, 'I don't feel'*] Nothing much really interests me. I spend the weekends on the sofa in front of the TV eating toast.'

Samantha, aged 14 (over-aroused): 'I hate my life. I'm angry all the time. I'm always in trouble because I've hit someone or smashed something.'

Ginny, aged 17 (optimally aroused): 'Wow, I love so many things about my life: my friends, and my hobbies – particularly rock climbing and swimming and I can't wait for sports day. I think it will be awesome!'

The teenage brain in relation to this life skill
In adolescence, the brain's alarm systems stay activated longer than in the brains of adults, which means they have a prolonged stress response. They also have higher levels of cortisol (a stress hormone) compared with adults. Furthermore, during adolescence, oestrogen and testosterone make girls more sensitive to the effects of stress, but only if there is a lot of stress around (eg bullying at school, fighting with parents at home) (Saluja *et al*, 2004). We also know, as we have seen, that due to the frontal lobes (involving impulse control) still being under construction, the teenager can't regulate moods as well as an adult. These are all key factors in terms of why teenagers can handle stress so badly and suffer from persistent states of anxiety, depression or aggression, and why suicide is so prevalent among teenagers.

What we can do to empower teenagers with this life skill
Basically, stress regulation that will really hold in a crisis is not something that can be taught. A teenager will establish good stress-regulating systems in the brain, or not, according to how many effective self-regulating interactions (soothing, validating feelings) they have received from calm, emotionally regulated adults over time. Hence we see just how important parents are in the teenage years in terms of whether the young person will thrive or mess up (*see Parent–teenager relationships: how to get them right*).

It's easier for effective stress-regulating systems in the brain to be set up in childhood as the brain is so malleable at that time. However, it is not too late in the teenage years to establish good stress response systems in the brain. But this requires emotionally regulated adults to sit down with the teenager repeatedly over time, stay calm when the teenager is erupting, soothe them, validate their experience of an event, and then, when the teenager is calm enough, help them think about what has triggered their stress reaction. Then listening empathically to what they have to say, and conveying that empathy, means new synaptic connections will develop in their frontal lobes, establishing capacity for emotional regulation.

Each positive, soothing and validating adult–teenager interaction can be an important brain-developing event:
- establishing top-down brain pathways key to the effective management of stress – frontal lobe pathways connecting to the more instinctual parts of the brain will naturally inhibit primitive fight, flight or freeze behaviour (Cozolino, 2002, 2006)
- developing pro-social systems in the brain

- regulating brain and body systems
- decreasing negative effects of stress on the brain
- significantly improving functioning of the immune system.

What parents can do

Any intervention that gives parents and teachers skills in empathic listening is a huge help. In fact, some fascinating research shows that teenagers are still emotionally regulated by the presence of their parents. The study found that after teenagers were put in a stressful situation their stress levels went down when they sought help from their parents. Also, their bodily arousal levels calmed. This highlights the continuing importance of the parent–child relationship in adolescence for affect regulation and mental health (Willemen et al, 2008). Furthermore, research shows that most teenagers do value their parents' opinion when making important decisions (Ackard et al, 2006). Interviews with more than a thousand teens showed that they were yearning for more time and more communication with their parents. This was often not explicitly said to the parents. Nevertheless, teenagers were emphatic that the message they wanted their parents to get was this, 'If we push you away we still want you, so hang around' (Galinsky, 2000).

Parents need to model being stable under stress. If they can't do this, they would do a great service to their teenager to go and get counselling or therapy. They also need the skills to take the emotion out of the picture when a teenager is stressing them out. The common pitfall with a stressed-out teenager is to be pulled into being like them and to scream back. But this means those stress-regulating brain pathways will not develop as they should. Consequences for unacceptable behaviour should be given in a factual, non-emotional way. This is why Cline and Fay's (2006) writing about good and bad choices, and consequences, is vital reading for any parent wanting to discipline teenagers in a way that develops their higher-functioning brain instead of strengthening primitive, 'reptilian' responses of fight or flight.

Example

Parent: 'Shame you called me a xxxx and threw the vase across the room. The consequence is xxxx. Hope you make a better choice about how to express your angry feelings next time.'

Also, punishment is stressful; the teenager often feels ashamed and their self-esteem suffers. Consequences delivered in a calm, measured voice do not have to be at all stressful.

In addition, when the teenager dares to tell them about something in which they have messed up, parents should avoid going into shock or flying into a rage. As this teenager says so aptly, 'Don't say, "You can tell me anything," and then freak out and lecture us when we do' (Faber and Mazlish, 2006). If parents don't adhere to this, the teenager will simply decide not to go to their parents again for help.

What schools can do

Schools also need to ensure that teachers are trained in empathic listening skills and in responding to teenagers with challenging behaviour, by taking emotion out of the picture. The last thing a troubled teenager needs is a teacher who shouts.

Psychoeducation

Schools should inform teenagers about why their brains trigger so much stress and how, in terms of brain development, it will get easier as they get older. They need to be informed about how the reptilian part of their brain can hijack the good, thinking part of the brain, leading them to primitive fight, flight or freeze behaviour. It is useful for teenagers to talk about when they have 'lost it' and if they moved into fight, flight or freeze, and what helped them to get back to their good thinking self.

Teenagers also need to be informed that they can develop stress-regulating systems in their brain and that the best way of doing this is to talk to an adult who they find soothing, empathic and compassionate. They should be given statistics about how many teenagers try to manage stress states by using alcohol, smoking or taking drugs. So, in short, talking to adults about their stress states develops the teenager's brain; taking substances to de-stress damages their brain. At least by choosing the former over the latter they can make informed choices.

Physical activity has been found to be very important for stressed-out teenagers. A research study involving over 7,000 teenagers showed that while family conflict increased the likelihood of depression in teenagers, physical activity decreased the likelihood of depressed mood (Sigfusdottir *et al*, 2011). Meditation and yoga are also excellent.

When counselling or therapy is necessary

Some teenagers are so hyperviligant, hyperaroused for too much of the time, that they are constantly losing control. By and large this is due to unprocessed trauma or loss; this may have been successfully defended against in childhood but, as already stated, defences often cannot hold with all the hormonal changes in the teenage years. When outbursts go beyond what we expect of the average teenager and result in harm to self, others or property, then it's time to call in the counsellor.

Life skill 3: capacity to reflect and be self-aware

The resilient teenagers [realised] that their inner world requires as much skill as the external environment; they look for the rocks that shipwrecked them before ... In that search, they are willing to look inward.

(Hauser *et al*, 2006, p271)

About this life skill

This skill means that you are able to think well under stress or when faced with a difficult decision, instead of rushing into impulsive ill-thought-out action. As Harold Macmillan aptly said, it is the ability to 'hurry slowly'. The skill also involves being able to consider why you are reacting as you do – and sometimes overreacting – by referring to how painful past experiences might be colouring your perception of the present. This means a curiosity about your inner world and those of others. If you are self-aware and able to reflect in this way, you are far less likely simply to blame others for all the painful things that happen to you.

Example

Ben, aged 15: 'Wow, I really overreacted there. I guess that guy reminded me of how I felt so powerless when my dad smacked us.'

The skill also involves the ability to reflect on interpersonal complexities, considering another person's inner world as well as your own and being aware of feelings you are defending against.

Example

Tim, aged 16: 'I hate him. I guess it's because I feel so hurt by him. But thinking about it, he must have been really hurt by someone in his life, to call my mum names like that.'

The particular suffering of teenagers who haven't mastered this life skill

Brian, aged 13: 'I'm going to get him. He was dissing me. See how he looked at me.'

Stephen, aged 14: 'I'd be fine if it wasn't for all these rubbish people in my life; having to listen to all those rubbish teachers.'

So many teenagers mess up because they don't have this skill. Instead of reflecting, they move into impulsive ill-thought-out actions – for example, hitting someone because they 'looked at me the wrong way', having sex without contraception, taking a dangerous drug and mixing it with alcohol because someone suggests they do, binge drinking. All these can cost them dearly, not just now but for life, particularly in terms of brain damage (*see* below). British young people are involved in more drug taking and binge drinking than teenagers in any other European country (Unicef, 2007). In the UK, one in four teenage girls binge drinks every week.

The teenage brain in relation to this life skill

The problem is that the teenage brain is in a very vulnerable state as it is in this stage of major growth. So as neuroscientist Jay Giedd (2002) says, 'What you are doing this weekend may not just affect you on Saturday night but for the rest of your life.' In the teenage years there is a major increase in synaptic connections in the frontal lobes (a process known as synaptogenesis). Some of the key executive functions of the frontal lobes are the capacity to reflect, impulse control, and the capacity to plan and think ahead. So it is easy to see how teenagers, with their undeveloped brains, mess up with this life skill in terms of their typical impulsive behaviour. Just think of Romeo and Juliet (aged 13). They met and, four days later, through massive emotional intensity and poor impulse control, they were both dead!

There is also another part of the brain involved in teenagers' poor impulse control and bad decision making. In the teenage years, there is exaggerated activity in the nucleus accumbens, one of the brain's reward centres. In effect, this means that, when doing something exciting and novel, the teenager will get a massive dopamine (reward chemical) hit, far stronger than that in the adult brain. This can lead to increased novelty seeking, risk taking and pleasure seeking. This, coupled with the impulsivity and poor capacity for reflection from immature frontal lobes, means that teenagers often don't take care to do a proper risk assessment of a situation. Hence the awful statistics of teenage deaths, three quarters of which result from accident or misadventure. Also, because of the big dopamine hit, nicotine, alcohol and drugs have enhanced rewarding effects in adolescence. This can lead to dependence.

What we can do to empower teenagers with this life skill

In a longitudinal study, Hauser and his colleagues (2006) interviewed teenagers and asked them to speak about their lives. They followed them up when they reached 30 years of age. The ones who were doing well were distinguished from the ones who were doing badly by several key factors, including self-awareness and the capacity to reflect. They were interested in psychological experience and the process of relationships. They paid attention to how they were with other people. The ones not doing well had no such interests. As Hauser says, 'All of the kids are impulsive at times. But the resilient ones also give their lives and problems steady and serious attention.'

What parents can do

Parents could be empowered to model reflection and good listening in the face of conflict with the teenager.

So rather than, 'You will clean the cat litter tray. I got you that cat and you just don't look after it. You are so selfish …' parents can try, 'We have a problem here. Let's play the "When you …" game.'

The 'When you …' game – instructions

This game will give parent and teenager a safe structure in which to reflect on what are really bugbears for both of them. Parent and teenager number themselves 1 and 2. Number 1 starts by finishing the sentences below. Number 2 must stay silent. They must keep very strictly to the four sentences. Number 2 just listens.

- When you …
- I feel …
- So what I want is …
- Will you … ?

Example
Parent:
- When you always leave me to clear out the cat's litter tray …
- I feel treated as a servant.
- So what I want is for us to take turns doing it.
- Will you do that?

Number 2 has to repeat back to Number 1 what was said, particularly focusing on what the person said they felt:

Teenager: OK, Mum. So you say you felt like a servant when I do that.

The two discuss the 'Will you …?' They each suggest ways that this could happen and write them down. Then number 2 takes their turn.

Example
Teenager:
- When you nag me all the time …
- I feel like leaving home and I feel like rubbish in your eyes.
- So what I want is for you only to nag me about the really important things and also tell me stuff I am doing well.
- Will you do that?

They then leave a day of reflection time before they come back together to finalise the change ... how they are with each other.

Important points

1 Both parties can only speak within this set format. This prevents them spiralling into yet more anger, hurt and miscommunication, as in the common attacks of, 'You are this/you are that', 'It's all your fault' and 'If it weren't for you ...'
2 With the 'So what I want' sentence, the temptation is just to say something unhelpfully general like, 'I just want you to be more helpful around the house generally'. Statements such as this are likely to be disguised blame. If you generalise, it also does not give the other person enough information as to the exact nature of your request or need.
3 With the 'Will you?' question, if the answer is, 'No I won't', the person will need to explain why not. They can be encouraged to give or compromise in another area of the relationship. Or they can say, 'I will think about it' and give the other person a time when they will get an answer. Or they may say, 'I am happy to do x but with the following conditions'. In short, you are empowering the two people to find healthier options for dealing with difficulties and conflicts that will inevitably arise between them.

What schools can do

My argument is that far more teenagers could be enabled to develop curiosity about, and interest in, human psychology and the psychology of human relationship. We need inspirational teachers to engage them in the fascinating study of how the human mind works, why relationships go wrong and the key skills to help them not to. If we engage them in this way, they will develop capacity for self-awareness and reflection. And again we turn to the importance of therapeutic conversations. If adults engage teenagers in creative ways to talk about how their past is colouring their perception of their present, teenagers usually find it fascinating. There are lots of ways discussed in this book to start such a conversation (see the worksheets in Part Two). Research shows that talking about feelings calms the brain's alarm systems and helps to stop impulsive actions (Hariri et al, 2000).

Psychoeducation

Schools should allocate time for teenagers to discuss and be informed about:
1 The teenage brain and how tenagers are vulnerable to making poor, impulsive decisions.
2 The high levels of teenage death from accidents in the context of the teenage brain, frontal lobe development and the reward chemical hit.
3 How their reptilian brain can be in the driving seat when under stress.
4 How the mind works with unresolved trauma and loss.

We should not be scared of venturing into this territory. Vaughan (2011) has found that traumatised teenagers are hugely relieved to hear about their brain as they realise they are not bad or mad when they mess up through some impulsive action. That said, ideally a psychologist should run these sessions, someone trained to handle what comes up. Ideally sessions should also be in small groups, so teenagers feel safe enough to talk about their lives.

In terms of alcohol, smoking and drugs and teenagers ending up with brain damage, heart attacks and other serious damage to their body, and even early death, you can't stop them, but you can help them make informed choices. Show them brain scans of the damage caused in the alcoholic brain. (In the alcoholic brain the ventricles are larger, which can impair memory and cognitive functions, the corpus callosum is thinner, adversely affecting social and emotional intelligence – and the frontal lobes have shrunk, affecting memory and the most sophisticated relational and cognitive skills we have.)

> It's a cruel irony, when the brain is most vulnerable [due to this dramatic period of change and development], it's a time when teens are trying drugs. Drugs may be not just affecting their brain for that one night, but affecting their brain for the next 60 years of their life.
> (Giedd, 2002)

Life skill 4: capacity to explore/be curious/have the passion and drive to make good things happen

About this life skill

This life skill is vital in terms of living a fulfilling life. If someone has this skill they want to explore new experiences, which are welcomed as opportunities rather than potential threats. They are able to play with new possibilities rather than moving into fixed and closed positions. And most importantly, they are able to start with a seed of an idea and find the passion, drive and determination to follow it through until something of real worth is born in reality.

There is a genetically ingrained system in the brain that supports all this. It is called the SEEKING system (Panksepp, 1998). Panksepp refers to this as a system of desire, of wanting to go and pursue the fruits of the world. The system is like a muscle; the more it is activated in childhood and the teenage years through access to stimulating activities and inspiring adults, the better it works. The key 'fuel' running the system is the brain chemical dopamine. 'When lots of dopamine synapses are firing, a person feels as if he or she can do anything' (Panksepp, 1998). Interestingly, at the top of the *Harvard Business Review*'s list of vital qualities for business success is 'a high level of drive and energy', or as Brown (1999) says, 'Everyone looks for that sparkle in friends and lovers to "make things happen". Most of all, everybody is looking for energy within themselves: the motivation and drive to get up and do something, the endurance, stamina and resolve to carry through ...'

The particular suffering of teenagers who haven't mastered this life skill

If someone has a poorly functioning SEEKING system, they will feel lethargy and frequent 'can't be bothered, what's the point' feelings. They will suffer from lack of motivation, lack of will, drive, and curiosity. Dopamine is being poorly activated.

Example
Amy, aged 15: 'I can't be bothered to do that', 'I don't want to do that.'

Over one in ten young people aged 16–18 are not in education, employment or training – so-called 'Neets'. (LSN Institute for Education, 2009)

One in five teenagers are not getting any GCSEs.

Your mind now, mouldering like wedding-cake,
Heavy with useless experience,
Crumbling to pieces under the knife-edge
Of mere fact. In the prime of your life.
(Adrienne Rich, from *Snapshots of a Daughter-in-Law*, 1963)

Many teenagers are difficult to motivate to do anything, other than lie on the sofa and play with their computer, Wii or PlayStation. They have a poorly activated SEEKING system. If the teenager's brain has not habituated to optimal levels of dopamine in childhood from sufficient positive relational interactions and stimulating activities introduced by energised adults, problems with the SEEKING system become very apparent at this stage of development. The teenager may simply not be producing enough dopamine to be bothered to really make something of their lives.

The teenage brain in relation to this life skill

As stated, due to the brain's major growth spurt at this time of development, the teenage years are very important and a real opportunity for mastering new skills quickly and efficiently. As Giedd (2002), who has been studying the teenage brain for years, says, 'An hour practising the violin as an adolescent may be worth many hours in contrast to that of an adult.' In this time of growth, brain connections used frequently will survive and flourish, but those that aren't will wither and die. So if you spend your teenage years with pursuits such as playing the piano, rock climbing, reading exciting books, getting fascinated with biology or history, and so on – in other words, with an optimally functioning SEEKING system – those synaptic connections will be reinforced. But if you spend your teenage years lying on the sofa watching the television, the only skill that will be honed, as Giedd says, is using the remote.

Furthermore, teenagers with a poorly functioning SEEKING system are also vulnerable to taking cocaine. This is because you can actually tap into the SEEKING system's supply of dopamine by taking cocaine. 'Psychostimulants give you the very sense of vigorously pursuing courses of action that they would get from a healthy SEEKING circuit' (Panksepp, 1998). On cocaine, the teenager feels energised, confident, motivated. This is a key contributory factor in why 780,000 people in this country use cocaine, and lots of them are teenagers and people in their 20s. The problem is that following cocaine use there is usually a period of depression for days afterwards, as the dopamine supplies, which have been so forcefully raided, are slowly replaced in the brain. There is also a long-term cost in terms of dopamine cell death (possibly leading to early Parkinson's disease in later life), as well as risk of heart attack (even in teenagers), respiratory failure, strokes, seizures, gastrointestinal problems, convulsions, nausea, blurred vision, chest pain, fever, muscle spasms and coma.

What we can do to empower teenagers with this life skill

What parents can do
Realistically, if parents haven't had the personal resources to strengthen the teenager's SEEKING system in his or her childhood, it is unlikely that the parents will suddenly start to do so now that their child is a teenager. Sometimes parents have received so little encouragement from their own parents when they were children that they simply don't know how to empower children in this way. Often, the best they can do at this stage, if they have money, is to buy in inspirational adult–teenager time or pay for their teenagers to go on really exciting community holidays. But the fact remains that a parent's praise continues to be as important for the teenager as it is for the toddler.

What schools can do
The more the SEEKING system is activated, the more the teenager will be able to find the curiosity, desire, will, drive and thirst for knowledge so key to living a fulfilling life. As already stated, it is always best for the SEEKING system to be optimally activated in childhood as this can then lead to the teenager staying motivated even over times of typical teenage scepticism, depression and doubt. Hence, there is an argument that the very best teachers, as opposed to novices, need to be teaching in the early years. This would ensure that all young children repeatedly experienced a sense of achievement and competence, a sense of, 'I did it', 'I can do it', 'I want to do it' and later, 'I can do it for myself and for other people'.

But if the SEEKING system has not been optimally activated in childhood it is not too late. One of the most powerful ways of activating the SEEKING system is through inspiring and encouraging teachers or youth workers. In other words, if home has not helped the teenager to develop an optimally functioning SEEKING system, they will need the school and adults involved in extra-curricular activities to make up for this relational deficit.

Ideally, demotivated teenagers can form an attachment with motivated adults in regular one-to-one or small-group time. The adults will be prepared to put the time into introducing them to, and inspiring them with, pursuits such as fishing, skating, rock climbing, and so on. So schools would be well advised to do an audit for each poorly motivated teenager of the adult the teenager feels close to and inspired by. If there is no one, they need to think about a mentoring system or outsourcing to specific youth workers. The current situation, in terms of this life skill, certainly leaves a lot to be desired. As

Claxton (2008) found, 'A third of 11 to 16-years-olds interviewed for the Work Foundation report [exploring the health and well-being of the educated workforce in the UK] were bored by school.'

Schools also need to assess this life skill in each teenager in turn by asking:
- How do we prevent this teenager from living an unremarkable life because they have been unable to envision something better? How do we help them resist the comfort of the ordinary?
- How can school life support this teenager to develop and sustain the passion and persistence for creative endeavour throughout their adolescence and into adult life?
- How can we help this teenager to envision an expansive life, one that is far more than just a fulfilling career? As Brown (1999) says, 'Too many people live life as if they have another one in the bank'.

In addressing these questions, we need to consider the anxiety and fear levels of each teenager, because fear blocks the SEEKING system. The relational experiences for many children at school are:
- fear of being bullied
- fear of not fitting in
- fear of falling out with friends
- fear of having no friends
- fear of being told off by teachers
- fear of being shamed in class
- fear of looking stupid
- fear of what might happen in the playground
- fear of what might happen on the way home from school when no teachers are there to supervise.

It is only when we start thinking psychologically about all teenagers in this way that we can really support them to thrive in this particular aspect of emotional health.

Psychoeducation

Schools should allocate time for teenagers to discuss and be informed about *blocks to the SEEKING system*:
- self-sabotage
- put-downs from peers, siblings, parents
- negative self-talk
- negative internal working models (eg 'I'm not clever')
- parental modelling of frustration avoidance, giving up, lack of dreams, lack of self-belief
- early programmed negative messages
- peer pressure or culture pressure not to achieve, not to do well at school, not to create
- insecure attachment leading to lack of curiosity or lack of self-esteem.

This knowledge will then provide them with the self-awareness and insight often needed for them to seek help to master this life skill before it is too late.

Example

In one PSHE (personal, social and health education) lesson I observed, the teacher asked the teenagers to write down their goals and ambitions. The lesson was not relationally engaging. The energy in the room was flat and dull. Such a cognitive task will not impact on a teenager with a poorly activated SEEKING system who has had a diet of criticism and commands in childhood. For such teenagers, it will take repeated, emotionally charged relational experiences with a teacher or mentor over time, to reverse their negative programming, change internal working models, and for their brain to habituate to optimal levels of dopamine. For such teenagers, occasional encouragement and praise in a class of 30 is very likely to be too weak an intervention to withstand all the discouraging forces they have experienced in their lives. Hence the need to think about nurture groups or other small home groups or mentoring systems as early as possible for these teenagers.

Leon Feinstein and colleagues (Institute for Public Policy Research, 2006b) found that if teenagers had attended an adult-led youth club, they were doing far better in their 30s, financially, socially and emotionally, than teenagers who had attended a youth club that was not adult-led. Certainly, the teenage years are a crucial time for adults involving the teenager in shared adventure, and modelling the spontaneous, the exploratory, the creative and novel use of resources. Such relational interventions in schools are needed more than ever now, when television is the new nanny and where the child *passively receives* rather than *actively creates*. On average, children spend 28 hours a week in front of the television and only about 45 minutes in meaningful conversation with parents.

When counselling or therapy is necessary

Sometimes the level of lethargy becomes extreme. Often, when things have deteriorated to the point where the teenager has no motivation to do anything but sit all day on the sofa, no impetus for personal hygiene or for conversing with anyone in the house at all, parents need to consider the possibility of clinical depression. If worried, parents should seek professional help and not make the mistake that this level of inertia is 'just something teenagers do'.

Life skill 5: capacity for conflict resolution, diplomacy and negotiation

About this life skill
This life skill involves sophisticated interpersonal awareness, such as negotiation and diplomacy, and the ability to accept that problems in a relationship are often co-created. This means that the person will not immediately go to a place of blame in a conflict but look at their part in things. Furthermore, if they feel particularly upset by an argument, they will be able to consider what painful memories from their past might have been triggered. They will focus on resolution not blame.

The discount matrix (transactional analysis) is particularly useful in assessing this life skill in teenagers. The list goes from 1 (a position held in poor mental health) to 4 (which shows very good mental health).

The discount matrix
When something has gone wrong, the attitude is:
1 There isn't a problem.
2 There is a problem but it's nothing to do with me.
3 There is a problem, it is do with me but I can't do anything about it.
4 There is a problem, it is to do with me and I can do something about it.

Many troubled teenagers adopt positions 1, 2, and sometimes 3.

The particular suffering of teenagers who haven't mastered this life skill

---

Tracey, aged 14: 'It's not my fault I got in trouble at school today. It's all your fault, Mum. You're a rubbish mum.
My life would be great if it wasn't for you.'

Billy, aged 13: 'Mum, please don't meet me any more at the school gates. I am embarrassed because you are so overweight and look so old. And I need a lift to the skating rink tomorrow.'

It is normal and healthy that teenagers start to go off their parents in a big way. If teenagers didn't enter a period of fairly major disillusionment about their parents, they would never want to leave home. Hence there is a genetically programmed falling out of love with parents and in love with peers at this developmental stage. This can lead to teenagers insulting parents often on a very personal level: about their clothes, their face, their smell, how they speak, what they say. It is not unusual for parents to put their teenagers into care because they are so lacking in this life skill, acting like a toddler tyrant in an adult body.

Figures show that around 40 teenagers a day go into care because parents have had enough. Steve Goodman, assistant director of children's services at Hackney Council in East London, says that parents become desperate and approach social services to ask for their teenagers to go into care: 'They've really reached the end of their tether. They've usually done quite well in bringing their children up to teenage years, and either the children's behaviour is very difficult or the parents haven't got a good sense of how you need to change your parenting behaviour as the child goes through the teenage years.'

The teenage brain in relation to this life skill
As we have seen, the frontal lobes are still developing in the teenage years. A key function of this part of this brain is concerned with interpersonal skills. We know, for example, that in people with Alzheimer's, cell death in the frontal lobes can leave them very socially inept. As the teenage frontal lobes are still

---

under construction, this gives vital context to such instances as a teenager calling their mother a bitch one minute and then asking her to give them some money the next.

Also, the cerebellum (*see* below) is still developing in the teenage years and continues to do so right into the early 20s. The cerebellum has strong links to the frontal lobes. Scientists used to think it was just about physical coordination. They now know it is also about thinking coordination (Schmahmann and Caplan, 2006).

Furthermore, Deborah Yurgelun-Todd's research (2006) shows that teenagers are not good at accurately gauging emotion on people's faces or reading social situations. She found that teenagers are 20 per cent less accurate in gauging emotion on faces. Studies show that teenagers react emotionally, not rationally, to faces. When reading emotion, teens rely more on the amygdala (one of the roles of which is to detect threat), while adults rely more on the frontal lobes. Hence the commonality of the somewhat paranoid stance of many teenagers who think someone is looking at them disrespectfully – 'Stop dissing me'. People can be beaten up as a result of this inaccurate emotion reading.

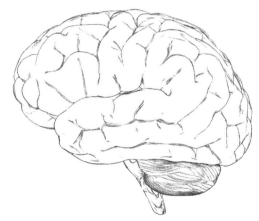

What we can do to empower teenagers with this life skill

Of course, for adults on the receiving end of all this, the temptation is to attack back. But teenagers will not learn this skill for conflict resolution, diplomacy and negotiation unless teachers and parents model it well (*see* skills in *Parent–teenager relationships: how to get them right*).

What parents can do

Example
Mother: 'There was so much bad feeling between us. But as soon as I ... really listened to her point of view and accepted all her feelings she turned into another person. Suddenly she was telling me things she never would have told me before' (Faber and Mazlish, 2006).

Parents need to model how to negotiate. This includes really listening to their teenager's point of view. If they don't do this and model submission/dominance instead, lashing back with hurtful words, they will miss vital opportunities to help the teenager to learn about conflict resolution.

Example
Parent (shouting): 'Turn that awful music off now. Ben, I have had enough. You are so selfish and you do nothing to add to this household. You just slob around all day at the weekends. I have had enough. I will confiscate your CD player if you don't stop now.'

Parent (negotiating): Hey, Ben, we have a problem. You like loud music and I find it jarring. I think if we think about it together we might come up with a solution, which means we both feel OK. Then I don't go on nagging and doling out punishments and you don't keep saying it's lousy living in this home. Would you think with me about it now?

(Parents can then use the 'When you ...' game, as detailed above.)

What schools can do

In order to achieve position 4 on the discount matrix (*see* above), teenagers again need the support of psychoeducation at school. They would benefit from knowing about how their brain's developmental stage leaves them vulnerable to social ineptness, and that such ineptness often comes with a heavy price. They need to be taught actual skills of negotiation and diplomacy. They can learn about events in history when such skills have stopped horrific bloodshed. And, finally, they need to be taught the discount matrix itself so they can recognise when they take refuge in the easy positions 1 and 2 and when they achieve the superb sophistication of position 4.

Life skill 6: capacity for fulfilling relationship

About this life skill

Many people are able to fall in love, but being able to sustain and develop that relationship over time, once the honeymoon period is over, is the difficult thing. It involves being able to listen well to the other person, have curiosity and interest in the other person over time, being able to be vulnerable and share personal feelings, particularly feelings such as hurt or fear, being able to own your part when things go wrong, being motivated to resolve rather than blame, and being able to be empathic, warm and kind.

Developing and sustaining a close, fulfilling relationship over time is a real art, not mastered by many. The statistics bear this out. One in two cohabiting couples split up before their child is five years old (Centre for Social Justice, 2007), and one in two children or teenagers will see parents split up by the age of 16 (Centre for Social Justice, 2011). It costs the taxpayer £20bn a year to pick up the pieces of family breakdown. Then there are those who stay together but their relationship and quality of connection is poor. So we need to ensure that far more teenagers leave school versed in the art of fulfilling relationship or we will continue to see the level of family breakdown and common human misery caused by unfulfilling or downright abusive relationships that we see today.

The particular suffering of teenagers who haven't mastered this life skill

Alfie, aged 17 (a computer geek): 'I don't need anyone. I don't care. I far prefer just being on my computer all day.'

Sally, aged 15: 'I was so hurt last year by my boyfriend, I slit my wrists. Someone found me. I wish they hadn't.'

So many teenagers who have not mastered this skill are happier with 'just having sex' or using the opposite sex for physical sexual pleasure. Others are happier being with their PlayStation or the internet than with people. They have no sense that there is anything better. As Sylvia Plath says, 'I cannot see where there is to get to'. They have no idea about the profound sense of fulfilment, well-being, inner calm and warmth that can be gained from a loving relationship.

Many other teenagers who have not mastered this skill think about relationship in terms of power and control.

This can come to an awful head at this stage of development, with violent verbal or physical bullying at school and/or sibling and parent abuse at home. Parent abuse is not just shouting at a parent or refusing to do things, it's when there is actual repeated and persistent verbal, emotional and/or physical abuse. Teenagers can abuse parents emotionally or physically by hitting, pushing, swearing at them, stealing money, damaging the home, furniture or precious objects, punching holes in walls, purposefully breaking things, threatening to hurt the parent or themselves, using a parent's credit card, and so on. Teenagers can abuse siblings by kicking, shoving, punching, biting, choking, verbal put-downs, threatening with knives, and so on. This is actually very serious, as peer bullying can cause brain damage in the teenager's developing brain and leave them vulnerable to developing a psychiatric illness, such as clinical depression or anxiety disorder (Teicher, *et al* 2010).

Teenagers abusing parents

Up to a third of teenagers are abusive toward their parents, Robinson *et al* 2004). In 82 per cent of these cases, the mother is the victim.

Fourteen per cent of parents are assaulted by their teenage children at some point (Cottrell, 2003).

One in 10 calls to the Parentline helpline are from parents abused by violent teens (Parentline Scotland, 2010).

Parents need to accept that parent abuse is domestic violence. Professor Lynn Jamieson, professor in sociology at Edinburgh University's Centre for Research on Families and Relationships, said: 'Violence has become normalised and part of the family experience. Parents who have been frightened by being hit by their teenage child have often had no other recourse for assistance but to phone the police. The child will be sad and sorry and everyone traumatised.'

What we can do to empower teenagers with this life skill
We know that if teenagers are to develop the capacity for a fulfilling relationship, they need to be offered warm, empathic relationships consistently over time in which they feel understood, accepted, validated and valued. It is only by experiencing such relationships at first hand that teenagers will value human relationship (over the allure and delights of technology).

What parents can do
We know from Gottman's 1998 research and all the attachment literature (*see* Cassidy's *Handbook of Attachment,* 2008) that children who are empathised with by their parents are far more emotionally secure and able to empathise with others, obviously a key factor in the capacity for fulfilling relationship. It is not

too late for parents to learn this skill even if they haven't been empathic previously (*see Parent-teenager relationships: how to get them right*).

In addition, one of the best ways for the teenager to learn this life skill is to see how a parent behaves in a relationship: to be able to witness arguments that are resolved, to hear negotiation, diplomacy, support, compassion, shared laughter and delight between parents or partners. But for many teenagers this is never going to happen – their experience is of the kind of parental relationship that ends up contributing to soaring divorce rates and the now relative normality of parents splitting up before the teenager's sixteenth birthday. And so, for these teenagers, we must look to schools.

What parents can do about parent abuse
It can be hard for some parents to accept they are being abused by their teenager. They can feel too ashamed. Others just pretend to themselves that the violence (verbal or physical) is normal. It is not. Doing nothing is giving a message to the teenager that the abuse is a normal and accepted part of a human relationship. Parents need to tell someone, for example, the doctor, a friend, a therapist, the police. Often, just like in domestic violence, the abusing teenager tells the parent not to tell anyone. But the parent must tell someone. The teenager, the parent and the parent–teenager relationship need help and, in particular, help to stop the escalation of violence. If nothing is done, the parent is in danger and the teenager may do something worse that leaves him or her with a criminal sentence.

Sometimes the support that parents need is with parenting skills: help to establish clearer and firmer boundaries delivered in a way that is not angry, shaming or blaming. But parent abuse is not always about this. Sometimes teenagers attack their parents because of unprocessed loss or trauma, for example, parents splitting up or becoming emotionally unavailable ... to worry or depression (*see Life skill 1*).

What schools can do

As already stated, the art of relationship is complex and will come naturally to very few teenagers – those few who have had parents who have offered excellent models in conflict resolution, empathic listening, being stable under stress, and so on. So schools must provide a lot of input with this skill. Yes, in reality we can be so busy testing teenagers that their *relational* journeys at school get little attention. As Geddes (2005) says, 'The pressure on schools and on teachers to focus on measurement and comparisons of performance can obscure the interpersonal experience at the heart of teaching and learning'. We are neglecting the teenager's relational journey at school if we focus so much on their academic journey, when in fact the former can so often predict the success of the latter. Many primary schools offer lovely relational experiences, which then cease when the fun goes out of schooling with the looming of SATs in Year 6, and fear and anxiety increase in secondary schools.

Nurture groups are very rare in secondary schools, and yet they provide a wonderful arena for troubled teenagers to develop the skill of being able to enjoy fulfilling relationships, when the home environment is unable to do so. This is because such groups provide a small, close-group environment like a family group, in which the teenager can form secure attachments to their peers and nurture group staff (Cooper and Tiknaz, 2007). Only about 500 schools in the country currently run nurture groups. So all too many teenagers are set adrift in the school community of, say, around 1,000 pupils.

Psychoeducation

Schools would allocate time for teenagers to discuss and be informed about:
- the psychology of trust and mistrust
- the psychology of betrayal
- the psychology of defence mechanisms and their cost to self and others
- the psychology of fighting in family and intimate relationships
- the psychology of feeling unnoticed or overlooked
- the psychology of belonging or not belonging
- the psychology of shame and humiliation

- the psychology of cruelty and kindness
- the psychology of guilt and blame
- the psychology of revenge
- the psychology of trying to mend the people we love
- the psychology of hating and loving the same person
- the psychology of 'worried about Mum or Dad'
- the complexities of sibling rivalry.

Teenagers need to learn some of the basics of attachment psychology: why intimate relationships break down in terms of the relational skills that so many people don't have, and the key relevance of each partner's attachment history (Johnson, 2006). They would learn that moments of attachment rupture in intimate relationships activate primitive pain systems in the brain and that relationships often break up because such moments are never fully reflected on and worked through. They would learn how intimate relationships often evoke unmet childhood needs where the partner is hated for 'the original failure' (Winnicott, 1971). They would learn about Gottman's highly respected longitudinal research (2007) and how he can predict a separation or divorce with a 97 per cent success rate. They would learn about the key factors involved, and how to interact in far healthier ways, which would not put the relationship at risk. All this would be enriched with references to art and literature and use of film clips.

In short, if teenagers are to master this skill we are not talking about a few useful relational skills but a serious study of the psychology of relationship. If these changes were implemented, many more teenagers would enter into relationships with a substantial body of knowledge of human psychology, enabling them to have far more thoughtful responses to relational difficulties, instead of the usual teenager journey in intimate relationship from 'very, very happy to very, very hurt'.

And if we don't start to empower our teenagers in this way? Well, one may ask what on earth are we doing, and how utterly irresponsible (knowing the statistics regarding relationship and family breakdown as we do), sending our teenagers off into adulthood knowing they will experience just as much heartache and misery as all the past generations who were not privy to this vital body of knowledge.

When counselling or therapy is necessary
Sometimes the intervention needed is for someone to facilitate a therapeutic relationship between parent and teenager. This is because, like any intimate relationship, a parent–teenager relationship can suffer from a build-up of resentments, misunderstandings and mistaken beliefs about not being valued by the other. If a teenager takes part and remains emotionally present during a therapeutic conversation, is it an excellent learning experience for this life skill of developing fulfilling relationships.

Life skill 7: capacity for empathy and compassion

About this life skill

This is the capacity to be moved by the distress of another person and to then to offer solace in words or deeds.

Let's face it, no one can be empathic all of the time. When we are feeling angry, frightened or distressed empathy can be blocked. But this capacity is about being able to be empathic as a common response to human suffering, not just to certain people (the Nazis were very empathic to members of their own family) but extended to all human suffering, whether within or outside one's own social group. We know that all mammals have the potential to be distress averse (feeling pain at the pain of another). Many experiments with chimps and now even chickens (Edgar, 2011) show this. The problem is that many teenagers are actually distress excited. This means they like to inflict pain on others as opposed to feeling pain at the pain they have caused.

The particular suffering of teenagers who haven't mastered this life skill

Sarah, aged 13, to Milly, aged 13 (text message): 'Hi Milly, just texting to say we don't want you in our group anymore. We are all really glamorous, you know. You are kind of just too plain and odd to really fit in. Sorry and all that. The others asked me to tell you. Bye.'

Bill, aged 14: 'We sometimes beat them up because they are a different post code or skin colour to us. Yes, I've bullied a lot in my life – can't stand wimps and then there's so many weirdos at school. I often tell them how pathetic they are. I guess it makes me feel good.'

Simon, aged 16 (a text sent to his girlfriend): 'You are so dumped.'

Many teenagers are extremely cruel, as the quotes illustrate, with not an ounce of empathy. We know, for example, that cyberbullying and texts can be so hurtful that teenagers can end up feeling suicidal. In younger teen boys toughness is such a status card, and so weakness and vulnerability in others often gets attacked as they may see in others what they hate in themselves. Later on the cruelty tends to diminish as status moves from toughness to coolness.

The teenage brain in relation to this life skill

Lack of empathy is due in part, once again, to immature frontal lobes. One of the executive functions of the frontal lobes is empathy. When we are feeling the pain of others, a particular part of the brain called the anterior cingulate lights up (Zubieta *et al*, 2003; Singer *et al*, 2004). If, on the other hand, a teenager takes pleasure in hurting, the reward centres in their brain are likely to have lit up instead (Singer *et al*, 2006). We know a lot more about empathy now in terms of the systems activated in the brain.

What we can do to empower teenagers with this life skill

Angry teenagers don't need punishment, because it doesn't mean anything to lots of them. What they need is to be helped to feel again.
(Batmandghelidji, 2008)

We all have the genetic potential to be empathic and compassionate. There are genetically ingrained systems and particular brain chemical activations for these wonderful human capacities. As Panksepp (1998) says, 'Brain oxytocin, opioids and prolactic systems appear to be the key participants in these subtle feelings that we humans call acceptance, nurturance and love ... warmth'.

These capacities, however, will only be fully awakened through relationship. Research shows that we cannot expect a child or teenager to develop the capacity for empathy unless they have been on the receiving end of repeated empathic responses from a significant adult over time (Davidov *et al*, 2006; Hoffman, 1984; Steele *et al*, 2002). The enormous body of attachment research also bears this out. Similarly, we cannot expect a teenager to be consistently kind unless they have been treated with kindness. So, once again, the development of this life skill for teenagers is a relational task.

For some teenagers, who are cruel rather than empathic, it takes therapy or counselling to help them to be able to feel again. Without this intense one-to-one experience over time, it can be difficult for a teenager to give up their defences. Defences stop us feeling our own pain and the pain of others. Defences are often incredibly difficult to give up without the powerful input of an effective therapeutic relationship. The therapist empathises with the hurt and pain under all the teenage bravado. Over time, a good enough therapist will get through. Sometimes using the worksheets that are in this book helps start a conversation about the hurt and the pain underneath.

Moreover, teenagers who act cruelly in a totally blind way often do so due to unresolved trauma. Research on post-traumatic stress disorder shows time and time again that one common symptom is revictimisation. This means that 'I treat others as I have been treated' but this is often delivered in a very cold cut-off way. It is only when the teenager is helped to feel the pain of his trauma or loss that he starts to have compassion for the pain of others. Brain scans show that it is possible to act in a totally cut-off way, with no emotion systems activated in the brain (Lanius *et al*, 2003). This is called dissociation, a very common defence resulting from childhood trauma.

What parents can do
Parents need to be empowered to have empathic responses to teenagers, even when the whole of their being wants to shout and hit out and the last thing they feel is compassion. There are some wonderful books on this – see in particular

How to Talk So Teens Will Listen and Listen So Teens Will Talk (Faber and Mazlish, 2006)**.**

Example
Miserable scenario
Teenager: 'You are a rubbish mum. You are never there for me. I hate you … You are so selfish.'
Mum (wrong answer): 'How dare you talk to me like that? You are so ungrateful. OK, that is half your pocket money gone.'
Teenager (storms out of the house): 'Fxxxxxx bitch.'

Scenario far more likely to engender a capacity for empathy
Teenager: 'You are a rubbish mum. You are never there for me. I hate you … You are so selfish.'
Mum (knowing no point in taking the outburst personally and that the teenage brain leads to much emotional volatility): 'Hey Sally, so sorry to hear you feel that way. I didn't know you felt like that.'
Teenager (bursts into tears): 'That is all I needed you to say, Mum.'

What schools can do
There is no point in schools trying to teach teenagers to be more empathic through PSHE (personal, social and health education) lessons, and yet this is often all the input teenagers get regarding developing this life skill. Are we in education so naïve that we think we can get a teenager to take down their defences and melt their hardened heart over a set of PSHE lessons, a good peer mentoring or buddy system? Similarly, you can't transform a teenager who is 'distress excited' by bullying into one who is 'distress averse' simply by teaching about the impact of bullying and that bullying and intolerance of difference in particular is wrong. Bullying and cyberbullying, for many teenagers, is very exciting. They get addicted to the adrenaline buzz. As already stated, for teenagers to develop this life skill they need a relational intervention.

Moreover, lessons in 'teaching empathy' won't positively impact on teenagers who are in survival mode due to a very difficult home life. The acute level of stress hormones flooding their system and their flight or fight reactions block any interpersonal sensitivities. For the most part, we must be feeling safe and secure to feel empathy. You can't just say to a frightened teenager, 'Feel safe please, so the empathy centres in your brain can activate.' As stated, teenagers will change in the most profound and positive ways, not through cognitive understanding of emotion but through emotional arousal in the context of relationship. This again points to the need for them to be on the receiving end of empathy in exchanges with parents and school staff, and to have the time and space to reflect on their painful life story. Again, nurture groups or equivalent would be an excellent intervention. Attachment research clearly shows that if teenagers successfully develop a capacity for empathy, it is because someone has been consistently empathic to them, not because they have 'learned' that it is good to be empathic.

There is an abundance of studies showing that what prevents teenagers *in extremis* from treating others in the traumatic abusive ways they themselves have suffered is a positive relationship from an emotionally regulating adult (Sroufe *et al*, 2005; Hauser *et al*, 2006). The Minnesota Study of Risk and Adaptation (Sroufe *et al*, 2005) followed 180 infants born into poverty from birth to the age of 30, focusing on risk factors for abuse and neglect. The key factor for non-perpetuation of maltreatment was *relationship,* but not necessarily therapeutic relationship. The children who went on to thrive had all experienced an emotionally responsive relationship. For some, it was a minimum of six months in therapy, for others it was a reflective, empathic adult at some time in their life. In addition, Fosha (2000) states, 'Research shows that whilst personality is shaped by experiences with attachment figures over time, it is also shaped by intense emotional experiences of often short duration'.

In short, for teenagers who cannot empathise, or worse, who are excited by hurting (insecure attached), the question must be not what we should teach them about empathy, but how do we relate to them?

All this said, although it is not possible to teach empathic response, it is possible to heighten a teenager's awareness and understanding of the plight of others. For example, one girl at the end of a PSHE lesson said, 'I understand more now what a person in a wheelchair goes through'. So the aim of 'heightening awareness' would be a far more reachable and honest aim on a PSHE curriculum in place of the word 'empathy'.

When counselling or therapy is necessary
When a teenager is 'distress excited', enjoying seeing another human being in pain, as opposed to 'distress averse', feeling pain at the pain of another (ie empathy), we should be concerned. Being distress excited usually points to dissociation, an emotionally numbing defence resulting from some past unprocessed trauma. Sometimes it points to revictimisation, a symptom of trauma where a teenager often blindly treats another person in the ways they have been treated by someone and that resulted in the trauma. This can be made worse by watching lots of television, internet and video game violence. Research shows that television violence is linked to verbal bullying in teenagers (Kuntshe *et al*, 2006). Research also shows that when teenagers watch violence on television, PlayStations and the internet it can increase aggressive behaviour. This is partly due to the fact that the part of the brain to do with the motor rehearsal of aggressive movement lights up. Also, new memories are encoded that are similar to those encoded after traumatic events in post-traumatic stress disorder (Murray, 2001). Teenagers who are distress excited are a danger to others. In order for them not to ruin their lives and those of other people, they need counselling or therapy in order to process past trauma or loss and to be enabled to feel again.

Life skill 8: capacity to savour the pleasure/beauty of the moment

The quality of contact determines whether life 'passes by' or whether it is lived to the full.
(Clarkson, 1989)

About this life skill

This life skill, a key factor of emotional health, is the ability to be fully present in the moment. That means being able to be with the sunset, the cuddle, the smell of the daffodil, the beautiful music or the moment of meeting with another person, rather than being worried about something happening in the future or thinking about some painful past event. It is the ability to savour, to be aware of sounds, sights and smells in the present moment, and to slow down enough to do so. It is about contentment, as defined by Frederickson (2004), 'The urge to sit back and savour in ways which can result in new views of self, others and the world'. It is about the capacity to drift and let go. To quote Nietzsche (1911), 'All good things have something lazy about them, and lie like cows in the meadow'. Many of us are so busy, stressed, preoccupied or neurotic that this wonderful human capacity is too seldom lived.

The particular suffering of teenagers who haven't mastered this life skill

Simon, aged 16: 'I'm always thinking about who I hate and why and how I can get revenge. I love watching war movies and doing killing and smashing on my PlayStation.'

Sally, aged 15: 'I spend loads of time worrying about what I look like. I can never really enjoy being out, because I always think my clothes are wrong and my hair is wrong and that people are looking at me.'

As Seamus Heaney says, 'We live amongst the marvellous', but all too many teenagers are so crippled by teenage angst that they don't really spend many of their waking hours seeing or hearing or tasting or savouring the marvellous. Arguably, in the world of technology and computer games it is increasingly difficult for teenagers to enjoy an embodied, impassioned response to this beautiful planet. Instead of sitting in a grassy meadow, by the side of the river, drinking in the beauty of the buttercups and feeling the sun on their skin, many teenagers are far more likely to be in their house on the internet, texting, on their PlayStation or in some internet chat room. Arguably, more and more teenagers are becoming disconnected from this beautiful planet, from the awe of the natural world and what it is like to be really engaged with it rather than away from it.

This life skill rarely comes up on the agenda when we talk about teenagers, but it needs to. Of course, we should be concerned about the teenager who cannot control their emotions, is anxious or depressed, but we should also be concerned about the teenager who can only understand cognitively about beauty, and is unable to feel it viscerally, who is great at maths but doesn't have the capacity for exhilaration, so can't roll down grassy banks with glee, or spontaneously give someone a compliment. If we don't think in these terms, and particularly in education, we are in danger of providing schooling for 'excellence without soul' (Lewis, 1966).

What we can do to empower teenagers with this life skill

What parents can do

Parents need to limit computer, internet and other technology time. Then they are well advised to make space in their life for one-to-one time with their teenager each week. This will entail getting out of the house and ideally doing something that involves nature or something that is sensorially rich – for example, a picnic in the park, going fishing, going to the theatre. There are also some wonderful holiday organisations, where computers and so on are not allowed. When parents have the money, these community-based holidays, where teenagers build, sing round fires, rock climb, canoe, and so on, can give sceptical teenagers a huge 'jolt' back into being able to savour their life on this beautiful planet (see, in particular, Superweeks al www.ate.org.uk

What schools can do

We need a personal, social and health education curriculum and a whole-school culture that touches teenagers' souls as well as their minds. Teenagers should have regular sessions in school to reflect on the good things that have happened to them in their life, rather than quickly rushing on to the next thing, hence experiencing the power of positive reminiscence. We must ensure, in secondary as well as primary schools, that we offer an optimal environment where teenagers experience 'The kind of thinking that makes them catch their breath and lean forward with interest. This has the power to connect them with the deepest in nature and with the deepest in themselves' (Petrash, 2003). This is in part to do with adults inspiring teenagers in this way.

Schools should think far more about how to develop a teenager's capacity for awe. Fox suggests people showering each other with stories of awe: 'When there is no awe, everything becomes a consumer object. Where is our awe? What hole has it been sucked into? Awe is a source of strength making the heart strong. Awe enlarges the heart. We should be showering each other with stories of awe. We take the awesome world for granted. The awe of the plant world. The body is awesome. 18 billion years to prepare the earth for us. 100 billion galaxies. How can we be bored again? How can we put up with boring institutions? We can argue about the meaning of the universe. We cannot argue about the beauty of the universe, the wonder at just being here. Awe awakens, we are asleep. How do we help children choose awe over cynicism? We don't live in a pretty universe; we live in a beautiful one' (Fox, 1983).

The other part involves, yet again, *Life skill 1: capacity to grieve and process painful life experience*. The inevitable anxiety, depression and angry fallout from unprocessed trauma or loss means that it will be extremely difficult for a teenager to savour the moment. This is because the negative 'mind-noise' will drown out the moment, or, on a neurobiological level, too high levels of stress hormones block the positive arousal chemicals such as opioids and oxytocin. With neurosis you are not in the present moment but preoccupied by the painful past or worried about events that might happen in the future. So, once again, we come back to those vital therapeutic conversations with teenagers, which will enable them to work through unresolved trauma or loss.

Psychoeducation

Schools should allocate time for teenagers to discuss and be informed about the following:

- The difficulties of running after happiness as opposed to long-term satisfactions. 'We are … [happy] … just for as long as our relevant neurochemistries are aroused to sustain the neurodynamics of [happiness]' (Panksepp, 1998).
- Activating positive emotion circuitries in the brain, as opposed to negative ones, leads to 'broadened mindsets … contrasted to the narrowed mindsets sparked by many negative emotions (eg specific action tendencies such as attack or flee)' (Fredrickson, 2004). These broadened mindsets 'promote discovery of novel and creative actions, ideas and social bonds, which in turn build that individual's personal resources, ranging from physical and intellectual resources, to social and psychological resources' (Fredrickson, 2004).
- The concept of 'flow' and how to achieve it. A flow state is characterised by 'an almost automatic, effortless yet highly focused state of consciousness. It ensues when one becomes so deeply focused on a task and pursues it with such passion that all else disappears, including a sense of time or the worry of failure. The person experiences an almost euphoric state of joy and pleasure in which the task is performed, without strain or effort, to the best of the person's ability … Any activity, mental or physical, can produce flow as

long as it is a challenging task that demands intense concentration and commitment, contains clear goals, provides immediate feedback and is perfectly matched to the person's skill level' (Dietrich, 2004).

- How neurotic anxiety, depression and aggression can block our capacity to 'breathe in life' and what we can do about it.
- The brain chemicals that block the positive arousal chemicals, why and what you can do about it.

Life skill 9: capacity to be assertive

A person who knows – perhaps without ever having thought about it – that if the situation demands it he can assert or can defend himself, is and feels strong. A person who registers the fact that he probably cannot do this is and feels weak.
(Horney, 1977)

About this life skill
This life skill is about being able to say no and to establish clear boundaries. Without it, we are open to being abused and used. It is too easy for people to disregard or play down bad treatment in a relationship as 'something that just happens', or to pretend to themselves and others that it really isn't that bad. Underlying this skill is the ability to know your own mind, what you want and don't want. It is this that forms such a key part in feeling psychologically strong and resilient.

The particular suffering of teenagers who haven't mastered this life skill

Their friends were so important to them that some of them were willing to give up a part of themselves in order to be part of the group.
(Faber and Mazlish, 2006)

Tess, aged 15: 'With boys, it's easier just to say yes. But I don't like myself afterwards.'

Flo, aged 17: 'I didn't want to take the drugs, but they said I was a wimp if I didn't, so I just went ahead and did it. Now I really regret it. I have flashbacks and loads of headaches and stuff.'

Sam, aged 18: 'When my boyfriend asked do I want white or red wine, my first thought was which does he want me to have. I keep doing that. I don't really know what I want, only what I think others want me to want.'

Many teenagers end up doing things they don't want to do; often risky, dangerous things that cost them dearly not just in the present but in the long term (eg teenage pregnancy; brain damage or early death from peer pressure to take drugs, smoke, binge drink). They often do these things just to get other teenagers to like them or to prevent a relationship with them from ending. A classic is the boyfriend who says tells a girlfriend that they must take drugs with him or have sex, otherwise he will go off with someone else. In fact, many teenagers give their power away and agree to do something they don't really want to do, due to their urgent need to belong, to be included in the group. Teenagers without this skill are also very vulnerable to being bullied or abused. They can then suffer in adulthood from all manner of bad treatment from partners, relatives, friends and work colleagues. Other teenagers look assertive but they are actually just feeling more of a power buzz from being negative or blocking. They need skills to be reflective instead of just coming up with a 'no' or 'shan't', like toddlers.

What we can do to empower teenagers with this life skill

What parents can do
- Authentic appropriate assertiveness in a teenager (as opposed to stroppy power over behaviour) usually comes from having parents who are prepared to listen, to encourage, who value the opinion of the child and then the teenager. Parents need to be properly informed, therefore, that if they over-control and demand compliance and obedience from their child in forceful

controlling ways, when reaching adolescence, the teenager will not know who they are, want they want and what they don't want. Without this as a base, they will then be unable to find any authentic assertiveness. As Sam, aged 15, the daughter of a very controlling mother said, 'I don't know what I want, only what other people want me to want.'

- Parents also need to know that some teenagers have no assertiveness because their healthy anger was punished in childhood rather than acknowledged. An example of the latter would be this response to an angry infant, 'I am not going to let you travel with us out of your car seat but I can see how angry you feel about having to be put in it. Not just a bit angry but really, really angry.' Gottman's (1998) research found that repeatedly validating children in this way is crucial for them being able to develop a sense of self, and from this a sense of appropriate assertiveness in the teenage years and beyond. In contrast, if parents discipline in ways that are shaming, or from a place of anger, the teenager will learn not about assertiveness but about submission/dominance. All too many teenagers with no assertiveness have been shamed as a part of discipline in childhood.

- Parents should praise as much as they can the 'sensible thinking part of their teenager', so that the teenager begins to believe in herself as someone who really can make really good decisions, for example:

Parent: 'Listen, daughter of mine, if I could, I'd follow you around day and night to make sure that nobody ever gives you or sells you anything that could do you harm. But that would be pretty crazy. So I have to count on you to be smart enough to protect yourself from all the garbage that's out there. And I believe you will. I believe you'd do what's right for your life – no matter how much people pressure you' (Faber and Mazlish, 2006).

- Parents need to model assertiveness themselves. So they should not be a doormat for their angry teenager, just putting up with being hit or sworn at. Neither should they be angry or shaming or call their teenagers names

such as slob or selfish. As stated, parent voice is key – factual and firm but not punitive, for example:

Parent: 'Hey, you know what? I'm not available to you to be shouted at. So I am going to walk away now. When you are ready to negotiate in a different way, I will be really happy to talk. Just text me when you are ready and I'll come back' (leaves the room/house).

In short, if we are to empower teenagers with this skill, parents need to be informed about what supports the skill in terms of child development, and how easy it is, with the wrong discipline or mode of interaction, for the teenager not to find her own voice, opinion, boundaries and her 'no', leaving her very vulnerable to giving in readily to negative peer pressure.

What schools can do
Role play in PSHE lessons can really help heighten a teenager's awareness of the negative impact of peer pressure and how, because of their need to be liked and included, they often find themselves in a situation where they end up saying yes to something harmful. Role plays can involve scenes of teenagers being pressured to binge drink, have sex, smoke, smuggle drugs, and so on. Role play is particularly useful for practising this life skill in terms of body language and voice and coming over with conviction. The pushy teenager can come in with usual phrases such as, 'You gotta try this', 'Trust me, you'll like it', 'This stuff is really great', 'It feels sooo good!', 'Helps you relax', 'Come on, don't be a wimp' (Faber and Mazlish, 2006). The teenager role playing being assertive will often need to be given clear assertive phrases, such as 'I don't want to do that' or 'I will go away and think about your offer and let you know later what I've decided.'

Here is an exercise for a group of teenagers to do and then discuss:

- Think of a relationship you have with a sibling, parent or friend that often gives you that heart-sinking feeling because you know that person has all

the power in this relationship. Draw what it feels like to be with that person.
- What can you do to stop yourself being treated in this way?
- What beliefs about yourself, other people or life in general do you need to challenge?
- What support and help do you need?
- Who would you like to give you this support?

Psychoeducation
In addition, schools can allocate time for teenagers to discuss and be informed about the following:
- Examples of the awful consequences suffered by teenagers who agree to something harmful because of their lack of sense of self, yearning for acceptance in the peer group or from a boyfriend or girlfriend, and the fear of saying no.
- Appropriate anger as a boundary-setting emotion.
- The difference between appropriate assertiveness and inappropriate expression of anger.
- The power of saying, 'let me think about that and I'll get back to you in a few days' instead of saying yes.
- The right to change your mind.
- The best way of supporting yourself is by saying what you feel.
- Parenting that supports this skill and parenting that doesn't. In terms of the latter, teenagers could be informed about the subliminal messages that some parents give their children. These are called 'injunctions', taken from a school of psychology called transactional analysis. Injunctions include:

- Don't succeed
- Don't grow up
- Don't be important
- Don't be someone in your own right
- Don't be
- Don't be you (Don't exist)
- Don't make it
- Don't be a child
- Don't
- Don't think.

When counselling or therapy is necessary

In states of shame, images of the self as weak, defective, pathetic, exposed and violated come to the fore.
(Mollon, 1993)

Teenagers who lack this skill often need one-to-one work with a school counsellor or equivalent. Assertiveness, in a teenager lacking any sense of self, self-worth or confidence, is not something you can just teach through a few lessons. If a teenager feels weak and frightened, we are not suddenly going to make her not feel like this. Such teenagers need help from a school counsellor or equivalent, through therapeutic conversations, to talk about their childhood. They need to focus particularly on the relational events that led to them today giving their power away. They need help to find their voice and their natural anger. Many teenagers who have no assertiveness say they never feel angry. This is the problem. They need first to find their rage or anger about past events, under that often over-compliant exterior. They need to talk about the discouragement and shaming they have experienced and the bullying and abuses of power (from peers, siblings, parents). They need to talk about the times in their life when they have felt unimportant and/or invisible.

Part Two

The worksheets

About the worksheets

The worksheets in this section address feelings and concerns that most teenagers grapple with at some time or other. Yet, shockingly, statistics show that of all the teenagers in the UK struggling with emotional problems (and what teenager doesn't?), a mere 30 per cent receive any sort of intervention or treatment. The other 70 per cent simply struggle through the pain and emotional turmoil, doing their best to make it to adulthood (Brown University, 2002). When teenagers fail to get the help they need to address painful feelings and events in their life, they tend to make mistakes, some of which can cost them too dearly in terms of hurt and harm to self and others.

So these worksheets are designed to offer vital support for practitioners who are helping teenagers to talk about and address what is troubling them. The worksheets provide really easy-to-use structures that enable adults to be with the teenager in a confident, non-embarrassing and effective way, so that the conversation flows rather than flounders. We have also provided up-to-date psychology pertinent to each issue, which can be talked about with the teenager. They usually find it both fascinating and very useful.

If a teenager is to develop the capacity to reflect, in place of impulsive, ill-thought-out action, then quality conversation time with a listening, non-judgemental adult is essential. This adult can help them work through their life experiences in an insightful and informed way. Through this process, the teenager will be able to clarify what they think and feel. In fact, it's really difficult to do this on one's own – for anyone of any age. It's true that, 'Often enough, we do not know our own mind. In the process of dialogue with another person, we are able to clarify what we think and feel'(Fonagy, 2006, p118). If they are not talked about, the teenager often discharges the emotional tension from painful feelings and difficult life events in destructive or self-destructive behaviour.

How to choose which worksheets to use

If you have engaged with Part One of the book you can choose worksheets relevant to *The teenager well-being profile*. You might like to do this in conjunction with the questionnaire on the page 43, *Common emotional themes in the life of a teenager*. If you are just using Part Two, again it is advised that you begin with the questionnaire. This is to be filled in by the teenager. In the questionnaire, if there is more than one tick in a particular category, and there are lots of ticks in some, this means that the teenager would really benefit from engaging with the corresponding worksheets. There is a worksheet for each of the categories in the questionnaire.

You will also find a more general section of worksheets after this. For some teenagers, and particularly those who are somewhat defensive about talking about what is bothering them, these will be a better place to start. These worksheets are divided into the following sections: *All about me and my life*, *About my relationships* and *About me and my Mum/Dad*. They serve as an easier warm-up before venturing on to the more potentially troubling topics of the emotional themes worksheets. They are designed to open up a conversation while hopefully engaging the teenager's curiosity and interest in the act of reflecting on their life. Many teenagers will never have sat down and given their life this sort of attention. Many love it and are fascinated. It is the beginning of a personal journey, which can have a profound positive impact on how they live their life.

Sandplay

Sandplay therapy is ideal for teenagers. They can use the sandbox as a quasi film set. Where they get very stuck with words, teenagers often make breathtakingly powerful images about their life in the sandbox.

Ideally, what you need is a sandbox about 23 x 29 x 3 inches (57 x 72 x 7cm). It should be painted blue on the bottom to represent water. The box becomes the frame or forum for the teenager's symbolic statement about some important aspect of their life. Of course, teenagers can draw something instead, but lots of them like the three-dimensional environment of the sandbox. Because of the sand, they can bury things or bomb things, and everything stands up easily. When the sand is wetted, they can mould it into a fort, an island, a cave, and so on.

Then you need a big choice of miniature objects. Your aim is to represent most key objects in the world. This is one reason why sandplay therapy is known as 'the world technique' (*see* Lowenfeld, 1991, for more on sandplay therapy). Having said that, I started off with about 30 miniatures with teenagers and they still made some amazing sandplay 'filmscapes'. The important thing is to have some miniatures from each of the following categories:

- transport (must include emergency service vehicles) as well as train, aeroplane, helicopter, car, bus, and so on
- people (to include figures of aggression or cruelty and figures of love or warmth, and so on, mythical figures such as trolls, witches and fairies, and family members)
- people in professions (for example, police officer, nurse, lollipop lady, teacher)
- monsters
- farmyard animals
- jungle animals
- buildings (for example, houses, prison, fort, and so on)

- furniture (for example, bath, bed, armchair, toilet) and food
- outside man-made world (for example, gate, road, fence)
- outside natural world (trees, flowers, hedge, stones, shells, cliffs).

How to explain sandplay to a teenager

Show the teenager the miniatures and the sandbox. Some may look at the images and say indignantly, 'I'm not playing with toys'. If this happens, simply explain that they are not to be used as toys. Rather, each miniature can stand for something. 'For example, someone might use this monster figure to represent their anger, or this very little duck to stand for their weak small feelings.' I have never had a teenager refuse to engage in the activity after this explanation. Show them how you can then put miniatures in the setting to make up a story, or a play or a film set. Prior to this, you might also demonstrate putting your hands in the sandbox to show the blue on the bottom for water, and how you can wet then mould the sand into a building, a wall or a dam, and so on, so you have a setting. After the teenager has made their image, you can talk about it. The conversation often changes perspectives on things, so it is always useful to ask the teenager at the end of your conversation, 'Is there anything you want to change in your film set now that we have talked about it?'

Questionnaire: Common emotional themes in the life of a teenager

Please tick any of the statements in any of the categories that are what you sometimes feel.

Sometimes I feel:

1 Others have all the power
- I can't change things
- I'm scared to say what I really feel
- I can't say no
- I'm living a life of lost battles
- The grown-ups have all the power
- People do to me, I don't do to them
- I feel like giving up

2 I'm rubbish
- Being me is hell
- I hate how I look
- I'm not happy with what I do
- I'm my own worst enemy
- I feel ugly/stupid/unlovable
- I feel unspecial
- I feel unloved
- My head is full of critical voices
- I'm not happy with who I am
- I feel like hurting myself
- I don't feel special to the people who matter to me

3 Worried
- I'm worried that something bad will happen to me
- I'm worried that I'll be found guilty of something
- My worries mean I can never have fun
- I'm worried that something bad will happen to the people I love
- I'm never really able to relax, I've too many worries
- I'm frightened of losing everything
- When Mum/Dad wobbles, the whole world wobbles

4 Not belonging, feeling on the outside
- I don't belong
- Unwanted
- On the outside
- Pushed out in the cold
- Shut out
- A stranger in my own world
- Bullied

5 The people I miss/the people I've lost
- Like my world ended that day
- I'm not going to let people in any more
- There's no point getting close to anyone because they just leave
- I spend so much time missing them
- Being in a world with no warm faces in it
- Being in a world where it's always winter

6 Family stuff

- I've a mum who got broken but didn't get mended
- I'm trying to mend Mum/Dad but never managing
- Our family can't seem to save each other
- I'm trying so hard to make Mum/Dad happy again
- Full of silent screams at having to watch stuff
- Stuff at home's doing my head in
- I hate my brother/sister
- Like a person in a crazy film
- There's no one to make the hurting stop
- Like Mum/Dad don't want to be with me much

7 Mum and Dad split up

- Home isn't the same any more
- Lost family rituals – we used to do that together
- Lost my Mum/Dad to her/his pain
- Lost too much time with Mum/Dad
- Lost my sense of belonging
- Lost my sense of trust
- Lost so many good things in my life
- Living in an upside down world

8 Nag, nag, nag

- I'm always being got at
- I'm always waiting for the next criticism
- I can't seem to do anything right
- I live with constant nagging
- Discouraged, not encouraged
- I'm just waiting for the next telling-off

9 I did this bad thing

- I did this bad thing
- I think I was born bad
- Like I'm to blame for the bad stuff that happens
- Like the bad in me could destroy the good
- Who I am is wrong
- Feeling like a criminal
- Feeling rotten inside
- Like I'm the cause of people's unhappiness

10 Leave me alone

- My parents don't give me any space
- Enclosed, confined, hemmed in
- My privacy is not respected
- Suffocating
- Imprisoned in my parents' life
- My life is not my own/it's what they want me to be/do
- Like everything I do is watched and judged

11 Life sucks

- It's all too difficult
- Worn out from being me
- Like I'm very, very old
- Like I'm living in a world where it's always winter
- It's all too much
- Stop the world, I want to get off
- Seen too much, heard too much, thought too much
- I feel like giving up

12 Kind of numb

- Don't care anymore
- Closed down
- Dull
- Just going through the motions of my life
- Emotionally numb
- Frozen inside
- Cut off
- Too painful to feel what I feel
- No one cares for me, so I care for no one
- In the prison of the life I've made for myself

13 Not doing much with my life

- I'm a lazy slob
- I want to want something
- I can't decide stuff
- I can't decide what to do with my life
- I am so unsure of things
- I'm unable to choose between one thing and another
- I don't finish stuff I started
- I'm in a rut
- I can't make anything good happen

14 After the bad thing happened

- The world ended that day
- Like a nightmare got stuck in my brain
- I'm living in a world of broken people
- As if everything got smashed up
- Full of silent screams
- Like someone shot me full of holes

15 Why so angry?

- Like I've got a volcano inside me
- I want to smash things
- So deep in anger that sad won't come out
- Frightened I'll destroy all that matters to me
- Full of bottled-up feelings
- I want to scream and scream
- I'm like a walking time bomb
- Frightened I'll damage the person/people I love the most

16 Mistrust

- Rarely feel at ease with anyone
- Got to get through this on my own
- There's no one to catch me if I fall
- There's no one there to help me with my problems
- No one really understands me
- Often the world feels out to get me
- I can't trust anyone
- Don't want to let anyone in

17 Jealous/possessive/clingy

- I get really jealous
- Can't stop texting him/her and phoning him/her
- Worried about where he/she is and who he/she is with when not with me
- Terrified of losing him/her
- I make sure she/he does what I say
- I wouldn't cope if I lost him/her

Others have all the power

She did not expect to be seen, recognised, or understood.
(Balint, 1993, p48)

Objective
This exercise is designed to help teenagers reflect on how they may be giving their power away in relationships. It is for those teenagers who cannot find their voice, who give in too easily to what others want them to do and be. It is hoped that this exercise can become an important step in the teenager finding their appropriate anger and natural assertiveness. As a result of this and more work on the subject, they may then be able to stand up to their parents appropriately and refuse to be in relationships with peers or partners where they feel pushed around, put down or shamed.

Instructions for the teenager
When you feel that your life involves grown-ups and/or other people having too much power and you feel that you have very little, it is useful to think about what you might want to change. It can help to stand back for a while and think about the whole power thing. So take a look at the pictures and captions below. If you sometimes feel like any of the following, please tick the box or colour in the relevant pictures. If it's not any of these things, draw or write in the empty box what you feel inside when it seems as if others have all the power and you have none or very little.

Development
Exercise: How big are you in your family?
This exercise provides the teenager with a lot of information when they reflect on the size they have drawn the other people in their life, the positioning they have chosen for them on the page (eg central, sidelines) and how that contrasts with how they have drawn themselves. It may, in fact, reveal that the true power base lies with someone other than a parent – a sibling or grandparent for example.

Instruction: Draw all the important people in your life, friends, family, teachers, and so on, and yourself, as animals. When you look at what you have drawn, what have you learned about who has power and who hasn't? Then ask yourself, do they abuse that power or use it well to help and support you and others? Speak to each of the animals in turn. Finish the sentence: 'What I would you like to say to you is ...' or, 'What I would like to do to you is ...' Discuss your answer.

Exercise: The belittlers
Instruction: Draw the people in your life who make you feel small. Draw how small they make you feel. Now draw the people who make you respect yourself/feel good about yourself. Draw what size they make you feel. Find sandplay miniature people to represent all the 'belittlers' you have experienced in your life (see page 42 for an explanation of sandplay). Put them in a row and express your anger/other feelings towards them in turn. Start the sentence for each one of them: 'What I want to say to you is ...' or, 'What I feel about you is ...'

Discussion
(Pick one or more of these topics to discuss with the teenager, as appropriate.)

Give reassurance that this feeling is very common at this of stage of development
You might say something like this: It can be very painful to feel you have no voice, and not much confidence to say what you really feel or think. It might feel as if you still have the powerlessness of a child when, as a teenager, people expect you to feel more potent and with rights that a child doesn't have.

Things are very likely to change as you go through these teenage years. This stage of development is often difficult as it's a time when you are still finding out who you are and what you want and what you feel, as opposed to what your parents want and what they feel about what you do and don't do. It is difficult to have a voice if you are not sure of what *you* feel about things, I mean deeply feel about things. But, for a lot of teenagers, as they get older, all this becomes far clearer. They find a voice and opinions and feelings that are very much their own and not someone else's. And with a stronger voice and stronger opinions, they find they are far more able to stand up to people.

When teenagers are not sure what has happened in their life to make them feel like this, it can be useful to give them common contributory factors to see if they relate to any of them:

- feeling small or unimportant in the family
- older siblings taking up much of the emotional space in the home and having far more confident voices
- parents who are emotionally volatile taking up much of the emotional space in the home
- strict parents who have needed the teenager to comply and conform all the time in their childhood and teenage years
- parents and who haven't made the shift in the teenage years to there being some give and take and shift in the power base
- people who have shamed you at home or at school.

Talk about shaming experiences and how they can knock a teenager's confidence

A person who knows ... that if the situation demands it he can assert or can defend himself, is and feels strong. A person who registers the fact that he probably cannot do this is and feels weak.
(Horney, 1977)

When introducing the concept of shame to a teenager, you might say something like: 'Shame makes us feel very weak and small, exposed and violated because it feels like an assault on the self, on the very core of who we are.'

Teenagers who feel powerless and without a voice can find it an immense relief to consider the concept of shame. Often they are shocked and relieved to realise that this is what they have been experiencing, often for years. They are also relieved to hear how being shamed at home or at school – for example, told off in a humiliating or belittling way – can have a long-lasting effect on confidence, making them feel weak and pathetic and utterly valueless. The teenager then needs to know that the way to stop this becoming a way they see themselves is to get angry about the shaming. The anger will always be there, because under shame there is always shame rage. Once shame rage is expressed, ironically the teenager will find resilience against being shamed in the future. They will find their stature and emotional strength in doing so.

You can rehearse with the teenager putting up their hands in a firm stop sign and saying, 'I will not let you shame me.' Don't give up until you hear real strength in the teenager's voice.

Example
Millie, aged 15, was asked by her counsellor to imagine her dominating father was in the room and to talk to him.
Counsellor: 'Let's pretend your dad is on that chair over there. Tell him what you've never told him and each time you say something bang on this big drum here.'
Millie (banging on a very loud drum): 'How dare you make me feel so small. I hate you for that and for not being interested in my thoughts and feelings.'
Millie breathed deeply and said she felt emotionally strong for the first time in her life.

I can't change things

The grown-ups have all the power

I can't say no

I feel like giving up

I'm scared to say what I really feel

People do it to me. I don't do it to them

I'm living a life of lost battles

Talk about the subtle subliminal messages about staying small and voiceless

It may be useful with some teenagers to talk about 'injunctions', a concept from the field of psychology called transactional analysis. In this model, the idea is that parents, teachers, siblings and other key figures in the child's or teenager's life can intentionally or unwittingly give them non-verbal messages (*see* below). It may be that the parents' parents might have given them these messages too. Hence the power of what is known as 'intergenerational transfer'. The effect, however, of such 'injunctions' can be that the teenager feels they have no right to have a voice, an opinion, an identity, success, and so on.

Injunctions include:

- Don't succeed
- Don't grow up
- Don't be important
- Don't be someone in your own right
- Don't be
- Don't be you (Don't exist)
- Don't make it
- Don't be a child
- Don't
- Don't think.

Talk about standing up to parents

> *Having access to her anger spontaneously allowed her to feel for the first time that she was living in her own life rather than adjusting to others' lives.*
> (Orbach, 1994)

Discuss how it is common for teenagers to feel powerless at this time in life. This is particularly the case when parents don't take on board the fact that it is appropriate to make adjustments to the power base at home at this developmental stage, even more so if the teenager is responding to events in a mature manner. The teenager should be given autonomy now in terms of taking responsibility for some of the choices they make, even if they make some bad choices. In light of this, I like what Sue Fish, an eminent child psychotherapist, said: 'Two-year-olds must lose the two-year-old battle gracefully. Parents must lose the teenage battle gracefully.' Where this has not been the case, the teenager may be totally right in their perception that, 'Others have the power, not me.' This can be detrimental. They can go into adulthood and then make really bad choices, as they have never had practice at independent thinking, acting and taking responsibility for their decisions in the teenage years. They can continue through life, taking submissive or overcompliant roles in relationships that are more appropriate for a young child. This can lay them open to being abused in teenage partner relationships. It is also vital that there is a shift in the power base at this time, when a vital developmental task is for the teenager to form a clear identity of their own, separate from that of their parents. This is why the rebellious, defiant, disagreeing voice that parents find so trying is often so key to the process of the teenager finding their own voice, opinion, views and sense of self.

Talk about when feeling voiceless is due to a poor sense of self

Teenagers with this issue can feel relieved when they express a sense of not really knowing who they are and understanding that, if you don't know that, it's hard to have a voice or an opinion. It should be explained that this is not their fault. Sometimes teenagers don't know who they are because grown-ups in their life have been too eager to be in charge, to lecture rather than listen, and get over their opinions about the 'right' way of being and doing. It can also happen when parents are preoccupied by demands in their life, and so are unable to provide enough quality, one-to-one time in which they could really listen to what the teenager has to say about things. This is not in any way to blame the parents, but rather for the teenager to stop blaming themselves (eg 'I am just pathetic, I can never seem to be able to say anything or to say what I want or don't want.'). You can explain that your time together now is all about listening, not lecturing. It is an exploring together of who the teenager is, until they feel confident in that themselves, and respectful of who they are.

Talk about fears of failure and fears of success

Sometimes teenagers find it a relief to talk about how they dare not say or initiate something because of fear of failure, or of being shamed or humiliated as they have been in the past. But with others it may be equally important to talk about fears of success; how they might be keeping them small and unnoticed because to feel successful or special or powerful might mean they would be even more exposed, with an even greater risk of being shamed or laughed at.

I'm rubbish

We can find a lot of different ways to express how much we hate ourselves.
(Williamson, 1992)

Objective

For teenagers with low self-esteem, life can all too easily lose its magic, its fascination, its excitement. Each day can be met with dread of yet more failure, feelings of inadequacy, fears of feeling shamed, and feelings of being unacceptable or that there is something fundamentally wrong with you. Also, when a teenager feels that they are worthless it can have a marked wearing-down effect, a draining on their natural resources of energy and enthusiasm. They can believe that anything they do will be worthless – schoolwork, homework, anything they make, say, invent, dream of. As a result they often give up easily or don't even start something new at all. This is in contrast to a child with good self-esteem who will persevere and often triumph in the face of adversity.

Research has shown that self-esteem in the childhood and teenage years is vital for success in the workplace, far more so in fact than academic ability. Leon Feinstein, at the Centre for Economic Performance, assessed data through the 1970 British Cohort Study. Self-esteem was monitored at age 10. He then looked at what these children were earning when they were in their 20s. The data showed that self-esteem and friendships at the age of 10 were very important indicators of high earnings in their 20s, far more than their academic ability (Feinstein, 2000). Many very rich celebrities, like Richard Branson, Alan Sugar and Max Clifford, did poorly at school but, having been enabled to feel very confident about themselves from an early age, became highly successful.

Low self-esteem in the teenage years can also be very worrying and should be taken seriously by the adults in the teenager's life. It can be a major contributory factor in clinical depression. We also know that half of all mental health problems start at the age of 14 (HM Government, 2011). Given that in the UK, on average, every 22 minutes a teenager tries to kill themselves, and that the teenage brain is far more geared for impulsive action than the adult brain, we should be doubly concerned. Sometimes a period on antidepressants is needed for a teenager to be able to function and enjoy life again, ideally in combination with some conversation therapy, which is what this book is all about.

Most importantly, we know that positive self-regard can only be attained relationally (Sunderland, 2006), so this exercise and the development and discussion are designed to help the teenager:
- to consider different ways of seeing and treating themselves
- to feel encouraged and valued by you the practitioner (authentically and appropriately given)
- to find value in themselves
- to be given help to sort out the common confusion of I *feel* worthless, therefore I *am* worthless and replace it with 'People in my life haven't been good at valuing me in the ways I needed them to'
- to understand the concept of negative self-talk.

Instructions for the teenager

When you feel bad about yourself for too much of the time, it can be really important to think about what has made you feel like this and what you can do to stop suffering in this way. It might help to think about it with some pictures. So look at the pictures and captions below. If you sometimes feel like any of the following, please tick the box or colour them in. If none of the pictures say what you feel when you are feeling bad about yourself, draw or write in the empty box.

Development
Exercise: Your life as a film set
Instruction: Draw your life as a film set with you and the main characters in your life (home and school). They are not necessarily the people you want to be in your life; for example, there may be a school bully in there. Then use red to colour in or mark the people who have made you dislike yourself and use green for the people who have made you like yourself. If it's neither, leave these people blank.

Exercise: The negative voices in your head
Instruction: Write down what all the critical voices in your head say. Usually these are things that have been said to you at some time in the past, or they haven't actually been said, but you know that a person has thought it about you. In other words, think about all the negative messages that you have heard or felt from the people in your life: the ones you have just taken in unquestioningly and swallowed whole, so to speak. Write them on a bit of paper. Now tear them up and put them in the bin. We do have control over what we say to ourselves in our heads. Next time you start to say this negative thing to yourself just say, 'Stop. Calm.' Keep doing it. Soon the negative voices will stop.

Discussion
(Pick one or more of these topics to discuss with the teenager, as appropriate.)

Helping teenagers understand the causes of their low self-esteem
When teenagers are not sure what has happened in their life to make them feel like this, it can be useful for them to consider common causes. Let them look at the list and ask any questions they may have:
- Parental depression/post-natal depression. (This means your parent may not have been emotionally available to give you the praise and feeling that you were very special in early infancy and later throughout your childhood.)
- Overtly spoken childhood messages about being of little value. (For example, 'I wish you'd never been born' or 'You're so stupid'.)

- Non-verbal childhood messages about being of little value. It can just be a sense that you were often found to be annoying, irritating, provoked anger or made your parent feel tired.
- Parents too preoccupied with their own troubles to voice enough appreciation, praise, encouragement in your childhood and now teenage years.
- Too much discouragement at home and/or at school and not enough encouragement.
- Parents with very high standards. (As one teenager said, 'I realised that the reason I felt ashamed and inadequate so often was because I failed to live up to the expectations of my parents' voices inside my head.')
- Life experiences when you felt shamed.
- Being bullied by someone at home or at school – a teacher, a sibling.
- Being rejected by a friend or group.

(A note to the practitioner on the link between post-natal depression and low self-esteem in the teenage years:
Research shows that post-natal depression (when the mum didn't get enough help) can affect a teenager's mental health. Sixteen-year-olds whose mum suffered from post-natal depression are four times more likely to suffer from depression at this age (Murray *et al*, 2011). It is important for teenagers with low self-esteem to establish whether or not their mum did suffer from post-natal depression. If they suspect that they did, it will be an important conversation to have with their mum. This can really help, not in any sense of misplaced blame, but in terms of building up a coherent narrative of their personal history. We know that having a coherent narrative about their life is key to teenage mental health.)

Talk about the common muddle with feeling rubbish rather than seeing the lack of warmth and generosity in the people who judge you so negatively
Example
Teenager: 'I am rubbish.'

Adult: 'I disagree. I think it's that grown-ups haven't been good at letting you to know how special you are.' Or,
'I think people haven't done a good job at helping you to know how special you are' (Hughes, 2001). Or,
'Perhaps it's not this but rather that the adults in your life weren't very good at speaking about all your qualities and lovely things about you because they were too busy, worried about something or emotionally preoccupied, or no one had told them lovely things about them in their childhood.'

When teenagers in a peer group are being horrible
You might say, 'Teenagers are hugely affected by whether their friends or group like them. The trouble is that some teenagers are very cruel and so, if you feel rejected, put down or bullied, it is actually that something is wrong with them because they are cruel.'

Talk about the importance of finding anger towards people who have made you feel so bad about yourself, in order to find your self-respect: 'Anger helps us reassert our sense of power and maintain our dignity and self-respect' (Bar-Levav, 1988, p171).

Talk about finding people who believe in you
The best thing is to find people who believe in you and also remember the people in your life who have believed in you and then think about them at least once a day.

Quotations that the teenager may find useful

When people think they're rubbish it's often because people in their lives haven't been good at loving, sometimes because when they were children, no one was good at loving them.
(The author)

We all need love but who can do the loving?
(Mitchell, 1997, quoting Oscar Wilde)

We may choose to grow, to stagnate or to decline and in a world where there is little encouragement to grow, most of us may not do it very much or at all.
(Rowan, 1986, p13)

His love of his mother in the face of rejection at her hands ... is equivalent to discharging his love into an emotional vacuum. By virtue of these experiences of humiliation and shame [the baby/child/teenager] feels reduced to a state of worthlessness, destitution or beggardom.
(Fairbairn, 1940, p113)

The mother, then reveals by the light and expression on her face, the nature of the baby in her mind, which is there to be read by the baby and which forms the basis for his developing self-image from the beginning of life.
(Reid, 1990, p48)

A note about reassurance
If you say to the teenager with low self-esteem, 'But I like you', this can sometimes backfire. Some teenagers will secretly think, 'Well if you like me, that must mean there is something wrong with you' or, 'Praise does not fit with the person I know I am inside'. Or 'He can casually discredit anybody who loves him, for there is evidently something wrong with a person who loves somebody who is unworthy of love' (Watzlawick, 1983). So keep your emphasis on empathy for the pain of low self-esteem and then, if you are going to compliment the teenager, find something really specific instead of a general liking.

Worried

Objective

Due to the huge hormonal changes at this stage of development, a worried child can all too easily become a very anxious teenager. The common causes of this tend to be:

- parents who themselves are anxious
- parents troubled by depression, violent outbursts, alcoholism, financial difficulties, or unprocessed trauma or loss
- parents who were unable to provide the teenager with sufficient emotional regulation during overwhelming emotional states in infancy and childhood
- teenagers parenting their own parents
- unresolved trauma and loss
- mum being stressed in pregnancy (maternal stress during critical periods of foetal brain development, particularly the third trimester, can reprogramme the child's stress response system, in such a way that he or she can develop as a worried personality (Field *et al*, 2002)

So this exercise and discussion are designed to enable teenagers who worry a lot to understand what neurotic anxiety is, how it forms in the first place, what it protects people from, and how to get rid of it. It is also designed to enable teenagers to stand back from their worries for once in order to look at how they might do things differently, and to understand more about what past experiences may be fuelling their anxiety.

Instructions for the teenager

When you find yourself worrying too much in your life, you may find it useful to think about it in terms of what it feels like, how much of your time it takes up, and what you might want to change in order to worry less. It might help to think about it with some pictures. So look at the pictures and captions below. When you worry, if you feel like any of the following, please tick the box or colour them in. If it's not any of these things, draw or write in the empty box what your worry feels like or means to you.

Development
Exercise: Head space

Draw a big head. Draw on the head the amount of time each day you think you take up worrying, and then the amount of space left for:

- fun and laughter
- carefree times
- love
- enjoying life.

Concentrating on things that interest you

Having done this, if you think you spend too much time worrying, the first thing to do is to think about what is fuelling your worries. Very few worries are actually based in reality. In fact, the statistic is that 90 per cent of what we worry about doesn't happen (Jeffers, 2007). Worries tend to be fuelled by a feeling other than worry – for example, anger, fear or feelings about a trauma or loss in your past. Can you think of anything that happened in your past, like a big loss or shock, that you haven't really ever talked to someone about? Is your parent a worrier? Sometimes teenagers are worriers because their parents are worriers.

Another approach to this might be:
If you seem to be always worrying, in the sense that as soon as one worry goes another one comes in to replace it, it often points to the fact that something happened in your past that you have not resolved. To resolve it means talking through the painful things in your past and feeling them again in the presence of someone who can really listen. Once that happens, the pain of whatever

I'm worried that something bad will happen to me

Worried that something bad will happen to the people I love

My worries mean I can never have fun

I'm frightened of losing everything

I'm worried that I'll be found guilty of something

I'm never really able to relax. I've too many worries

When mum & dad wobbles, the whole world wobbles

happened to you gets a lot less or goes away completely. So when people say, 'The past is past – forget it', they don't know that the mind and brain don't function like this. The brain keeps triggering stress hormones, which make us feel anxious until we have talked about and felt the painful past experiences. Once we have talked about them and felt them, then they won't haunt us.

Discussion
(Pick one or more of these topics to discuss with the teenager, as appropriate.)

Talk about what is happening in the brain when we are worrying too much
The brain has natural anti-anxiety chemicals that stop you worrying about things that are very unlikely to ever happen. If a child has parents who are very good at calming and soothing them, and who are calm themselves, these chemicals tend to work really well. This is known as the brain habituating to these chemicals. Some of the main chemicals are called opioids. With optimal activation of opioids in your brain, you feel like this:
You do not feel aggressive or anxious.
You feel calm and psychologically strong.
You have a sense that everything is well in your world, a deep sense of well-being.
You feel safe in the world.
Your immune system works better.
Your stress hormones will drop to the right level.

Pleasurable opioids can be found in the baby's bloodstream from the seventh week of pregnancy.

Parents who are not very calm people themselves, and/or who have not managed to soothe and calm the child, can result in that child growing up to be a teenager whose brain activates levels of stress hormones that are too high. These block the anti-anxiety chemical hormones, making the teenager likely to worry unnecessarily. Too high levels of stress hormones colour perception with a sense of danger and threat. They also block the body and the brain's natural calming chemicals.

It is not too late to change things round and wake up the anti-anxiety chemicals in your brain. You can do this with an adult who is calm and who helps you talk about things. It is great to do this now in your teenage years rather than entering your adult years blighted by painful past experiences that put clear limits on your ability to enjoy life and enjoy carefree times.

Talk about neurotic anxiety and what it is
With neurotic anxiety, the imagination is overactive in a negative way. The imagination can feature a sort of ongoing horror movie, such as feeling convinced that 'they're all dead in a ditch'. This is because worry and anxiety interfere with the perception of reality. So, teenagers suffering in this way are often not really in the present moment, so to speak, but rather are thinking about their regretted past or fearing something bad happening in the future.

Talk about whether their parent needs help
Teenagers can worry about a parent because the parent seems not to be doing life well. Perhaps they are depressed, or drinking too much, very worried about money, unhappy at work, or something else. When this is the case, teenagers can end up parenting their parent; this means worrying about them, soothing and calming them rather than the parent doing that for the teenager. This is a burden that teenagers shouldn't have. It can get in the way of teenagers succeeding at school or enjoying their social life in a carefree fashion. If you think you are parenting your parent, the best thing to do is to ask at school for help for your parent, or go and see your doctor and talk about it. No teenager should have to live this way and there are always grown-ups who can help.

Talk about calming the body down
Yoga, Tai Chi, going for a run or any exercise are all good at calming the brain and body's stress hormones.

Quotations that the teenager might find useful

Worry gives a small thing a big shadow.
(Swedish proverb)

The axe that never falls batters you stupid.
(Murray, 1997)

Ninety per cent of what we worry about never happens.
(Jeffers, 2007)

The reason most people age at such different rates is that our society is full of 'big spenders' who overreact to harmless circumstances as if they were life-or-death matters.
(Waitley, 1985, p192)

Not belonging, feeling on the outside

Alienation carries ... complex loads of discomfort.
(Padel, 1995)

Objective

What we are talking about here often involves a painful lack of warm, validating human connection in the teenager's life. This can be accompanied by feelings of hurt, loneliness and lack of appreciation. Perhaps the teenager has made attempts to connect or get through to significant people in their life, but these have failed, leaving them feeling very alone.

The exercise will be particularly useful for looked-after or adopted teenagers. This, of course, can be an enormous shock to any sense of belonging. Even if the teenager knows it's for the best, because of birth parents not coping or being abusive, it can still feel like an unbearable rejection.

Feelings of alienation with parents

In the teenage years, feelings of alienation from parents are, of course, very common. This is epitomised by the well-known scenario of the parent enquiring, 'How was your day?', to which the response from the teenager is no more than a grunt. There is also the common complaint of, 'They just don't understand me', as the teenager spends hours in their bedroom, perhaps not even appearing for family meals. It is only right that relationships with parents do change at this key developmental stage, as the teenager becomes far more of a separate person in their own right, with a set of opinions, values and ideas of their own. For this reason, many parent–teenager relationships have to be re-established as if from the beginning, the parents adjusting to the person their beloved child is becoming. When a parent fails to adjust, the emotional distancing between parent and teenager can become entrenched, which is damaging for both parties.

Feelings of alienation with peers

When teenagers feel that they don't fit in with their peer group, or are being actively excluded, it can be particularly painful for them. This is because this stage of development is all about moving away from parents and making strong attachments with one's peers. So, if you have distanced from your parents and then you are not accepted by the peer group, what horrible no man's land do you find yourself in? The feelings of alienation can be so awful that it can lead to thoughts of suicide. Furthermore, we know that teenagers can be particularly cruel in terms of bullying tactics, such as non-inclusion and the silent treatment. As Donald Sutherland said, 'If you want to drive somebody mad, isolate them.' This can be doubly painful at this stage of development, because teenagers just hate feeling they are missing out.

Then there is the 'who's in, who's out' based on whether or not you have the latest fashion accessory or the right brand of trainers. As Warren, who was a quiet 15-year-old in a class of particularly loud boys, said, 'The moment I come into the room, it trips the spotlight onto me, as the odd one out. All I want to do is put out the spotlight and go away, sink into the floor or disappear.' Such experience of shame must be addressed, otherwise it can be carried into adulthood, leading to all manner of avoidance, phobic response and social withdrawal.

It is hoped that, through the worksheets, exercises and discussion, the teenager will:
- experience the opposite of alienation, in that they will feel your interest and curiosity in their painful feelings of not belonging and lost connections

- experience the opposite of alienation as they feel your genuine interest in learning who they are, what they feel, what they believe in, and as you validate their experience and empathise
- find hope as a result of your non-judgemental attitude and empathic listening, and from appropriate psychoeducation when hope has been lost – for example, 'If my mum can't understand me, then who can?'

'No one ever quite knows what it feels like to be me', said Art Garfunkel. One-to-one talk time with an empathic, good listening adult can come very close for some teenagers, so that they stop taking peer cruelty personally, are able to understand the wider social picture and have their pain eased by seeing the historical perspective on intolerance of difference and the unbearable pain it has brought to so many people over so many generations all over the world.

Instructions for the teenager

When you feel a sense of not belonging or being on the outside in your life, you may find it useful to think about things in terms of what it is like for you, what has made you feel like this and what you can change. It might help to think about it with some pictures. Have a look at the ones below. If you feel like any of the people in the pictures, please tick the box or colour them in. If it's not any of these things, draw or write in the empty box what you feel inside when you feel like you are on the outside or do not belong.

Development
Exercise: Aloneness and togetherness

What have been some times of best togetherness and worst aloneness in your life? Draw some quick pictures for both (stick people are fine).

Exercise: What's wrong with our relationship?

Think of an important person in your life from whom you feel emotionally distant at the moment. Tick which of the following statements feel true:

☐ They do not feel my pain.

☐ They don't want to know what matters to me.

☐ They are not interested in understanding how I see things.

☐ I worry about having to give up something important in terms of who I am, and what I believe in, in order to get along with them.

☐ I can't really be *me* with them.

Then think of a way that you might be able to tell them any of these things in a way they can hear.

Exercise: From distance to connection

Mark on this continuum where you put the most important people in your life (use their initials).

Painful
distance _____ Lovely
connection

Exercise: When someone tries to connect with you but makes it worse

Have you had times in your life when someone has tried to get through to you, maybe a parent or friend or partner, but they have been emotionally clumsy in some way and so you are left feeling even more alone? It can be hard sometimes to see why an attempt at a connection leads to a failed connection. Discuss why this passage below is a failed connection between a boy and a girl and so in the end the girl walks out.

'Why are you crying?' I asked, rather ineptly.
Annick didn't answer. Her shoulders kept heaving while she cried: was she just sobbing violently, or was she trying to throw my arm off her back? How could you tell? It was time to be sensitive, I thought. I did this by keeping a baffled silence for a bit. However, this became rather boring.

I don't belong

Unwanted

Shut out

A stranger in my own world

On the outside

Pushed out into the cold

Bullied

'Are you crying because I mentioned that girl?' No reply.
'Are you crying because you don't think I love you enough?' No reply. I was stumped.
'Are you crying because you love me?' It was always a possibility, I thought.
Annick walked out at that point.
(Barnes, 1980)

Discussion
(Pick one or more of these topics to discuss with the teenager, as appropriate.)

Talk about the common causes of feeling on the outside or not belonging
When teenagers are not sure what has happened in their life to make them feel like this, it can be useful to give them common contributory factors to see if they relate to any of them. Let them look at this list and ask any questions they may have:
- Parent–teenager misconnections, failed connections or broken connections.
- Feeling like a stranger in their own home.
- Parents not understanding who the teenager really is, their beliefs, passions, opinions, dreams, and so on.
- Parental conditional love (often unspoken) – for example, 'I will love you/approve of you if you are who I want you to be and if you do what I want you to do with your life.'
- Serious communication breakdown with a parent where once there was real closeness.
- Never felt really close to one or both parents, even as a child.
- Feeling like the unfavoured sibling.
- Feeling worthless compared to a clever, outgoing and/or very popular sibling.
- Being in a class or peer group with teenagers none of whom are like you.
- Being bullied.
- Being excluded by a group because of an intolerance of difference – for example, different social class, interest in learning, clothes (eg, not designer label), religion, nationality, temperament (eg, you are quiet while they are all outgoing), and so on.

- They have suffered a major loss – for example, mother died or is ill, father left or couldn't look after them, so they feel they have lost connection with all that is warm, safe and loving in their life.

Talk about feeling alienated from parents
The following quotations could be read out to see if the teenager relates to any of them:

Sammy, aged 15: 'When I am with my dad now, I realise that I have moved away from him so much because I'm my own person, rather than my dad's son. The worst thing is that when I'm with them, I often return to being who they want me to be, think that I am, just to fit in, and then when I leave, I feel empty and hollow, as if I have betrayed myself.'

Billy, aged 17: 'I want a mum like my friends have a mum. Not someone who constantly makes me feel like I am failing.'

Trudy, aged 17: 'In that moment, I suddenly saw my mum as just a woman who worries loads, instead of the all-powerful person she had been to me as a child.'

Polly, aged 19: 'My parents say they love me. I don't know what they love or who they love, but it certainly isn't me as they don't know me.'

Dan, aged 18: 'Mum and I argue a lot and then we don't talk to each other for days, but when that happens I feel like a stranger to myself as well as to her.'

Billy, aged 13: 'Dad and I don't talk anymore.'

Talk about how to improve their relationship with a parent
You can help the teenager to find the words to try to get on better with their parent. For example:

Teenager: 'Mum, it's like we have lost touch with each other. I don't feel as if you know me anymore.' And/or, 'Mum, you seem not to know me and the person I have become.'

Rehearse then what they might do if the parent isn't listening well:

Teenager: 'I don't have a sense that you are understanding what I am trying to tell you.' And/or, 'Will you just listen now and not comment until I have told you I have finished.'

Talk about what it can feel like to be a teenager who feels changed by a powerful life experience and whose parents don't adjust

Teenagers may do something amazing with their newly discovered independence. They may go travelling, become part of a very exciting group or start a new relationship. They change as a result, while their parents and that old familiar home base remain the same. If this is relevant for the teenager you are working with, talk about how sometimes parents find it difficult to adjust to sudden changes in their teenager. They move into a defended critical stance as a result, rather than adopting a healthy, enquiring, curious attitude. As a result there can be a gulf between parent and teenager and the things they can talk about and share. The teenager must decide how much they are motivated to heal the rift at this moment in time. If they are motivated, they may need help to find the words to open up the conversation about it with their parents.

Talk about common coping strategies when teenagers feel alienated, and what it can cost in the long term

> *There is something inherently noxious in the process of stepping back too far from life.*
> (Yalom, 1980, p478)

One common coping strategy for the teenager who feels alienated or not belonging at home and/or with peers is to take refuge in technology – the internet, internet chat rooms, video games. They might also move into a defensive position of 'Who needs people anyway?' and 'I am better off on my own.' But in giving up on human connection in this way, a teenager often gives up any real connection with life too. So distancing from people means distancing from life. We know this can lead to a deep sense of emptiness, meaningless and depression at some point. This is because, like it or not, we are genetically programmed to need relationships with people, and not just cyberspace relationships. Discuss this with the teenager who is using these social withdrawal strategies. Also consider whether the teenager is aware of any ambivalence, for instance, 'I always want to be on the outside, at the same time as feeling the pain of it.' Or, 'When I am with other people I long for time on my own. When I am on my own I feel lonely.'

Talk about bullying that means you are left out, excluded or not talked to

For some it started in primary school: 'We don't want to play with you. Go home. You are dirty and smelly', and so on. Teenagers need to know that children and teenagers are often particularly cruel because their social brains have not yet properly developed. So remind them, 'This too shall pass'. On reaching adulthood many people are far nicer and far less cruel than teenagers. This is because the emotional and socially intelligent parts of the brain mature further. The key message is, 'You will find people like you and who appreciate you. Give up ever trying to get accepted by people who are cruel. Find the open-door people who see the lovely things about you.'

Talk about being on the outside of a group due to feelings of not being good enough to belong

This is an important discussion point if you think that the teenager's low self-esteem is fuelling their feeling of being on the outside. They may be alienating themselves from being a part of a group because they don't feel special enough to belong. They put themselves on the outside because that is where they imagine the group wants them to be. Here are some of the painful

statements made by teenagers whose low self-esteem led to them excluding themselves. You may decide to read these out to the teenager you are working with:
- 'They are all thinking I shouldn't be here.'
- 'They belong and I don't. I'm a misfit.'
- 'I'm not good enough. I'll never be good enough to be part of their group, for them to want me to be part of their group.'
- 'Whatever I do, I never do that well, so they won't accept me.'
- 'They all want me to leave and not to come back.'
- 'There's no point me saying anything because I have nothing worthwhile to say'.

Teenagers who feel like this can be relieved to know that their perception is likely to be coloured by childhood experiences. Ask the teenager whether in their family they did not feel special enough. The feeling of not being significant or powerful enough to make an impact, of not having anything worthwhile to say in the group, can come from a childhood experience of being with older, more verbal, exciting, capable siblings or with a powerful parent who did not sufficiently encourage the child's sense of potency.

Talk about conversations that alienate and conversations that connect
A conversation that connects always has the following four factors:
1 I ask you questions about you, your feelings, your life.
2 You ask me questions about me, my feelings, my life.
3 I offer something personal about me.
4 You offer something personal about you.

A conversation that is empty and alienating will be missing one or more of the factors above.

Quotations the teenager may find useful

Sarah felt that her mother never saw her as she was; neither found an echo in the other ... The mother and child could not 'live an experience together'.
(Balint, 1993)

There are actually families in which nobody is present. The fact of living under the same roof is the only link between its members.
(Odier, 1956)

Trying not to catch each other's eyes because we might realise we were strangers.
(TS Eliot in the film *Tom and Viv*)

She had an instantaneous vision of herself as someone forever outside, forever looking in through glass at a bright human world, which had no place for her.
(White, 1979)

We cannot bear connection ... We must break away, and be isolate. We call that being freed, being individual. Beyond a certain point ... it is suicide.
(DH Lawrence, 1972)

The space between two people, the emotional distance, could be a space of miles and miles and miles. You might as well be on the moon.
(Pinter, quoted in Gussow, 1994)

The table was a large one, but the three were all crowded together at one corner of it: 'No room! No room!' they cried out when they saw Alice coming.
(Carroll, 1994)

Communication itself between people is so frightening that rather than do that, there is a ... continual talking about other things, rather than what is at the root of their relationship.
(Pinter, quoted in Esslin, 1982)

The tension of connectedness and separateness is present from the moment of conception.
(Polster and Polster, 1973)

Emma, aged 16: *I tried so hard to look as if I wasn't lonely. I tried so hard that probably everybody knew I was pretending.*

Lots of people complain that they never meet people or get invited out anywhere, and there they sit, wondering why they are so alone. They are alone because they're not making an effort to reach out to other people; instead, they are hoping and praying that someone will reach out to them.
(Jeffers, 1992, pp39–40)

The people I miss/the people I've lost

Objective

One in two cohabiting parents split up before the child's fifth birthday (Centre for Social Justice, 2011).

One in two children will experience family breakdown before the age of 16 (Centre for Social Justice, 2011).

Every 22 minutes the mother or father of someone under 16 dies (Winston's Wish, 2011).

Approximately two children under the age of 16 are bereaved of a parent every hour of every day in the UK (Winston's Wish, 2011).

Around 53 children and young people are bereaved of a mother or father every day (Winston's Wish, 2011).

Over 24,000 children are bereaved of a parent each year in Britain (Winston's Wish, 2011).

Every 22 minutes a teenager tries to kill themselves (Institute for Public Policy Research, 2006b).

Each year there are around 19,000 suicide attempts by UK teenagers while more than 2 million children attend GP's surgeries with some kind of psychological or emotional problem (Depression Alliance, 2011).

Suicide is the number one cause of death for 18 to 24-year-old males (Marr and Field, 2001).

Some 40,000 children and young people in the UK take antidepressants. The National Institute for Health and Clinical Excellence says that general practitioners should offer children psychological talking therapies instead of prescribing medications (National Institute for Health and Clinical Excellence, 2005).

Seventy-five per cent of men in prison have suffered a broken attachment in childhood (National Association of Crime Reduction, 2012).

It is vital that teenagers know about the pain of loss, its inevitability, and how to suffer well. So many adults have never learned to suffer well, and as a result they live a blighted adult life often using alcohol or another substance to dull the pain. Others get stuck in it, like Miss Havisham in *Great Expectations*, and are then not able to thrive or reach their potential. As the statistics show, at least half of all teenagers will suffer major loss at home by the time they reach their teenage years. Then add to this the common experience of short-lived teenage partner relationships and how so many teenagers get rejected in these years – moving from very, very happy to very, very hurt. It is frankly immoral that we don't empower them to know how to grieve well and to the point of resolution.

As part of the art of grieving, teenagers need to know about what is happening in the brain when we lose someone we love or lose their love. As a famous neuroscientist says, 'We are plunged into a terrible pain. Pain of loss is actually as painful as physical pain. This is because the pain of missing someone activates the pain centres in the brain. So the language of loss is the language of pain' (Panksepp, 1998). Panksepp also makes the connection that losing someone you deeply love is as painful as coming off heroin. What happens in both is that opioids (the chemicals that make us feel all is well in the world) are deactivated and re-uptaken in the brain. This can lead to mood swings, aggression, problems with sleep, crying, agitation, then withdrawal and lethargy. It really helps to know this when we consider teenagers who seem depressed, lethargic, aggressive at school and unable to focus on learning.

So this worksheet, accompanying exercises and discussion are designed to support the teenager in the following ways:
- To feel that you really understand the enormity of their loss.
- To normalise the grieving process and the feelings involved.
- To help them realise that the pain they are feeling is a natural response to loss and that indeed it can hurt so much.
- To enable the teenager to understand the importance of grieving and to learn what is vital in the art of grieving.
- To understand that 'It is not possible to properly grieve without the presence of another (Bowlby, 1978).
- To feel relief from entering the mourning process in the presence of a compassionate, understanding adult.
- To understand the common cost of not grieving and bottling up feelings instead.

Instructions for the teenager
When you are in pain because of people in your life that you miss, you may find it useful to think about things in terms of what it is like for you, what has made you feel like this and what you can change. It might help to think about it with some pictures. Have a look at the ones below. If you feel like any of the people in the pictures, please tick the box or colour them in. If it's not any of these things, draw or write in the empty box what you feel inside when you miss someone very much indeed.

Development
Exercise: The Museum of Loss
You may want to do this exercise in addition to the main one.

Instructions for the teenager
Think of all the people and things you have lost in your life. Sometimes losing a special toy in childhood can be very painful. Think also of lost opportunities, and lost places, any form of loss. Write them on the exhibit stands in the Museum of Loss. When you look at them all together what do they make you feel? Which of the losses do you still feel pain about today and which do you feel you have come to terms with?

Discussion
(Pick one or more of these topics to discuss with the teenager, as appropriate.)

When teenagers are not sure what has happened in their life to make them feel like this, it can be useful to give them common contributory factors to see if they relate to any of them. Let them look at the list and ask any questions they may have:
- Parent leaves or dies.
- Rejected by boyfriend, girlfriend or good friend.
- Parents separate or divorce.
- Moving schools.
- Losing a parent to depression or other mental illness, anxiety about finance, drugs or drink.
- A feeling of having lost their parent to a new partner or to a sibling or the new baby.
- A sense that their parent offers them on-off love or conditional love (conditional on them being someone their parent wants them to be or doing what their parent wants them to do).
- Feeling let down by a parent who says they will visit but doesn't.

Talk about the importance of reminiscence
Talk to the teenager about the fact that, even if they have lost the person they love, or lost their love, no one can ever take away the memories of the lovely times they had together. It is important to bring these to mind whenever you want. They can keep warming them with expansive life-energising feelings.

Like my world ended that day

I'm not going to let people in any more

There is no point getting close to anyone because they just leave

I spend so much time missing them

Being in a world with no warm faces in it

Being in a world where it's always winter

Talk about the pain for a teenager of being rejected by a girlfriend or boyfriend

Talk about the fact that, although this is common, it is often so painful, as many teenagers end relationships in a way that is crass and deeply hurtful. This is because their social and emotional brain is still developing. Hence the well-known text message in teenage relationships, 'You are so dumped'. It is important that teenagers don't mistake someone's lack of skills and knowledge about how to develop fulfilling intimate relationships with their own lovability.

Talk about how to get help with the pain of loss so you dare to love again

Talk to the teenager about the statement, 'Better to have loved and lost than never to have loved at all.' Explain that when some people get hurt, they dare not love again, which is a tragic waste in terms of the possibility of leading a deeply fulfilling life., They think, 'If I love, it will happen all over again, I'll feel that pain all over again, so I will not love again.' Such people often move into a personal crisis at some point where they find life meaningless. Indeed, without a loving relationship too much is missing from anyone's life. This is not a value judgement, but rather based on the scientific fact that we are all genetically programmed to need strong attachments with others. If we fight this, we will at some point become very unhappy.

Talk about the allure of the bad deal relationship

Some teenagers are drawn, as indeed are some adults, to what others can clearly see are bad deal relationships, or what is sometimes known as the 'the exciting-rejecting relationship'. What happens is that the partner is often found to be very exciting to start with, but then becomes either increasingly neglectful or abusive. Often, rarities are mistaken for pearls. So just because on night x, their partner was lovely and appreciative, they stay in the relationship waiting for him to be like that again. The waiting can involve days, weeks or months of abuse and neglect. They do not realise that they could get pearls, metaphorically speaking, in a relationship every day, and by this time

they are hooked, so end up, 'Wasting love on an unworthy object' (Wilde, 1949).

Teenagers who can relate to this often need the vital knowledge that the people who are particularly vulnerable to this are those who experienced their relationship with their parents as on-off. So they may have been locked in a life of yearning for that parent, just as now they are doing the same with their boyfriend or girlfriend. Others who are vulnerable have also just received 'crumbs' from their parents, but this has kept them hooked. If a teenager can make the link that they are repeating their troubled past, it is often enough for them to stop abusing themselves now in terms of staying in a bad deal relationship with the common misconception that 'my love will heal him'.

Talk about the common shift from the pain of grief to anger or violence

Teenagers all too easily think they are mad or bad. They do so because no one has given them the facts about how painful life experience, such as loss of a loved one or loss of their love, can affect brain, body and perception on an ongoing basis. As stated, we know that animals that are accustomed to high level of opioids (close relationships) then suffer a withdrawal of those opioids in their brain when they lose that loved one, and become very nasty with each other. This is because, when there is a withdrawal of opioids in the brain, opponent forces are activated – namely, high levels of acetycholine. This can make teenagers very angry, hostile and irritated. This gives the biochemical understanding for cases where grieving children and teenagers are thrown out of school. They are doing fine until the loss and then their behaviour becomes unacceptably violent. But no one asked about whether they have experienced a loss. The only way to bring acetycholine down to base rate is to grieve. Usually this means grieving in the presence of another, as the feelings are far too strong to go it alone The comfort of grief will release opioids and oxytocin in the brain – these block the toxic chemistry of acetycholine. This is why it is vital for teenagers who are suffering from loss to receive comfort.

Example

Henry is 14 years old. His mother took her own life after a bout of deep depression. Henry, who had always functioned really well at school, started to get very aggressive and his schoolwork when downhill. Teachers were talking about expulsion. Luckily he was referred to the school counsellor. Henry really liked the counsellor and could accept her comfort. As a result, the high levels of acetycholine in his brain returned to base rate, and Henry's behaviour was no longer aggressive. Some teenagers who are expelled as a result of traumatic loss are not as lucky as Henry and there is no such counsellor available for them.

Talking about loss with teenagers in the care system

It is important to take time to imagine the terrible catalogue of losses that so many teenagers in care have experienced.

Imagine this: You are separated from everyone you love; you are not sure when you will see them again; you suffer the loss of parents, school friends, familiar surroundings, home, pets, siblings – often over and over again. Inevitably, so much of your time is taken up in thinking about the people you don't see any more. You live in fear of moving on again and again, with the anticipation of more and more loss. It is not surprising that the statistics are as follows:

- Over 60,000 children in care in the UK.
- Only 6 per cent of care leavers in the UK enter higher education.
- Children in care are four to five times more likely to have mental health issues contributing to poor educational attainment, unemployment and criminality among care leavers.
- Over 20 per cent of female teenagers who leave (aged 16–19) become mothers within a year, compared to just 5 per cent of the general population.
- A third of homeless people were formerly in care.
- Children who have been in care account for nearly half of the under-21-year-olds in contact with the criminal justice system.
- Nearly a quarter of the adult prison population has been in care.

- Children in care and care leavers account for less than 1 per cent of the total population.

(*Couldn't Care Less: Children In Care Report,* Centre for Social Justice, 2008)

It really doesn't have to be this way, but to prevent it all teenagers must be allocated a counsellor or therapist who is very skilled in enabling them to grieve all that loss. All too often they meet with professionals who just fail to imagine the unbearable misery of having lost several mums, endured endless attachment ruptures and suffered awful neglect and abuse along the way.

Quotations the teenager may find useful

If there's no time for grief, there's no time for soul.
(James Hillman, 2006)

Man, when he does not grieve, hardly exists.
(Porchia, 2003)

Give sorrow words; the grief that does not speak, Whispers the o'er-fraught heart and bids it break.
(*Macbeth*, 5.1.5)

The sorrow which has no vent in tears make[s] other organs weep.
(Maudsley, 1918)

For some, a terrible experience of fear or loss seems to block off the horizon permanently; others manage to look past it.
(Hauser et al, 2006)

Longing for things that will never be, can obscure the things that are.
(Anon)

When you are sorrowful look again in your heart, and you shall see that in truth you are weeping for that which has been your delight.
(Gibran, 1991)

Family stuff

There are about 175,000 young carers in the UK who provide care or support to a family member who is disabled, physically or mentally ill, or has a substance misuse problem.
(Barnardo's, 2011)

Objective

Let's face it, even the best families can be difficult at times, but even more so when parents are emotionally or physically unwell. If something is wrong with Mum or Dad, it can be extremely anxiety provoking for the teenager because parents are still so important in the teenager's world. This is particularly the case when parents are mentally unwell, as often the teenager doesn't understand it. Physical disability is often far clearer. So, if a parent's emotional energy is chaotic or disturbing in some way, the world for the teenager can also feel chaotic or mad. They may also worry about their own sanity at times.

Some teenagers have lived for years with a parent who is emotionally and/or physically unwell..With the former, the parent may suffer from depression, anxiety or problems with anger. They may have an addiction problem or may have never properly grieved a traumatic loss. Others may be letting themselves be abused by a partner or spouse. Others suffered troubled childhoods themselves, so find it very difficult to parent. Consequently, there is a very chaotic family atmosphere with masses of negative emotion in the house, and very high stress levels.

As a result, the teenager may never have had the opportunity to merge with a parent's psychological strength and calmness until it has become their own strength and calmness, and so now they have what is termed an overburdened self (Kohut and Wolf, 1978, p419). This means that not only are they having to

manage and attempt to regulate their own feelings, they are also trying to manage the stress of their parent's emotions. This can, in turn, lead to them developing emotional problems in their own right.

Then there are the feelings of impotence when many teenagers in this position try in some way to heal their broken parents. The well-being of their troubled parent can become the focus of their life. They may be unable to focus on schoolwork as they are so worried about their parent. In some cases, school refusal is about wanting to stay at home because they are too anxious about what will happen to their mum or dad if they are not there to look after them: 'I used to stay off tae make sure my Ma did nae get drugs and all that ... 'cause I hate it ... I'd follow her and not let her doe it ... like I would make sure she stayed in the house with me' (Centre for Social Justice, 2011).

In light of the above, it is no wonder that the recent interim policy briefing, *Mental Health: Poverty, Ethnicity and Family Breakdown* (Centre for Social Justice, 2011), advocates a call for treatment to be more focused on helping the whole family unit as a way of preventing mental illness among children and teenagers.

So these exercises and discussion points are designed to provide information and psychology for the teenager to support them with this major infliction. It is hoped that the teenager feels empowered with a vital knowledge base and some practical ways forward.

Instructions for the teenager

When you feel that family stuff is getting you down you may find it useful to think about things in terms of what it is like for you, what has made you feel like this and what you can change. It might help to think about things with some pictures instead of just with words. Have a look at the pictures below. If you feel your life or concerns are like any of the pictures, please tick the box or colour them in. If it's not any of these things, draw or write in the empty box what you feel inside when you think about the difficult family stuff in your life.

Development
Exercise:
The following unfinished sentences can be particularly helpful for some teenagers. They can either practise saying them without the parent present or when the parent is present. If they do the latter, the parent must be asked just to listen and not respond until you ask them to. They should then be given the instruction of just to summarise what the teenager has said.

Mum, when you get sad I feel ...
Mum, when you get angry I feel ...
Mum, when you get scared I feel ...
Mum, when you need me to look after you I feel ...
Mum, when you ask me to listen to your problems I feel ...
Mum, what I would love to do with you is ...
Mum, I wish our relationship would change so that I felt like ...

Discussion
(Pick one or more of these topics to discuss with the teenager, as appropriate.)

Talk about the concept of parenting your parent
If a teenager is parenting their parent, they need to have this named, empathised with and talked about. They will need your help to consider the complexity of this with regard to fairness and reconciling two very different sets of needs – those of the teenager and those of the parent. They will need you to acknowledge that it can be very painful seeing a parent in physical or emotional pain and feeling that you can't do anything about it. They need to know that many teenagers never suffer in this way and are free to get on with their own lives and development, as they have parents who are clearly in the parenting role. They will also need to be given information about how to get help for the troubled parent instead of parenting the parent themselves. They need to know that children and teenagers often feel a huge relief when an adult takes over and looks after their parent, which is how it should be.

Talk about how to confront the parent
This could be by saying something like this:
'It feels as if you are using me as your counsellor.' Or, 'I am aware how unhappy you are for much/some of the time.' Or, 'I see how much pain you are in.'
Then:
'I feel impotent and useless in being able to help. I also find your pain very painful too and it takes up a great deal of my thought time. So I am asking you to consider getting professional help, by talking to the doctor about what you are going through. If you do that it would be a great gift for me, as I would feel free then to get on with my own life rather than spending so much time worrying about yours.'

If the teenager feels it is too much to ask this of the parent straight out, they might like to write this or something equivalent in a letter.

Talk about drugs or alcohol
Talk about how, with a parent addicted to drugs or alcohol, it is common to feel less important to them than their drugs or alcohol, but that this should never be taken personally because it isn't personal. The teenager can be helped by having the concept of emotional unavailability explained to them. This means that the parent is physically present but emotionally absent. The teenager can feel literally cast aside and secondary in importance, as expressed so well in the following statement: 'While she was alone in the light of the kitchen, I saw her drink her white wine and I wanted to be the wine, to do her some good, to make her happy, to attract her attention' (Cardinal, 1993, p68).

Talk about any misplaced responsibility
Correct any confusions over unwell people in the family – for example, 'Mum would be happy if it weren't for me.'

I've a mum who got broken and didn't get mended

I'm trying to mend mum/Dad but never managing

Our family can't seem to save each other

I'm trying so hard to make mum/dad happy again

Full of silent screams at having to watch stuff

Stuff at home is doing my head in

I hate my brother/sister

Like a person in a crazy film

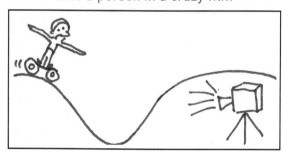

There is no one to make the hurting stop

Mum/dad don't want to be with me much

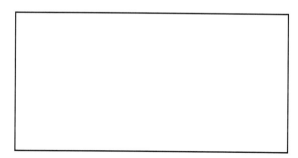

Talk about how important it is to get reparenting from other adults
Discuss how, because their own parents were unable to parent them adequately, reparenting from other adults as they go through life can make a huge difference. They can look to other adults to do some reparenting for them, to offer them the comfort, soothing and listening that their parent can't give them right now. Just bottling things up brings the risk of unhappiness and depression.

Quotations the teenager may find useful

He imagined wiping away his mother's black moods and sullen withdrawals. Once and for all he would restore her world, which he was forever being told, with a thousand cues, raised eyebrows, and turned-down corners of a mouth, had collapsed because of something he had done or failed to do.
(Stolorow *et al*, 1987)

While she was alone in the light of the kitchen, I saw her drink her white wine and I wanted to be the wine, to do her some good, to make her happy, to attract her attention.
(Cardinal, 1993, p68)

There are actually families in which nobody is present. The fact of living under the same roof is the only link between its members.
(Odier, 1956, p261)

The [teenager's mind] may be infected by the fears which the mother refuses to recognise as her own.
(Wickes, 1988)

Mum and dad split up

Objective

One in two children will see their parents split by the age of 16 (The Bristol Community Family Trust, 2006, and the Centre for Social Justice, 2011).

For every three weddings there are now two divorces, and one in four children will experience stress due to family breakdown (Centre for Social Justice, 2011).

The taxpayer is spending at least £20bn a year trying to repair the damage caused by family breakdown (Centre for Social Justice, 2011).

The statistics here are shocking, and as one in two teenagers will be adversely affected by family breakdown, it is vital that teenagers are helped with their feelings so that they don't have to go on to fail at school or suffer from mental health problems, low self-esteem or drug or alcohol problems (as shown below). In fact, research suggests that parental death is less damaging than parental separation and divorce. The former does not carry the same risks of poorer educational attainment, lower socio-economic status, poor mental health and long-term risk of substance abuse as separation and divorce (Kiernan, 1997). The problem is that, with separation and divorce, the teenager is in need of the best possible parenting at the time when parents may be least able to give it to them. In fact, research shows that it is the combination of hostility and detachment in parental communication that is the most damaging for the children and teenagers involved (Centre for Social Justice, 2011). Others see their parents breaking down, or falling into depression or panicked, desperate behaviour, which can be frightening for the teenager. All of this leaves the teenager feeling fearful, unsafe and emotionally dysregulated.

Some, like little children, cling to the hope of reunion. Others rush into partner relationships just as a way (often out of conscious awareness) of running away from the family situation. Many teenagers are not helped to work through the grief, guilt, anger, resentment and abandonment they are left feeling after their parents have separated or divorced. Some are pulled into taking sides and begin to place blame. Others are starting to develop more sophisticated thinking capacities, and so can see both sides when perhaps their parents are failing to do so. Hence professionals must support these teenagers with effective interventions. However, the statistics below clearly show that at present, we are failing to do so:

- After parental separation or divorce, children and teenagers:
  - are 75 per cent more likely to fail at school
  - are 70 per cent more likely to become a drug addict
  - are 50 per cent more likely to have alcohol problems (Centre for Social Justice, 2007)
  - are 50 per cent more likely have low self-esteem
  - are 50 per cent more likely to experience poor peer relationships, have behavioural difficulties or suffer from anxiety or depression (Centre for Social Justice, 2011)
  - have increased risk of behavioural problems, bedwetting, withdrawn behaviour, aggression, delinquency or antisocial behaviour
  - show higher levels of smoking, drinking and other drug use
  - are more likely to lack qualifications, be on benefits and suffer from depression (The National Child Development Study, 1970).
- Seventy-five per cent of children and young people who have experienced parental separation or divorce shift from secure to insecure attached (Murray, 2008).
- Twenty-five per cent of children watch parents screaming and shouting at each other (Rodgers and Pryor, 1998)

- Second marriages are twice as likely to break down as first marriages, so some teenagers in stepfamilies are just waiting to experience another family breakdown with another set of losses (Centre for Social Justice, 2011).
- Severe depression is three times higher among women and nine times higher among men who have been separated or divorced, compared with stably married and single people (Wade and Pevalin, 2004).

But won't PSHE in schools help?

PSHE (personal, social and health education) in its current form, with its emphasis on 'managing emotions', will not be sufficient to alleviate the negative affects of family breakdown for the teenager involved. A general exploration of anger or grief will not offer these teenagers the profound level of conversation they need to be able to heal. The pain is often far too strong and wide reaching. For the pain and shock of living with ongoing marital conflict and/or separation and divorce, a cognitive approach to healing, which activates cortical functions, simply doesn't work. This is because such pain is subcortical (Damasio, 2000). Thus a very different sort of intervention is required. Schools would need to invest in some form of intense, small-group support for these teenagers. In this way, schools could provide a 'family issues' group where pupils could discuss their feelings about family breakdown more freely in a small, safe group with a trained adult leader. Exercises such as those offered here would be a good starting place.

These exercises, development and discussion are designed so that teenagers can start to process their painful feelings about separation and divorce, knowing that you appreciate just how difficult it is to deal with all the mixed emotions – for many, including being torn between two parents – and the complexity of associated feelings.

Instructions for the teenager

For many teenagers, parental separation and divorce means major adjustment to a very different life and lifestyle, and with that can come all sorts of painful losses. Sometimes the remaining parent is struggling with half the income, so the teenager has to make lots of sacrifices: no more expensive fashionable clothes or expensive outings, for example. Or the remaining parent can't afford the tennis club any more or that Friday night ritual of a special meal out. Perhaps the teenager also feels they have lost a loving, warm, playful parent as that parent is now repeatedly angry or depressed. Sometimes the painful loss is a change to the teenager's home as they know it – for example, that chair isn't there any more or those plates you liked so much are gone because they belonged to Dad, or photos of Dad above the fireplace aren't there anymore. And, in addition to all this, there are stepfamilies and second marriages. For many teenagers this means just waiting for another family breakdown with another set of losses. It is all these losses that can make parental separation and divorce so very painful. In order that your parents splitting up doesn't affect you in the long term in a way that makes life difficult for you, it is very important that you talk about those losses now rather than carry them with you as emotional baggage into your adulthood. So look at the pictures below. Tick or mark in some way any of the losses you have experienced from your parents splitting up. Then put a number from 1 to 10 by each of the ones you have ticked, with 1 being painful but manageable and 10 very painful. In the three empty spaces draw or write other losses if they are not mentioned here.

Development
Exercise: Full of feelings

Look at this list of feelings on the next page. These are feelings often felt by teenagers who have experienced parental separation and divorce. Tick the ones you feel. Then grade them from 1 to 10, with 1 being manageable and 10 very painful.

The feeling	Tick if yes	The pain level (1–10)
No one understands what I am going through		
I'm living with split loyalties		
Shock: I had no idea that they were going to split up		
Having to watch Mum/Dad battling with their pain		
It's my fault they split up		
Like I've been abandoned by Mum/Dad/both of them		
I feel responsible		
Missing the parent who has moved out		
Like I've lost everything good in my life		
Like my house is no longer my home		
I used to talk to Mum/Dad about that but they're not here any more		
Lost so much 'just us' time with Mum/Dad		
Lost Mum/Dad to their new partner		
Nothing feels safe any more		
Lost my sense of basic trust		
The family photos feel like a lie/a con		

The feeling	Tick if yes	The pain level (1–10)
I'm not sure who I am any more		
Sick to death of all the fighting		
Angry with him/her/them		
Angry no one consulted me		
A real relief it's over		
I resent being used as a messenger between parents		
Hate it when Mum/Dad cries/loses it		
I don't care		
Caught in my parents' crossfire		
Worrying about Mum/Dad being all on their own now		
Who can I trust now?		
Who am I in this family now?		
Hating my stepfamily		
Not enough in common with my stepfamily		
Just waiting for the next catastrophe/the next break-up		

Home isn't the same any more

Lost family rituals 'we used to do that together'

Lost my mum/dad to her/his pain

Lost too much time with Mum/Dad

Lost my sense of belonging

Lost my sense of trust

Lost so many good things in my life

Exercise: Before, during and after it happened

Make a sandplay picture or drawing (*see* page 42 for an explanation of sandplay). Divide the sandbox or piece of paper into three. On one side, make an image of what life was like before your parents split up. In the middle, make an image of what it was like during them splitting up. On the other side, make an image of what it feels like now they have split up. Stand back now and look at your three images.

- What are you particularly aware of?
- What did you do well regarding this big life challenge?
- What do you wish you had done differently?

Now draw an image of what you would like your life to be like in one year's time and five years' time.

Discussion
(Pick one or more of these topics to discuss with the teenager, as appropriate.)

Talk about the research

Talk about the research that shows that it's not the separation or divorce per se that causes such fallout for the teenager in terms of emotional problems, rather it is the conflict in the family home. Discuss with the teenager the research (Hall, 2007) that shows that the ability of the parents to manage and process their own distress directly impacts on teenagers. Ask them to think about that in terms of their own parents. Ask them to think of other adults they know who can help them. Also, tell them that it can really help the healing process if you talk to other teenagers whose parents have also split up.

Talk about how vital it is to talk about the feelings

Without scaring them, we do need to find a way to let them know that research shows that, when teenagers bottle up their feelings about parents splitting up, it can have a bad effect on mental health, self-esteem, schooling and employment prospects.

Quotations the teenager may find useful

Ben, aged 14: 'I just wanted the arguing to stop, not for Mum and Dad to get divorced.'

Billy, aged 13: 'I knew Mum was miserable but mothers should put their children first.'

Judy, aged 12: 'How come my friend's parents aren't splitting up?'

Sophie, aged 14: 'When Mum keeps crying I hate it – I thought parents were supposed to be the big strong one – now I am having to be that for her.'

Toby, aged 14: 'If they can stop loving each other ... will they stop loving me?'

Some adults looking back on the times their parents split up: 'If only someone had helped us as children. No one talked to us about it.'

Tina, aged 17: 'I feel I have to look after Mum now after Dad left her. I can't cry because I have to be there for her when she cries. Yes, I guess I resent that. Who's there for me?'

Tom, aged 16: 'Just when I should be thinking of moving out, my Mum is so depressed she needs me. I resent it.'

Nag, nag, nag

Teenagers who are repeatedly exposed to negative ... interactions with their parents are likely ... to evaluate their own performance though a harsh, negative lens similar to that of their parents.
(Deblinger and Runyan, 2005)

Objective
If a teenager reports persistent nagging from parents, or any other adult for that matter, for example, a teacher, it is worrying as this is the time when the teenager is forming a separate identity. So all that negativity can too easily become internalised. This then becomes the teenager's negative self-critic resulting in negative self-talk. This in turn can lead to depression.

Sometimes parents get into a negative lock with their teenage children and, before they know it, they are nagging, criticising and issuing commands for much of their conversation time. This leads to a miserable household for both parent and teenager. Some parents were really good at praising their teenagers when they were children but now at this stage of development they just don't do so. It is as if they believe that praise, approval and encouragement don't seem to matter so much for teenagers. It is no surprise that such teenagers all too often don't want to come out of their bedrooms, share family meals or spend much time at home. For some teenagers, they may have no idea that life with their parent could be any different from this. They just feel low for a lot of the time, with poor self-esteem.

So this exercise, development and discussion are designed to empower the teenager with a heightened working knowledge of negative and positive human transactions. The underlying theory is from a field of psychology called transactional analysis. It is hoped that, as a result, the teenager will be more aware of a culture of negative parent–teenager transactions. From this more informed position, it is hoped that they will be more able to confront their parent or negotiate a better way of being together. They can ask for more encouragement and praise and less nagging. Throughout this exploration, the teenager may need you to empathise with the pain of the discouragement they have received in the past.

Instructions for the teenager
When you feel that you are on the receiving end of 'nag, nag, nag' at home and/or at you school, you may find it useful to think about things in terms of what it is like for you, and what you can change. It might help to think about it with some pictures instead of just words. Have a look at the pictures below. If you feel like any of the people in the pictures please tick the box or colour them in. If it's not any of these things, draw or write in the empty box what you feel inside when you feel nagged at or repeatedly criticised.

Development
Exercise: Saying it as it is
The following exercise is good to use when a teenager wants to confront a parent and find a different way of being together but doesn't want to do this on their own. It is designed to ease communication and to facilitate a deeper and more authentic level of connection between parent and teenager. But only do this exercise if you know the parent will be appropriate in their answers, provide the teenager with a good relational experience over all, and not burden the teenager with their own worries, anxieties or a barrage of unspoken resentments, anger, lectures on behaviour, and so on. You may speak to the parent before the session, to ensure they know what is expected of them, and to establish the necessary boundaries.

Instructions (to both parent and teenager): I'll give you both some unfinished sentences. I will ask A (teenager) to finish the sentences first. You can say your answer, or do a super-quick drawing for your answer, or a combination of both. If you don't want to finish one of the sentences you can just say 'pass'. B (parent) should just listen to what A says without speaking. At the end of the list I will give B some unfinished sentences to help you to respond to what A has said. Then we will begin again, this time with B finishing the sentences.

Here are A's (the teenager's) sentences:
- I like it when you ...
- I don't like it when you ...
- I love it when you ...
- I like it when together we ...
- I wish together we could ...
- I want you to know that ...
- I wish you knew that ...
- It feels like you don't understand that ...
- I am frightened of you when you ... (Don't give this sentence to a parent to answer as it can burden and worry the teenager.)
- I feel angry with you when ...
- I feel good when you ...
- I feel like rubbish when you ...
- I feel sad when you ...
- I feel sad that we never seem to do ... any more.
- If I had three wishes for you they would be ...
- If I had three wishes for me they would be ...
- If I had three wishes for us they would be ...
- One of my best times with you was ... (Good to finish on a positive note.)

B's chance to respond:
- I was surprised when you said ...
- I didn't know that you felt ...
- I was sorry to hear that ...

- I feel hurt that ...
- Thank you for letting me know that ...
- I am delighted to hear that you ...
- I agree with you when you said that ...
- I am really thinking about what you said about ...

As practitioner, it will be important for you to comment on the 'big feelings' in the session after both teenager and parent have finished the exercise, being most careful not to take sides. It may also be appropriate, after you have done this, to ask both people if you have failed to comment on something that was very important to either of them. It is also good to ask them before the end of the session if they want to say anything to each other, draw anything for each other or do anything with each other as a way of finishing. People often do amazing things at the eleventh hour. But don't ask this question if doing so would open up more pain that there isn't time to work through. Keep using the unfinished sentence structure right to the end of the session if you feel the two people need a structure to keep them interacting with each other positively, not negatively.

Discussion
Discuss with the teenager what they can do and their options
1 Talk to the parent on their own using some of the sentences above. (This conversation can be rehearsed with you.)
2 Ask you to facilitate a session between parent and teenager.
3 You talk to the parent on their own (*see* below).

Talking to the parents
Discuss with the teenager whether they would like you to see their parent in their presence or on their own to convey the effects of persistent nagging and the issuing of commands. If the teenager wants you to see their parent on their own, that's fine as long as you are comfortable with that and the parent agrees. The problem is then how to convey the findings of the research on the negative impact of nagging, without parents feeling patronised or that their parenting is

I'm always being got at

I live with constant nagging

I'm always waiting for the next criticism

Discouraged never encouraged

I can't seem to get anything right

I'm just waiting for the next telling off

being criticised. But the fact is that, in order to make informed decisions, parents do need to know about the research that shows that if a child or teenager receives a ratio of six negatives for every one positive, that individual is often going to become emotionally unwell, particularly in the form of aggression or depression in the teenage years or in later life (Jenner, 1999). Parents who themselves received little encouragement and praise from their own parents, and lots of commands and criticism, are particularly at risk of treating their teenagers in this way. Parents often really 'get it' and make a major shift in how they are with their teenager after reading an excellent book called *How to Talk So Teens Will Listen and Listen So Teens Will Talk* (Faber and Mazlish, 2006). It is based on empathic attunement with the teenager while still maintaining clear boundaries. One parent who was nagging all the time repeatedly had conversations with her teenager that went like this:

Teenager: 'I hate you, you don't understand me. You are a rubbish mother.'

Parent: 'How dare you talk to me like that. Now you need to go and tidy your room right now otherwise no more privileges and no more pocket money. I tell you time and time again.'

Teenager slams the door and doesn't come back until late that night.
After reading the book, the conversation the very next day went like this:

Teenager: 'I hate you, you don't understand me. You are a rubbish mother.'

Parent: 'Hey Sarah, I can see you are having a really hard time at the moment and probably made worse by feeling that I really don't understand you.' [Said genuinely]

Teenager bursts into tears and lets her mum cuddle her for the first time in years.

I did this bad thing

Objective
OK, who in their teenage years *hasn't* made a bad mistake of some sort? Teenagers do tend to mess up at some point, and often in a big way. This is partly due to what is happening in their brain. Brain changes mean that they are far more impulsive than adults (Giedd, 2002). Their capacity for reflective decision making is often poor because their frontal lobes, responsible for this capacity, are undergoing a period of rapid growth and development.

Common 'big' teenage mistakes include getting pregnant when you didn't intend to or getting someone pregnant, getting badly drunk and ending up in the police station, drug-taking that goes badly wrong in some way, selling drugs, and so on. Teenagers can feel so alone with their 'big mistake' rather than realising that it is very common for teenagers to make such errors. They can be helped to be more compassionate with themselves when they are given the information that the teenage brain is geared for impulsive, non-reflective action. The important question is, 'What do I do next?'

The parental response to the teenager's bad mistakes is crucial. If the parents are shaming and angry, it can confirm the teenager's feeling of badness. This process is beautifully described here:

> *If a [teenager] feels he has committed some terrible crime, and meets with [an adult] who does not share his self-appraisal of 'wicked', but instead meets an adult who is firm yet understanding and compassionate, then the [teenager's] terrible belief of himself is lessened, as there will be a mismatch between the persecuting parent in his head and the actual parent who is far more benign in his external reality. But if he feels wicked [or bad] and then meets [an adult] who hits him or looks at him with contempt, then he feels this confirms his inner reality. His fantasies about himself as a monster remain and are often strengthened as a result of this 'crucial exchange'.*
> (Greenberg and Mitchell, 1983)

There is a lovely example of a good parental response in the film *Juno*. Here the teenager gets pregnant. She is terrified of telling her parents but, in fact, they hear the news staying stable under stress and helping her to look at options. If only every parent of teenagers could see this clip. After all, Juno feels terrible about it anyway without having to cope with shaming, angry parental responses as well.

So this exercise, development and discussion will give the teenager an arena in which to discuss guilt about what they have done. As practitioner it is obviously important to help them to develop a compassionate response to themselves at the same time as helping them to think of ways to make reparation.

Instructions for the teenager
When you feel that you have done a bad thing, you may find it useful to think about things in terms of what has made you feel like this and what you can do, so that you don't feel so bad. It might help to think about things with pictures instead of just with words. Have a look at the pictures below. If you feel like any of the pictures please tick the box or colour them in. If it's not any of these things, draw or write in the empty box what you feel inside about this painful event or events.

Development
Exercise: Line down the middle – self-critic and self-encourager
Take a big piece of paper and draw a line down the middle. On the left-hand side, write the title, 'Self-critic'. On the right-hand side, write the title, 'Self-encourager'. Ask the teenager to write on the left-hand side the critical things that they frequently say to themselves. Then, on the right-hand side, ask them to write down the kind, encouraging, compassionate things that they frequently say to themselves. The latter can be over any timeframe, maybe when they have made other mistakes in their life.

This exercise is really useful to get an idea of the teenager's self-esteem and the work that needs to be undertaken on that front. It can be quite shocking, and often a real eye-opener, to some teenagers to realise that they are being so horrible to themselves and so hard and unforgiving with mistakes, and then how little praise and encouragement they give themselves. If appropriate, ask them who in their life has influenced the forming of their self-critic. Explain to them that negative things said by other people can be internalised and become even more fierce and condemnatory than the original critic.

Discussion
(Pick one or more of these topics to discuss with the teenager, as appropriate.)

Talk about inappropriate guilt
Teenagers need to know when guilt is appropriate or inappropriate to a situation. For example, some teenagers feel that they are responsible for their parent's drinking problem or depression. As Stella, aged 15, said, 'I am to blame for Mum's unhappiness.' Just like children, teenagers can still have irrational fantasies around causation – for example, 'I caused my parents to split up' or, 'My dad left home because of me.' Others, who are hit or smacked by parents, think they deserve it, even when they have been hit due to their parent's lack of ability to handle stress well, perhaps due to something like depression or a problem with alcohol. At least it keeps the notion that they have a good parent. It can be more awful to admit to themselves that something is wrong with their parent than with themselves. The logic can go like this: 'If I am good, how can you be bad to me if you are good? The reason you are bad to me is because I must be bad' (Armstrong-Perlman, 1995). Clearly, teenagers who formulate reality in this way need psychoeducation.

When the guilt is appropriate to the situation
If the teenager has done something that has hurt someone and/or broken the law, discuss options for reparation.

Talk about the parents' reaction to the 'bad thing'
When the parents found out about the 'bad thing', and other things the teenager does that the parents don't like, discuss with the teenager whether they were 'lie invitees' or 'truth tellers'. The concept of 'lie invitee or truth teller' is a very useful distinction devised by a therapist called Ellyn Bader, concerning how easy or difficult it is for teenagers (and others) to discuss sensitive issues with attachment figures. If, when teenagers try to discuss difficult issues with parents, the latter fly off the handle, the parents are 'lie invitees'. This means that these teenagers are likely to lie repeatedly to their parents because telling the truth leaves them feeling worse, not better; feeling shamed, guilty or awful in some other way. If the parents are 'truth tellers' the teenager is fortunate indeed, because even when they mess up, the parents listen and are focused on finding the best way forward. When parents are 'lie invitees', teenagers can be left battling with traumatic distress for years. It may not occur to them to go to a counsellor or other adult for help.

Talk about trauma and the concept of revictimisation
When the 'bad thing' has involved causing hurt, consider whether this is being done from a place of trauma. In other words, their cruel act may be an act of revictimisation. This means doing to someone else what has happened to them. You may be very well aware of the trauma particular teenagers have suffered.

If you think revictimisation is key to the teenager's 'acting out', explain this to them: When we have suffered a trauma, the mind often deals with it by treating someone else in a way in which you yourself have been treated. It may not be in exactly the same. For example, maybe you were hurt by the verbal assaults of someone's put-downs, so now you find yourself assaulting someone, but maybe in a physical rather than a verbal way. This is usually out of conscious awareness. For example, a teenager who was sexually abused when she was an infant went on to abuse a dog in a similar way to her own abuse. She felt awful, was suicidal with guilt until revictimisation was explained to her and she understood that this is just how the human mind operates. The only way to

I did this bad thing

Feeling like I'm a criminal

I think I was born bad

Feeling rotten inside

Like I'm to blame for the bad stuff that happens

Like I'm the cause of people's unhappiness

Like the bad in me could destroy the good

Who I am is wrong

prevent it is by getting help to feel and think about the original trauma (terror, disgust, shock, etc). Once this happens, the traumatic experience can be processed in more sophisticated parts of the brain. After this happens, the trauma no longer needs to be acted out blindly by the more primitive areas of the brain.

Talk about the difference between shame and guilt

Shame manages to derail [good thinking] ... [because of its] ability to act as a shock. In 1905, Freud talked of how 'shame acts as a psychic dam to the child's instinctual life' ... Shame transactions deactivate the dopaminergic circuits [feel-good chemicals] and activate ... low levels of endorphin [calming, soothing chemical] and high levels of cortisol.
(Schore, 1997)

Some teenagers say they feel guilty when in fact they are actually feeling shame. They can be helped to know the difference between the two.

You might say something like this: Guilt is your response to something you have done. Shame is a response when the whole of you feels not OK. So if you think that who *I am* is wrong, someone has shamed you. Shame is an awful feeling. Shame causes hormonal alterations in the brain – the feel-good chemical circuits are de-activated and high levels of stress chemicals wash over the brain, so you can't think properly. If you have been shamed:
1   Get to the childhood experiences that have been triggered. Who shamed you in childhood in the name of discipline? A parent? A teacher?
2   Find the rage under the shame.
3   Practise putting up a boundary so that you will not allow yourself to be shamed in the future. Literally putting up your hand in the sign of 'stop' and saying, 'I will not let you shame me', is often enough to stop the shamer in their tracks.

Talk about the human tendency to feel bad rather than good

Inform the teenager that this is just part of the human condition. This is why research shows that people need at least six appreciations for each criticism they receive (Jenner, 1999). For many people, what they receive is the other way round. This is the cause of so many people suffering from low self-esteem.

Talk about feeling alone with their badness in a good world

When parents continually exaggerate the goodness of their teenager and kindly overlook their faults, that teenager can feel far too alone with what they see as their 'secret badness'. This is particularly the case if they live with a parent who seems to be always good or who presents as perfect. Where this is the case, it is often a huge relief for teenagers to know about the underlying psychology.

Quotations the teenager may find useful

But she also had quite different feelings about her periods and felt that it meant that she had something dirty and smelly inside her. She was afraid that if this part of her was found she would be regarded as a dirty and smelly child.
(Barrows, 2003)

We are all criminals in phantasy.
(Segal, 1985)

If I wanted him dead, and then he dies, I must have killed him.
(Segal, 1985)

Leave me alone

Objective
Teenagers who feel emotionally suffocated by parents, or that they need more physical or emotional space, need to know that it is normal to want to move away from parents at this time; that teenagers are genetically programmed to want to be more separate from parents, to detach, in order to build up a separate identity and then to attach more intimately with peers. Some parents don't deal with this well and interfere or try to prevent this natural process from happening. Their anxiety and fear that they are losing their teenage child or their teenager's love, while very understandable, can result in them being invasive, intrusive and over-fussing. This can then lead to the teenager being even more intent on moving away physically or geographically, or moving away emotionally by being cold, monosyllabic and withdrawn when in the presence of the parent. They may 'drop out of sight' by not returning phone calls or text messages, or coming in late after their parents have gone to bed and getting up before their parents in the morning. It's all about protection against the perceived invasion of the parents.

Intrusive, needy or controlling relationships with parents, in these crucial years, can leave a negative legacy. It can put the teenager off being interested in developing committed loving relationships with potential partners, thinking they will just be like the relationship with their parents – a set of demands, a suffocating confinement, the fear of being trapped and losing their freedom and/or too many interactions that have been shameful, disapproving or intrusive. So, all in all, the teenager comes to associate relationship with pain rather than pleasure and hence the impulse to avoid.

So this exercise is to help teenagers to be more aware of the issue and then, as a result, to take a wiser approach – namely, engaging in conversation with the parent about the problem.

Instructions for the teenager
When you often feel frustrated or angry that your parents don't get it that you must have your own privacy, more freedom to be allowed to make your own mistakes and start to live your own life, you may find it useful to stand back, think about the situation and consider your options. It might help to think about it with some pictures and words. Look at these pictures. If you feel like any of the following, please tick the box or mark it in some way. If it's not any of these things, draw or write in the empty box what you feel inside.

Development
Teenagers need to know that getting the emotional distance right is not just an issue for parent–teenager relationships but for all important attachment relationships. But a key factor in getting it right is an awareness of what you might feel about that distance. So ask the teenager to fill in both of these tables and then discuss them. If they are already in a partner relationship they can fill in the tables with partner, parent and peer relationships in mind. Once they have filled them in, it is great to discuss what they have found out about themselves and their beliefs about relationships as a result.

Fear of closeness

Tick the statements that are true for you

Common core beliefs	Yes
If you let someone get close, they'll overwhelm you, control you, drain you or take from you in some way	
Close relationships mean loss of freedom and feeling trapped	
To be safe in intimate relationships you have be in control, not let them control you	
Intimate relationships mean so many emotional demands	
Closeness always carries obligations and pressures	
The more you give, the more they'll want	
Common fears	
Loss of self	
Feelings of powerlessness or helplessness	
Engulfment; being taken over or overwhelmed	
No escape routes or means of escape; nowhere to hide	
Your expressions of affection being taken as an invitation for the other person to move forward or intrude	
Insatiable demands that drain you or suck you dry	
Feeling used	
Behaviour that contributes to fears being realised (as it can provoke the other person to pursue, attack, demand or criticise)	
Being secretive or withholding	
Being tight or mean with shows of affection	
Primitive modes of flight or withdrawal	
Reacting to requests as if they were demands	
Frequently just not being there emotionally or in actuality	
Staying silent	
Common vocabulary and sentiment	
'I need more space'	
'Tied down'	
'No room'	
'Trapped'	
'Too demanding'	
'Feeling suffocated'	

Wants and needs	Yes
Long periods of time on your own	
Space away from people	
Respect for your need for separateness, withdrawal or alone time	
To be allowed to go and know that friends or partners will still love you, and be there when you return	
For people to understand that, after periods of closeness, you may need to move away for a while and for this not to be taken personally	
Use of space and movement	
The safety of a busy life or geographical distance, for example, being impossible to get hold of on the telephone; being 'unavailable'	
Spending a lot of time in the toilet	
Avoiding busy public spaces where you might experience a feeling of intrusion of personal space	
Withdrawal that leads others to pursue	
Always finding reasons for 'I must be going' or for delayed return	
Safety	
Retreats into one's own home, space or room	
Spaces without people	
Wanting to have people nearby to avoid loneliness, as long as there are no demands for contact	
Attachment to things, rather than people: computer, books and so on	
Solitary hobbies, for example, fishing or the potting shed	
Vital relational skills	
To know that if you let people get close, you can always negotiate your need for times apart	
To find a way of saying no rather than withdrawing or running away	
To state clearly what you feel	
To be able to set boundaries and be confident in your capacity to say no	
To be able to say, 'What I need now is...'	
To bring about negotiated withdrawals rather than sudden unexplained leavings	

Fear of distance or rejection

Tick the statements that are true for you

Common core beliefs	Yes
People you love will always leave you in the end	
I'm basically unlovable	
I have to try really hard to make someone want to be with me – seduce, control, coerce, always work on my appearance	
If he/she leaves me, I'll never find anyone else as lovely	
People will find me or my needs too much	
Common fears	
Being left	
Love going cold	
Aloneness	
Being unwanted	
Being uninvited	
Never having an intimate relationship again	
Dying alone	
Behaviour that can contribute to fears of distance or rejection being realised	
Repeated need for reassurances	
Rushing towards	
Repeatedly needing proofs of love	
Being very demanding	
Nagging, accusations, criticisms from a place of fear	
Persistent complaints of not getting enough, for example, love, appreciation, affection or attention	
Common vocabulary and sentiment	
'I need more from you'	
'It's not enough'	
'I want to spend more time with you'	
'Do you love me?'	
'What do you feel?'	

Wants and needs	Yes
To be taken care of	
To be pursued or sought after	
To be adored	
To be loved unconditionally	
To be seen as really special	
Frequent times of blissful union	
Use of movement and space	
Wanting togetherness	
Seeking out or pursuing	
Rushing towards then rushing away, then rushing towards again	
Waiting for them to seek you out or contact you	
Not trusting someone will move towards you, ring back, write back, return or stay, and so on	
Hating aloneness	
Safety	
Peopled spaces	
Someone you love telling you they love you	
Someone staying and not going	
Someone's arms	
Vital relationship skills	
To remember to stand still, rather than rush towards	
To get on with changing your own life, rather than trying to change them	

My parents don't give me
any space

Suffocating

Enclosed, confined,
hemmed in

Imprisoned in my parents' life

My privacy is not respected

My life is not my own.
It's what they want me to be/do

Like everything I do is
watched and judged

Discussion
(Pick one or more of these topics to discuss with the teenager, as appropriate.)

Talk about being clear with your parents about your needs for privacy and separateness

Explore with the teenager how getting the emotional distance right is not just an issue for parent–teenager relationships but for all intimate loving relationships. So if they can find ways to get it right with their parents, it's a great skill for their future relationships with partners. Discuss with the teenager that the most mature thing to do is not just to withdraw from a parent with an air of irritation or hostility, but actually to speak to them about their need for privacy, freedom, and so on, and then negotiate.

You might say something like this: Your parents need you to be clear with them about when you like to be with them and when you like to be separate from them, and how you like to be separate. Tell them how you feel when they do certain things – the feelings of invasion or suffocation. Many parents will be impressed by your use of sophisticated psychological language in this way and be more motivated to find a mutually satisfying way forward.

Empower the teenager to talk to their parents about being allowed to withdraw emotionally from them from time to time without pressure to reconnect, but to assure parents that they will reconnect in their own time when they are ready

Parents are often so impressed by the teenager's 'relational eloquence' around the negotiation of personal space that it can dissipate parental panic and disapproval.

Talk with the teenager about how, if you remain withdrawn and silent, often parents will invade you with even more questions, demands and needs

Sometimes parents just need the information about what you feel and what you need, and when you want contact and when you want to be left alone.

Talking to the parents themselves

Parents can also be resourced to have important conversations with their teenagers about emotional distance, so they don't lose their teenager to all manner of behaviours involving becoming secretive and distant, not answering their phone, just not being there, always finding reasons for 'must be going' and not staying.

Quotations the teenager may find useful

Some people don't know how to say No and stay. They only know how to say No by leaving.
(Resnick, 1993)

The idea of a lot of no one appeals to me. I'd like very much – why not? – to go on an excursion with a whole crowd of no one. Into the mountains, of course – where else?
(Kafka, 1981)

A great many [Casanovas] are uncomfortable immediately after sex, especially with a new partner. It isn't just the unease of sudden intimacy: they don't know what to do or how to feel in the postcoital hush ... One man said to me, 'The moment my penis goes down, my thoughts come back. And what they tell me is, 'Let's get the hell out of here, buddy'. (Trachtenberg, 1988)

*The distance is felt
already. You stir
in your sleep,
I fly away
across the bed. We
do not touch tonight.*
(Loydell, 1992)

> *They 'drop out of sight', not returning phone calls ... making themselves totally unavailable. This hiding is not the same as being alone or learning to feel comfortable in one's own company. Avoiding others, isolating oneself, while growth inhibiting, can be effective methods of protection.*
> (Blume, 1990)

Life sucks

Objective

This worksheet and discussion is all about teenage depression. Depression as an illness rather than a passing mood, at this developmental stage, must be taken very seriously. This is because it derails emotional development and the teenager's capacity to learn, relate to others and function normally. It is also a major cause of teenage suicide. In the UK, every 22 minutes a teenager tries to kill themselves (Institute for Public Policy Research, 2006b).

Ninety per cent of suicide among teenagers had a diagnosable mental illness, depression being the most common (Depressionperception.com, 2009).

Between 10 and 19 years old, the third leading cause of death is suicide, and suicide and depression tend to go hand in hand (Medicinenet.com).

Fifty per cent of all mental ill-health starts by the age of 14 (HM Government, 2011).

One in eight teenagers suffers from depression (HM Government, 2011).

Depression is the leading cause of disability and the fourth leading contributor to the global burden of disease. By the year 2020, depression is projected to reach second place of the global burden of disease for all ages, both sexes. Today, depression is already the second cause of the global burden of disease in the age category 15 to 44 years for both sexes combined. Fewer than 25 per cent of those affected have access to effective treatments (World Health Organization, 2011).

Of all the teenagers struggling with emotional and behavioral problems, a mere 30 per cent receive any sort of intervention or treatment. The other 70 per cent simply struggle through the pain/emotional turmoil, doing their best to make it to adulthood (Brown University, 2002). Yet untreated depression in the teenage years can lead to depression in adulthood, anti-social behaviour and, once again, suicide.

In light of these shocking statistics, it is vital that anyone working with teenagers is able to distinguish between depression as a mood and depression as an illness. The latter derails thinking and functioning and erodes any self-esteem. The too high levels of stress hormones block all the positive arousal chemicals, which means there is not one moment of joy, delight, excitement or pleasure. It's a living nightmare.

Emma, age 15, remembers starting to feel depressed about age 13 when she felt fat and spotty and so jealous of all the pretty girls in her class. 'I put on a happy face and people are taken in, even my parents. They have no idea that underneath I don't want to be alive. Life is just too hard. I often dream of dying so that I can make the pain stop.'

Teenage depression also makes teenagers vulnerable to drug abuse in their desperate attempts to change their agonising biochemical state: 'Taking drugs just helps you not to go too far down. I would be dead now, if it wasn't for drugs.' (Teenager)

Worryingly, research also shows that many parents do not recognise when their teenagers are depressed – as an illness not just as a mood. This is the case even with parents who have a good relationship with their teenagers (Brown University, 2002).

So this exercise is designed to give an important and focused listening space to the depressed teenager, so that they feel met and no longer alone in this painful state. This can make a huge difference.

We all have emotional needs that must be met for us to thrive and enjoy life. Without exception we find depressed teenagers are not having these needs met. Key emotional needs include attachment needs – that is, the need for meaningful emotionally regulating human connection – and doing something worthwhile with your life. We know these are genetically ingrained hungers (see Panksepp, 1998 on SEEKING and CARE systems). So therapeutic conversation with you in the context of an ongoing meaningful relationship can go some way to healing depression. This is because what you are offering is authentic human connection with warmth, encouragement and concern. A key outcome is that the teenager internalises you as an empathic presence to accompany them in their head, so to speak. In order for this to happen, as you talk with them about the pictures and images and words they choose, this is what they need from you:

1 It is important that you stay stable under stress on hearing the teenager's despair and hopelessness. Some people can't hold their own anxiety about this and so their empathy is compromised. Instead, they move into a state of alarm. Consider over-reaction or under-reaction on your part (good to have a supervisor to talk this through).
2 It is very important not to try to jolly the teenager up, but to empathise with how difficult life is for them at the moment. They need to know that they can trust you enough with their pain without you over-reacting or getting anxious, or talking them out of the feelings they are having – this is also part of the process of hope.
3 They may need your help to find their hope, but only when they are ready to hear it. This is hope of a warmer, kinder, more compassionate world. If you offer warmth, empathy and understanding you will give them a real experience of that world and often through it engender hope.
4 They need you to keep in mind their 'hidden resources that have been buried beneath the avalanche of despair' (Watchel, 2008) and to help them

find these when the time is right. If they are depressed as an illness, not just as a mood, they may insist that no other reality is ever possible. All you can do is listen and empathise.
5 Some teenagers who are really low need antidepressants alongside therapeutic conversation (see referral to GP, below).

If you are seriously worried that the teenager might take their own life
You will have to tell the teenager that you will need to tell their GP, and then do so. If you feel they really understand the whole issue they are what is known as 'Gillick competent'. This means you don't need to tell their parents (if they don't want you to) that you are informing their GP (Gillick competence is a legal term involving whether a child (16 years or younger) is able to consent to his or her own medical treatment, without the need for parental permission or knowledge). But it is worth holding the following in mind: There are others … for whom the mere idea of suicide is enough; they can continue to function efficiently and even happily provided they know they have their own, specially chosen means of escape always ready …' (Alvarez, 1971).

Instructions for the teenager
When you feel really low about things, you may find it useful to take a look at your life in terms of how things got to be like this and what you might want to change. It might help to think about it with some pictures as well as words. So look at the pictures below. If you feel like any of the following, please tick the box or mark it in any way you like. If it's not any of these things, draw or write in the empty box what you feel inside when you are feeling really low.

Development
Below is a useful table on the prime causes of why teenagers get depressed. The table is made user friendly for the teenager, but it is worth you knowing two of the key areas of research. They are:
1 There is a very clear link between depression and parents who are persistently interacting with their teenager through anger, irritation, criticism or commands and where there are lots of arguments at home

It's all too difficult

It's all too much

Worn out from being me

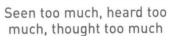

Stop the world, I want to get off

Like I'm very old

Seen too much, heard too much, thought too much

I feel like giving up

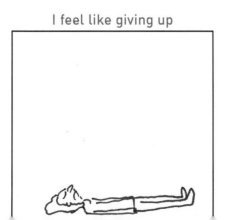

Like I'm living in a world where it's always winter

(Pikó and Balázs, 2010; Lewandowski *et al*, 2009; Sweeting *et al*, 2010). Higher levels of parental aggression predicted higher levels of both depression and anxiety symptoms in adolescents over two-and-a-half years, whereas higher levels of positive parental behaviours prospectively predicted lower levels of depression symptoms only (Schwartz *et al*, 2011).

2 When parents were themselves depressed there was more likely to be depression in the teenagers. Mothers with a history of depression exhibited greater sadness during their interactions with their teenagers (Jaser *et al*, 2008).

Exercise: Why do I feel so low?

In order to stop feeling low it is important first and foremost to work out what is getting you down. From knowing this it is far more possible to work out what to change and how to help. Here are the most common reasons why teenagers get depressed. If you think it is one or more of these, tick it and then add a score from 1 to 10, with 1 being a bit of a problem and 10 a huge problem.

The problem	Tick if yes	The pain level (1–10)
Parents who seem angry with you for a lot of the time		
Parents who are themselves depressed		
A home life with lots of stress and argument		
Feeling you can't live up to what teenagers are supposed to look like, wear or own		
Feeling lonely in your life		
Nothing much interests you		
Pressure about exams		
Bullying		
Trouble with friends		
Wanting someone really lovely in your life who is kind and warm and fun but not having someone like that		
No one in your life you can really turn to		
Doing difficult stuff in your life for far too long all on your own		
Something bad happened in your childhood that you think is still affecting you		

DISCUSSION
Talk about the symptoms of depression
Some teenagers don't know the symptoms of depression as an illness, rather than just as a mood. They just feel awful. If they can recognise themselves in the list of symptoms for depression as an illness, however, they are often far more accepting that they need help. Many will acknowledge that a visit to the doctor is important. If they accept this, it might be appropriate in some cases to inform them that the GP may prescribe antidepressants alongside a talking therapy. So if you think the teenager with whom you are working is suffering from depression as an illness, show them this list and ask which, if any, of the items they can relate to personally. If they say none of them, it may be that they are depressed as a mood not as an illness, or are instead being very defended with you.

Common symptoms of teenage depression (one or more of the following):

Eating – too much or too little; weight changes – lost or gained weight.

Restless, agitated (pacing, wringing hands) or the opposite – slowed down, loss of energy, feeling tired all the time.

Doing nothing (eg spends hours just staring, finds it hard to move).

Feelings of worthlessness.

Feeling that life is not worth living.

Aggressive or irritable.

No longer interested in favourite things or hobbies.

No longer interest in friends or wanting to make contact with them.

Looks sad, flat affect, flat voice – more monosyllabic than normal.

Poor concentration and attention.

Fails to show up to things or meetings with friends.

Drug or alcohol abuse.

Can't make decisions.

Drop in academic performance.

Physical symptoms (eg headaches, problems sleeping or sleeping too much).

Spending lots of time alone.

Talk about their despair, wanting it all to stop
Some things you could say or adapt:
- Seems like so many people have disappointed you, seems like so many people have let you down.
- Like one day you lost hope of there ever being a better time in this life for you.
- You have lost the 'around the corner'.

Talk about the depression that comes from not asking for help
Some things you might say or adapt:
- Doing painful or hard stuff on your own would make anyone miserable.
- Managing difficult feelings on your own without getting help is too miserable.
- People can face anything if supported by people who are warm, kind and understanding.
- Finding someone to do 'together' with makes everything feel far easier and more manageable.

Talk about how depression can come from an early childhood belief that difficult things are to be done on your own or having no concept of help or asking for help
Often doing far too difficult things on your own starts in early childhood. The research shows that at age one some children are already bottling up feelings. Not going to a parent for help with painful events, or indeed any other person, such as a friend or teacher, would be likely to make anyone feel depressed. But, for some people, it doesn't even occur to them to ask for help. Ask the teenager if they relate to any of this.

Talk about the biochemistry of depression
There are positive-feeling emotion chemicals in our brain that, when firing, can make us feel all is well in the world. In depression, stress hormones fire so strongly that they block the positive-feeling emotion chemicals and colour our perception with a sense of threat and misery. (This is particularly important for the teenager who has been prescribed antidepressants or is likely to in the future.)

Talk about how grief can get trapped in the mind and body

Once it does, it can get stuck and turn into depression. A lot of depression is fuelled by unmourned grief. It needs to be cried out, or even better, howled. Once this happens, life can seem far more bearable. Ask the teenager if they think that they are carrying around any unmourned grief as emotional baggage.

Quotations the teenager may find useful

(Only use the ones you feel are appropriate for the teenager you are working with.)

I never did anything. I just like went to school, and was totally withdrawn from my family. I just came home and sat around. I didn't do anything. I wasn't happy … I wasn't in control of myself. I could never understand how they kept telling me, 'Things will get better,' and I couldn't see it, you know. I never had seen change before, and they kept telling me, 'You will see it,' and I didn't even know what it was. And then I started seeing things change and stuff, and it really made me happy and it made me keep going.
(Hauser et al, 2006, p128)

People usually kill themselves to escape what they see to be an intolerable and otherwise inescapable situation, not necessarily because they want to die.
(www.clinical-depression.co.uk/dlp/depression-information/teen-depression)

People become really quite remarkable when they start thinking that they can do things.
(Norman Vincent Peale, 1994)

Hope is the thing with feathers
That perches in the soul
And sings the tunes without the words
And never stops – at all.
(Emily Dickinson, 1999)

But there are some knights on this earth, posing as people
Knights are fearless in fighting for fairness.
Knights take you by the hand and don't let go,
Knights take on the King not just the pawn.
Knights will be with you along the way, until you feel safe again.
(Sunderland, 2009)

And still we rise.
(Maya Angelou, 1994)

Kind of numb

The way I dealt with the mess of my feelings was by shutting off ... but shutting off was just another mess.
(Gemma, aged 13)

Objective
'Martin found any feelings of warmth, closeness, tenderness so painful that he had to dispose of them very quickly' (Barrows, 2003, p114). Emotional numbing is a way of dealing with painful feelings, particularly when you don't believe anyone can help you with them. Some teenagers shut off from painful feelings and even try to do life without emotion. They can then be wrongly labelled as having Asperger's. Other teenagers shut down on some feelings but not others. Most common here are those perpetually angry teenagers who have numbed all feelings of the hurt that lies underneath. Others cut off on attachment needs as they have felt too hurt by relationship in the past.

The costs of emotional numbing are often high. If you numb your hurt it can sometimes be difficult to feel that of others. This can cause all manner of heartache in relationships, with many teenagers getting ditched by partners for being too cold or cut off. As Polster (1987) says, 'A person who does not feel, is one not sought out by others.' It's easy to see why, because, if you don't have feelings, who are you?

Emotional numbing means that you can be violent and hurtful because you are not 'distress averse'. This means that you don't feel pain at the pain of others. The human capacity for cruelty is all about this. We have the genetic programming to be distress averse but many teenagers who have felt too much emotional pain and so have cut off are 'distress excited'. The pain that they cause to others excites them.

For others, cutting off on feeling leaves them feeling something is missing – as indeed it is. If you emotionally numb, you don't feel much pain, but you don't feel much life either. And by cutting off any passionate response to the world it is often very difficult to know what you want from life. Desire simply isn't strong enough. Some teenagers feel so deadened as a result of cutting off feelings that they self-harm in order to feel something again.

So this exercise, development and discussion are designed to empower the teenager to think about their defence mechanism of emotional numbing, how it helps or hinders them and what it costs them. It is hoped that the teenager will also understand which feelings they are defending against, for example, rage, hurt, fear or grief. Additionally, the exercise provides a time to reflect on the life events that were so painful or so lonely that they could not be tolerated.

Instructions for the teenager
If you think that you cut off from certain feelings sometimes or feel emotionally numb or empty in ways you really don't like, then these pictures and captions might help. If you feel like any of the following, please tick the box or mark it in the way you want. If it's not any of these things, draw or write in the empty box what you feel inside when you feel cut off or emotionally numb in some way.

Development
Causes of emotional numbing
When teenagers are not sure what has happened in their life to lead to them feeling emotionally numb it can be useful to give them a list of common contributory factors to see if they relate to any of them (see below). The list includes not only trauma and loss but also troubled parents. It is, for example, common, where a parent has suffered from depression, for a child to find that the parent's deadness becomes their deadness in some way. Allan Schore talked eloquently of the parent who suffers from post-natal depression, as a result or which the baby stops crying and stares into space because no one

Don't care any more

Closed down

Dull

Just going through the motions of my life

Emotionally numb

Frozen inside

Too painful to feel what I feel

In a prison of life I made for myself

responds quickly enough or at all. It's known as, 'The dead spot in going on being' (Schore, 1997). Now while this is probably too much detail and maybe inappropriate for the teenager, it is worth bearing this in mind when offering this reflective space.

Instructions for the teenager: Look at the list below. When you feel emotionally dead, dull or cut off, do you think anything in the list is contributing? (Research shows that these are the most common causes of emotional numbness.)

	Yes/No
Some traumatic happening in the past that has never been properly worked through	
Some traumatic loss to someone the past or traumatic loss of their love that has never been properly worked through	
No one to help you with some really painful event in your life	
Parents cut off from their feelings	
Deadening atmosphere in the family home	
Childhood memories of times at home of understimulation, boredom nothingness and aloneness	
Mother suffered from post-natal depression	

You might also say something like this: Perhaps, at some time in your life, it wasn't safe for you to feel your feelings because you were too alone with them. Perhaps, at some time in your life, it was too hard for you to feel your feelings. Perhaps you put them away because they hurt you too much. Maybe when your world went cold, your heart went cold.

Discussion

Talk about how, when we can't manage painful feelings and no one is helping us to manage them, we can go one of two ways – defence or discharge

The latter is to let the feeling out, but often it comes out in ways that hurt self or others – for example, angry attack, hitting someone, or self-harm. Defence, on the other hand, doesn't get you into trouble but often the price is feeling empty, dulled or deadened. You may also not have enough passionate feeling to know what you want or don't want, like or dislike. As a result, you may lack drive and will to make something happen.

Quotations the teenager may find useful

Our walls are our wounds – the places where we feel we can't love any more ...
(Williamson, 1992)

Walls to keep others out, keeps you safe, but it keeps help, warmth and kindness out too.
(Sunderland, 2009)

We must ... love in order that we may not fall ill, and we must fall ill if ... we cannot love.
(Freud, 1914)

He has little understanding of how the very ways he goes about feeling more secure moment by moment contribute to the chronic sense of dissatisfaction that plague's him.
(Watchel, 2008)

Not doing much with my life

Will left school at age 16 and now sits in the flat all day smoking dope. He says he doesn't really want to leave the flat. He says life's OK like this. He has endless arguments with his mum. She says there is far more to life than this. He disagrees with her.

Objective

The number of young people aged 16–18 not in education, employment or training – so-called 'Neets' – is over 10 per cent. (LSN Institute for Education, 2009)

This exercise is to empower the teenager with the psychoeducation they need to better understand their lack of focus, lack of direction, lack of motivation, or other factors preventing them from fully engaging in life. This will include knowing about the brain systems responsible for the opposite of 'not doing much', namely those systems responsible for drive, will and passion. From this new place of awareness and insight, teenagers often decide to take a different direction, to do things differently and get the help they need. The great thing is that it is never too late to activate our brain's genetically ingrained SEEKING system (system of desire, drive, will and curiosity), even if it has been poorly activated for a long time. As practitioner, your carefully worded and carefully timed encouragement and praise can also enhance the process of the teenager being able to find a more creative and energised response to their life and what they want to do with it.

Instructions for the teenager

When you feel that you are not doing much with your life and want to feel differently and do things differently, it can be useful to think more about things and, in particular, about what is stopping you using your life in ways you would like. It might help to think about it with some pictures. So look at the pictures below. If you feel like any of the figures in the pictures, please tick the box or mark it in some way. If it's not any of these things, draw or write in the empty box what it feels like when you think about not doing much with your life.

Development

When teenagers are not sure what has happened in their life to make them feel like this, it can be useful to provide them with common contributory factors (research-based), to see if they can relate to any of them. Let the teenager look at the list below and ask any questions regarding any of the categories:

Common reasons why teenagers don't feel motivated to do more with their life	Yes/no
Home life now or as a child – not enough encouragement or praise	
Home life now or as a child – too much criticism or too many commands	
Childhood where parents rarely offered 'playing with'	
Too much stuff happening at home, so can't think about what I want to do or what interests me	
Parents who don't really model 'Let's …' or 'Yes, you can' or any passion for learning	
Feel that I'm not really good at anything	
Not liking myself	
Being bullied	
Stuff happened in my past – loss or traumatic things that I think are still bothering me	
I feel depressed	
I don't want to try anything new because I might be no good at it and then feel lousy again	

Exercise: For people to achieve things in their life they need two capacities: capacity for will and capacity for dream (Yalom, 1980)

Explain that capacity for dream means capacity to imagine something, and capacity for will means the determination to make it happen. Ask the teenager to think about these in relation to themselves. Then ask the teenager to dream right now. Ask them to make a sandplay picture or write a short paragraph (first person, present tense) of what they want to be doing in one year and in five years.

Discussion

Talk about the brain systems that are key in terms of drive, motivation, will and desire

Explain the following to the teenager in language they can understand and then ask them to comment in light of their own life experience: If a person wants to feel an energetic impulse to explore, to follow their curiosity, to go after something they want to do, the SEEKING system in the limbic part of their brain must be optimally activated. The SEEKING system is a system of desire (Panksepp, 1998). The key biochemical for this brain system is dopamine. Dopamine locks you into something and helps you go from the seed of an idea to its birth in reality. Dopamine is required for 'vigorously pursuing courses of action' (Panksepp, 1998).

The SEEKING system is like a muscle: the more optimally activated by parents and schools in childhood, the more energetic engagement in life becomes part of the personality. This means the adults in the child's life offering really engaging experiences – physical, sensory, imaginary and cognitive experiences. Relational play with an adult is one of the best forms of this experience. Also, of course, masses of encouragement from parents is often the key to engendering a child's passionate interest in things. In this sense, the parent is the first teacher. In contrast, the longer the SEEKING system remains poorly activated prior to the child reaching school age, the harder it is to activate it in school. Moreover, a child can have a well-activated SEEKING system only for it to be deactivated by adults who discourage, criticise or who issue lots of commands and 'don'ts'. A poorly activated SEEKING system means desire isn't strong enough. Hence the teenager not knowing what they want to do, and suffering from procrastination and a lack of explorative urge that can be truly debilitating.

Talk about family and school cultures that do not support well enough the optimal activation of the child's SEEKING system, and what the teenager can do about it

It is not difficult to see that family cultures that do not sufficiently support the activation of the child's SEEKING system, coupled with a school life that fails to make up for this developmental deficit, can result in a lethargic, poorly motivated teenager. This is then made all the worse when transacting in the name of discipline means far too many criticisms and commands, such as, 'Don't' and 'Stop that', and too many experiences of discouragement, shame and humiliation. The following quotation may speak very powerfully to some teenagers in this position, but with the clear message that it is never too late to activate a SEEKING system. It just needs the right person, who encourages, inspires and supports that teenager.

> *Punishing causes [people] to close themselves in, freezing and withdrawing from their surroundings. Reward causes [people] to open themselves up and out toward their environment, approaching it, searching it ... This fundamental duality is apparent in a creature as simple ... as a sea anemone .... devoid of brain and ... little more than a gut with two openings. The circumstances surrounding the sea anemone determine what it does: open up to the world like a blossoming flower – at which point water and nutrients enter its body and supply it with energy – or close itself in a contracted flat pack, small, withdrawn, and nearly imperceptible to others. The essence of joy and sadness, of approach and avoidance, of vulnerability and safety, are as apparent in this simple ... brainless behavior as they are in [we humans].*
> (Damasio, 2000)

I feel like a lazy slob

I want to want something

I can't decide stuff

I can't decide what to do with my life

I'm so unsure of things

I'm unable to choose between one thing and another

I don't finish stuff I started

I'm in a rut

I can't make anything good happen

Talk about what to do when unmourned grief or unprocessed trauma is blocking the teenager's SEEKING system

As we have seen, one in two teenagers will experience their parents splitting up by the time they reach the age of 16. Many are left depressed and angry and we know that 75 per cent of teenagers who were secure become insecurely attached after this. Insecure attachment means you don't have the secure base that makes you feel safe in the world – safe enough to want to go off and energetically explore the fruits of the world.

We know that unprocessed trauma often leaves teenagers with lots of feelings that they can't manage, so they repress them. But as Freud found out all those years ago, with this comes repression of life force, resulting in neurotic symptoms. Energy is then taken up in phobias, obsessions and worrying and so is no longer available for passion for life, insatiable curiosity and explorative urge.

Explain to the teenager that you can't really be in the present in a fully engaged and positively energised way if you haven't properly mourned the past. Inform them that, at some time, they will need to grieve in order to free up all the energy caught up in the unmourning.

Talk about the link between low self-esteem and a poorly activated explorative urge

If relevant, discuss this with the teenager in terms of their particular childhood experiences. Explore whether they have built up a 'fear of doing' because past experience has led them to believe that it will only bring yet more painful feelings of failure and inadequacy.

Quotations the teenager may find useful

We may choose to grow, to stagnate, or to decline, and in a world where there is little encouragement to grow, most of us may not do it very much or at all.
(John Rowan, 1986)

Your mind now, mouldering like wedding-cake,
Heavy with useless experience,
Crumbling to pieces under the knife-edge
Of mere fact. In the prime of your life.
(Adrienne Rich, from *Snapshots of a Daughter-in-Law*, 1963)

Here I am getting on for seventy...
At that awkward age now
between birth and death
I think of all the outrages unperpetrated, opportunities missed.
The dragons unchased.
The maidens unkissed.
The wines still untasted.
The oceans uncrossed.
The fantasies wasted.
The mad urges lost.
(Roger McGough, 1990)

When lots of dopamine synapses are firing, a person feels as if he or she can do anything.
(Panksepp, 1998)

Everyone looks for that sparkle in friends and lovers to 'make things happen'. Most of all, everybody is looking for energy within themselves: the motivation and drive to get up and do something, the endurance, stamina and resolve to carry through ...
(Brown, 1999)

After the bad thing happened

Objective
This exercise is for teenagers whose life has been turned upside down by a painful event. Painful events often include such things as: parents announcing they are splitting up, divorcing or leaving; change of schools; someone dying; moving to a new area and so losing all your friends; making a bad decision and so ending up in trouble with the police; taking a drug, which messes up your mind; finding out you are pregnant or have made someone pregnant. Basically, these teenagers need help with the shock and this exercise, development and discussion are designed to do this.

Often, teenagers who have experienced some painful and often unexpected event just feel awful. They don't realise that they are in shock. They don't know what shock does to the body and the mind. Some teenagers develop post-traumatic stress disorder (PTSD) symptoms after a shocking event, particularly if no one helped them with their feelings at the time. They have no idea they are suffering from it, so don't go and seek out appropriate treatment.

Practitioners working with teenagers suffering from PTSD symptoms need to recognise what these are – in particular, the hypervigilance, stress states, and flashbacks that can dramatically derail emotional and social development, schoolwork and relationships. The body can also be unable to regulate its internal systems properly, resulting in physical symptoms or problems with one or more of the following: sleeping, eating, breathing, digestion and elimination. As Van der Kolk, a famous trauma expert working with teenagers says, 'The trauma keeps them rigidly fixated on the past, making them fight the last battle over and over again' (Van der Kolk et al, 1996, p17). So it is vital that teenagers have a place to talk about what has happened to them and to get help to process and work through their feelings about it. Sometimes people worry that by talking about the trauma the teenager will get re-traumatised. The difference this time is that, in the original event, the teenager developed PTSD symptoms because there was no one helping them with their feelings; this time, they tell you what happened and the healing is in the fact that you are emotionally regulating their feelings through your empathy as they talk about what happened.

The practitioner needs to be able to be psychologically strong and calm enough so that the teenager feels sufficiently safe to be able to release shock that has often been locked up in their body. They may need to shout, scream and howl. As Panksepp, a leading neuroscientist, says, 'We are deeply feeling creatures. We must come to terms with the human condition.' If the teenager senses that you are too emotionally fragile they just won't go into this level of discharge. They will instead stay defended and may not even want to talk about it.

Example
Max, aged 16, was in shock after his parents announced that they were splitting up. Shortly afterwards, his dearly beloved dad moved out. Max's schoolwork went downhill and he spent days on end alone in his bedroom. Max was with a counsellor who offered him real empathy and who was very at home with strong emotion. As a result, Max was brave enough to howl and howl, saying, 'Dad will never live with us again. Dad will never live with us again.' After such intense mourning with his counsellor, who soothed, calmed and contained Max, his schoolwork improved and once again he enjoyed a lively social life.

Please note: If you feel the teenager is actually very mentally unwell, not able to function at all and dissociating, you will need to refer on to a specialist or to their GP (that is, if you are not trained to work at this level of distress with severe post-traumatic stress disorder). Dissociation is a defence where the thinking and feeling mind can shut down and the teenager can enter states of depersonalisation, acute emotional numbing and sometimes amnesia. This can often be first recognised, in part, by the teenager staring blankly into space, as they are literally absent from the here and now. With dissociative identity disorder, even simple everyday tasks cannot be carried out as their mind is not in a sufficiently integrated state for this. Consider making a referral to a GP or CAMHS.

Instructions for the teenager

It is easy to think that your life will carry on down the same path, with roughly the same people and in roughly the same way. Then one day something happens that changes everything. Often the change involves some form of loss: loss of a loved one; loss of a place like your school; loss of something very known in your life that has made you feel safe in the world; loss of self-respect; loss of a sense of your sanity; loss of the respect of others; loss of feeling secure and confident in being in the world. Whatever it is, things are literally never the same again.

Terrible shocks are something the vast majority of us will have to manage at some time in our life. Without help to talk about the shocks, however, sometimes people suffer from long-term psychological problems. Sometimes the shock gets locked in their body too, resulting in illness and/or physical symptoms. Shock states can also affect your relationships and your schoolwork, and sometimes even your ability to do simple everyday tasks. So this exercise is designed to protect you from these things happening or to help you if they have already happened. It is designed to enable you to find words for feelings linked with the shocks, so that the memories of the painful events lose their power.

Look at the pictures and think of a shock or shocks you have suffered in your life. Did any of them make you feel like any of the figures in the pictures? If so, tick the appropriate picture or mark it in some way. If none of the images feel right enough for the shock you have felt, draw your own images or write your own words in the empty boxes. Then give your boxes titles. What was the worst thing for you about the shock? What words describe it? How do you think the shock is still affecting you?

Development
Exercise: Before, during and afterwards
Instructions: Ask the teenager to divide a piece of paper into three. On one side, use words, lines and images to describe life before the shock. In the middle section, draw and write words (single words or short phrases) to describe what it felt like when the shock happened. On the other side, draw and write words to describe what the shock feels like now. Alternatively, if you have musical instruments, you could ask the teenager to play out the energy of the shock. As shock can leave a teenager feeling helpless or impotent, it can be very healing to take power back, through drama, drums or voice, in terms of making an energised protest in this way.

Discussion
Talk to the teenager about post-traumatic stress
Let them know the common symptoms: angry outbursts, problems sleeping, hyperactivity, nightmares, problems concentrating at school, anxiety attacks, generalised anxiety, agitation, depression, hypervigilance, flashbacks, startle reactions, social phobias, inappropriate flight or freeze responses (suddenly finding your thinking, feeling or doing is frozen or blocked). Ask them whether any of these things happened after they suffered the shock. Also let them know what is happening in their brain. A simple explanation will do. The amygdala (a small walnut-shaped structure located on each side of the brain, in from the ear) stores powerful emotional memories. If anything happens that is like your traumatic incident or reminds you of it, even some small aspect of it, then the amygdala activates and triggers high levels of stress hormones in mind and body. Other alarm systems in the brain also join in. This then derails good thinking and colours your perception of the here and now with a sense of danger and unsafety. You can start to see threat everywhere, even when there isn't any.

Reassure the teenager that if they talk about their traumatic experience they no longer have to feel this way. Let them know that the painful energetic charge not released at the time of the shock often stays in the body, causing

The world ended that day

As if everything got smashed

Like a nightmare got stuck in my brain

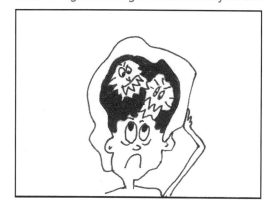

Full of silent screams

I'm living in a world of broken people

Like someone shot me full of holes

havoc in terms of feelings of anxiety and bodily states of hyperarousal. It is good to release this by shouting, screaming or howling in the presence of an understanding adult who can help them feel safe to have such intense feelings. Help them to understand with this quotation by a trauma expert:

> *When the reptilian [part of our] brain perceives danger, it activates an extraordinary amount of energy ... an 'adrenaline rush'. This, in turn, triggers a pounding heart and other bodily changes designed to give the [person] every advantage it needs to defend itself. The catch is that to avoid being traumatised, the [person] must use up all the energy that has been mobilised to deal with the threat. Whatever energy is not discharged does not simply go away; instead, it lingers, creating the potential for traumatic reaction to occur ... [If we are not to suffer traumatic symptoms] ... we must discharge the energy that has been mobilised, thereby allowing the nervous system to return to its accustomed level of functioning.*
> (Levine, 2006)

You can give them drums or cymbals if they want.

Talk about the particularly pain from suddenly being dumped by a girlfriend/boyfriend

Teenagers need to know that, sadly, many partner relationships in the teenage years are an experience of going from very, very happy to very, very hurt. This can be a real shock. Teenagers need the information that before adulthood it is likely that they will be deeply hurt on one or more occasions. Because of the stage of brain development, teenagers often end partner relationships in insensitive ways that can, at times, seem very cruel. The important thing is how you deal with it. Hurt is so painful that we often choose to deny or repress it instead of facing up to it. Some teenagers deal with it by drink or drugs to ease the pain. The teenager needs to know that the best way of soothing pain is to talk about it with an empathic adult.

Quotations to discuss with the teenager

This is me, this is my life and this is going to be my future. But, sometimes we get it wrong – and in comes a big shock.
(Dorothy Rowe, 1988)

But our minds were still out of breath...
(Siegfried Sassoon, 1996)

When young lips have drunk deep of the bitter waters of Hate, Suspicion and Despair, all the Love in the world will not take away that knowledge.
(Rudyard Kipling, 'Baa Baa Black Sheep', 1987)

When my house burnt down I could see the rising sun.
(Anon)

In traumatic stress we become frightened, unthinking animals.
(Van der Kolk, 2009)

The hushed network of nightmare. You have lost touch with the sustaining ordinariness of things.
(Fanthorpe, 2005)

Why so angry?

Objective
This exercise is for teenagers who keep getting angry and want to stop. They recognise that it is costing them too much, in terms of relationships with friends and family. They are motivated to change. Some are also frightened by their level of rage and need you to help them speak about that fear.

We are talking here about teenagers who may be unable emotionally to regulate their intense feeling states, so, like a toddler, they just lash out impulsively when stressed or irritated. With teenagers like this, usually their intense emotional states have not been emotionally regulated in infancy and childhood. This means that vital stress-regulating systems in the brain have not been set up. It is still possible to do this in the teenage years. Also, when teenagers are locked in anger, it can point to a history of trauma. This exercise will be particularly helpful where this is the case.

Teenagers are, of course, renowned for their angry outbursts and there is indeed a hormonal basis to this. Boys aged 10 and 11 have 50 times the levels of testosterone of younger boys. Teenage girls also have an increase in testosterone levels. But over and above this, we know that key contributory factors tend to be unresolved trauma or loss, stressful home environments, conflictual parent–teenager relationships, and parents who themselves use anger as a response to stress.

Additionally, for many teenagers, anger can be so much easier to feel than so many other feelings. So they get angry instead of letting themselves know that what they are really feeling is hurt, fear, low self-worth or impotence. Because of this, their emotional development is often at a standstill. Moreover, feeling anger can be like a drug for some teenagers in that the adrenaline rush makes them feel powerful, very alive and excited. Sometimes anger gives a teenager an identity, a sense of who they are. As Barrows (2003) remarks about a teenager he was working with, 'He was afraid that if he stopped his cruelty and noisy games, he'd be too empty handed.'

So this exercise, development and discussion are about the teenager having their anger heard and validated. It provides the teenager with an opportunity to make connections between past and present and which life events have led to them being so angry today. This important reflective process is key for those stress regulatory systems to be established in the teenager's brain. The exercise is also about helping teenagers to know when their anger is adaptive and when it is maladaptive. When feelings of anger are reflected on in this way, rather than just discharged, major positive changes occur in terms of brain as well as mind.

Instructions for the teenager
When you keep getting angry but really don't want to, it is possible to change. But to do that, certain things about your angry feelings need to be talked about and thought about in particular ways. First of all, it might help to think about them with some pictures. So look at the pictures and captions below. If you feel like any of the figures in the pictures, please tick the box or mark them as you like. If it's not any of these things, draw or write in the empty box what you feel inside when you feel so angry.

Development
Exercise: Museum of Fighting
Instructions: Divide a large piece of paper into six. Ask the teenager to draw in each of the six boxes a different 'museum exhibit' depicting a time in their life when they wanted to smash, kill, blow things up or be violent in another way. Then ask the teenager to take you round the museum. Help them to address other feelings that they might have been experiencing at the time. They might need help to consider such feelings as disappointment, let-down or hurt.

Exercise: Image of war

Instructions: Show the teenager images of war by famous artists, such as Picasso or John Martin. Put the pictures next to each other. Ask the teenager which of the pictures they like and why. Which features of which painting can they most identify with? Then ask them to do some of their own. Finally, ask them to do a drawing of what their life would feel like if they didn't get angry or fight any more.

Discussion

Talking to teenagers about what happens in the brain and body when we can't stop being angry

Teenagers need to know what is happening in the brain when painful feelings to do with emotional baggage get triggered. You can say something like this and show them the picture, or one like it: When we overreact with anger to something other people take in their stride, often as not, it is the amygdala that has been triggered. This is a part of the brain which has a key role in detecting threat. This, in turn, triggers a cascade of stress hormones that can make us move into primitive states of flight or fight. The amygdala triggers because the brain sees something in the present that reminds you of something painful in your past that you have never really talked about fully or worked through. The really annoying thing is that your brain doesn't tell you that you are remembering something. You really think there is a threat in the present – for example, someone looking at you disrespectfully – even if there isn't. But there is a clue. If you react with over-the-top intensity to a situation that other people just take in their stride, it's likely that you are remembering something.

Then show them where the amygdala is in the brain, explaining how stress hormones cascade over the frontal lobes, colouring thinking and feeling with a sense of threat.

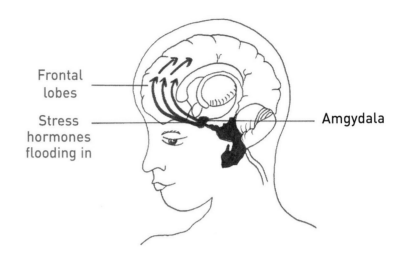

Finally, talk about how this trigger-happy amygdala can get you into trouble and really spoil your life. But if you work through your emotional baggage by talking about it with someone who can really listen and understand, the amygdala no longer reacts in this unhelpful way, and if it does, the frontal lobes (higher-thinking brain) activate and calm it down.

Talking about appropriate and inappropriate anger

Anger is appropriate when someone is trying to hurt you, shame you or bully you. In such circumstances, anger is a boundary-setting emotion. It helps you find the passion and psychological strength to say 'No' or 'Stop'. At other times, anger is not appropriate. Rather, it is a destructive overreaction to the situation, often triggered by emotional baggage you are carrying from your past (*see* above). As Aristotle said, 'Being angry is easy. It's knowing when, where, how, in what intensity and with whom to be angry that takes intelligence.' Inappropriate anger can hurt other people, get you into trouble and end up hurting the people who matter to you most. This table can help teenagers know when their anger is appropriate and based on the here and now, and when it is triggered by their emotional baggage.

I've got a volcano inside me

Full of bottled up feelings

I want to smash things

I want to scream and scream

So deep in anger that sad won't come out

Like a walking time bomb

Frightened I'll destroy all that matters to me

Frightened I'll damage the person/people I love most

Characteristics or anger triggered from painful experiences in the past (emotional baggage)	Characteristics of healthy here-and-now anger
Raw intensity of response The event has triggered in you raw, unprocessed feelings of hurt, rage, shame, feelings of betrayal and so on, from your past.	**The focus is on the resolution of the problem, not on the desire to hurt** For example, 'We have a problem, a difference of opinion here, so how can we resolve it?' This is completely different in tone and energy to, 'You are to blame because …' or, 'It's all your fault.'
A preoccupation with revenge You have a strong desire to make the other person feel what they have made you feel, or worse.	**Healthy anger is vibrant, active and soon over** Some people call it 'warm anger'. There is a 'clean' feel to it, although it can still be loud and passionate.
A desire to hurt With actions and/or words.	**Ordinary rather than extreme expressions and notions about the offending other** The offending other makes you angry, frustrated or very annoyed, rather than the extremes of archaic anger where the offending other is evil, an abuser, totally rotten or a psychopath.
The same angry, indignant or hating thoughts going round and round in your head You are preoccupied by what happened, and can't seem to let it go and move on.	
In-depth post-mortem examination of the event What you could have said or done.	**Little or no vindictiveness, sadism or vengeful purpose**
Negative responses to any apologies or attempts by the other person to make amends This is because you want to punish, not resolve – you are punishing this person for old hurts from people in your past.	**Healthy anger is finite, communicated clearly and effectively, and so you can move on**
	Rows, conflicts and arguments do not feel like catastrophic or dangerous events, just a normal part of life
Underlying deep sense of hurt Under all the anger or rage, a deep hurt has been re-triggered from relationships in your past – for example, not being responded to, being rejected, discouraged, shamed or humiliated, not being understood.	**You don't stay preoccupied with the incident long after it has happened**
Relief at having a core belief about yourself or others confirmed For example, 'See, this proves how unlovable I am', 'See, this proves that you can't ever really trust anyone', 'See, this proves that everyone is really out to get you.'	**Healthy anger leaves you feeling OK about yourself and the other person**

When teenagers are not sure what has happened in their life to make them feel like this, it can be useful to give them common contributory factors to see if they relate to any of them. Let them look at the list and ask any questions regarding any of the categories:

Common causes of teenager anger

Something happened in your past that was painful or traumatic. It made you sad, frightened or angry.

Your parents model using anger as a response to stressors.

Watching your parents argue or fight.

Strict parents who tell you off a lot.

Watching parental violence.

As a defence against feelings of impotence or helplessness.

'Love made angry and love made hungry'
(Guntrip, 1969). A parent who was loving but also emotionally and/or physically absent for too much of the time.

Talking to teenagers about revictimisation resulting from unworked-through traumatic experience
You might say something like this: When someone has hurt you badly in the past, it can leave you with an urge to hurt others in ways that bear some resemblance to how you have been hurt. This is called revictimisation. It is a common result of trauma; a common way that the mind deals with what has happened. It can get you into trouble a lot and you can feel you are bad when in fact you are not bad; you are traumatised. Talking about and feeling about that original trauma with an adult who really understands, can stop you from revictimising. You will find the urge to hurt just stops.

Example
Tommy, aged 16, presented as angry and a tough guy. He would beat people up when he felt they were looking at him in the wrong way. No one messed with Tommy. When Tommy was six years old, he saw daddy beating up mummy and

he couldn't do anything about it. When Tommy talked to a male teacher about how awful that was for him, and how he regularly had nightmares about it, Tommy lost all his impulses to lash out and hurt people.

Talking to teenagers about how being shamed or humiliated can trigger anger
Teenagers who have been shamed or humiliated need to know about shame rage. This is rage that is a natural response to shame. This is because shame feels like a brutal attack on the very self, so, like a wounded animal, it is a natural reaction to lash out, just as you would if someone attacked you physically.

Quotations the teenager may find useful

Human beings all prefer to be bad and strong rather than weak.
(Guntrip, 1969)

Anger is like raw garbage – banana peels, chicken bones, old brown lettuce. If you don't deal with it, you add to the pile, and over the years it loses its form and turns into sludge, until you no longer can say, 'I am angry because this or that happened'. You're left with brown yucky stuff without anything in it that you can name.
(Blume, 1990)

If hostility is repressed, the person has not the remotest idea that he is hostile.
(Horney, 1977)

Mistrust

In his play, people in the boats kept mistaking their enemies ... thought them less aggressive or dangerous than they turned out to be ... they saw the fin of the bog shark ... and they thought it was the fin of a dolphin. They got happily into the water to play with the dolphin and were torn limb from limb as they were eaten in silence.
(Hunter, 2001)

Objective

This exercise is for teenagers for whom trust is a real issue. Some are teenagers who did trust in the past but then were badly let down. Others have never really trusted because the people in their life have never felt trustworthy. As a result, they don't reach out for help. They just go through all the painful events in their life without asking for emotional support. The deep aloneness just becomes an unquestioned norm. They are known as 'insecure attached'. The parenting that results in teenagers becoming insecurely attached is mostly classified in the following terms, originated by Mary Ainsworth in the 1970s (Ainsworth *et al*, 1978):

Insecure-ambivalent attached: I need repeated assurance that the other will provide comfort and support because my parents were sometimes emotionally responsive and sometimes not (often needy, clingy, loving in torment).
Insecure-avoidant attached: I don't seek comfort and support because people won't be able to give it to me, so I'll do self-help. I tell myself I don't have attachment needs. This is because my parent was not emotionally responsive for too much of the time.
Insecure-disorganised attached: If I seek comfort, it makes me feel worse not better, so I'll do self-help. I can grow up to frighten others as I have been frightened. This is because my parent was a frightened anxious person or a person who frightened me by abusing me or being very angry (often in the name of discipline).

They are not securely attached:
Secure attachment: I have hope in a warm, caring world. I can trust people because my parents have been consistently emotionally responsive. (Grows up to love in peace.)

The key issue with insecure attachment is the incapacity to seek solace. So when life throws these teenagers something awful, by and large it doesn't even occur to them to ask for help from a friendly adult. Rather, they just try to manage the situation all on their own. This often leaves them very vulnerable to taking drugs or alcohol or becoming addicted to the internet in order to self-regulate. In other words, teenagers who don't trust don't simply do nothing when they are in emotional pain; they can do things that can cause long-term damage to their brain, body and quality of life.

So it is hoped that, through this exercise, the teenager will be able to link their current distrust to relational experiences in the past. From this newly discovered place of awareness and insight, it is hoped that these teenagers will realise that their need for psychological safety, in terms of going it alone, is very costly to them. In due course, it is hoped that they will find the courage to do things differently, dare to love, and get the help they need.

Instructions for the teenager

When you find you really can't trust people in life, and because of this, when things are bad, you don't ask people for help, you may find it useful to think about all this with the relevant psychology. These pictures can be a good starting point. If you feel like any of the following, please tick the box or mark it as you like. If it's not any of these things, draw or write in the empty boxes what you feel like when you are aware of your mistrust.

Development

Exercise: How I see me, other people and life in general

Ask the teenager to finish these sentences:

- I am …
- Other people are …
- The world is …

These are key questions in finding out a teenager's attachment style. If they say something derogatory about other people, and how they would never trust them, and/or about the world being fundamentally dangerous or difficult in some ways, just say something like this: Sometimes people feel safer with technology, internet games, chat rooms, films and books than real relationships because they have been too hurt in life – often in childhood. So they dare not trust again because they think the past will just repeat itself. They feel they can't afford to trust again – it cost them too much last time. Other people have never trusted anyone ever; never got really close to anyone. They often do not even know that they are missing out on the loveliness of people's empathy, compassion, warmth, kindness, deep concern and real help when life gets difficult.

Exercise: From trust to mistrust

Ask the teenager to think of a time in the past when they dared to trust, love and let themselves get close to someone and it went wrong.

When you dared to trust, love and let go in the past did it end in any of the following? Tick the ones that are true for you:

- feeling bad about yourself
- being let down
- feeling abused
- feeling used
- getting rejected.

If it is none of these, or some of your feelings are missing from the list, add your own.

Exercise: The origins of your mistrust

These are common reasons why people don't want to trust other people and/or get too close to them. Do you think any of these things have fuelled your sense of mistrust or your feeling that it is better only to trust yourself?

Reason	Yes/No
When you were little, you didn't go to your parents when you were upset	
You don't trust your parents to help you with a problem without responding badly (eg by not listening or by getting cross) so you've learned to deal with things on your own	
People in the past have been frightening	
People in the past have been disapproving or shaming	
People in the past have made you feel bad about yourself	
People in the past have needed too much from you	
You have trusted but then you were let down	
There was a major shock or disruption in the family, and you never trusted after that	

Rarely feel at ease with anyone

Got to get through this myself

There's no one to catch me if I fall

There's no one to there to help me with my problems

No one really understands me

Often the world feels out to get me

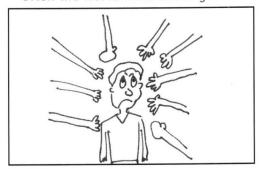

I can't trust anyone

I can't let anyone in

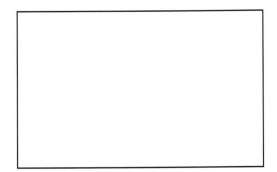

Discussion
Talk about the relief of 'what is sharable is bearable' (Siegel, 1999) and 'a trouble shared is a trouble halved'

The teenager needs to experience (hopefully with you) the 'felt knowledge' that having painful life experiences heard, acknowledged and understood is very healing and often a huge relief. At last someone else understands all that you have been carrying in your head, all alone, for so long.

Example
Tim, aged 13, had a very strict dad. He'd never told anyone before because he just thought it was normal to be shouted at every time he got a low mark at school, or spilt something, broke something or did something wrong. One day he talked to a teacher about it. The teacher told him that it wasn't normal and showed real feeling about how it must have made life far too tough for him at home at times. Tim felt a huge relief that he was no longer the only person on this earth who knew how he suffered. He ended up telling the teacher lots of other things too. If felt so good, like putting down massive boulders he'd been carrying all his life.

Quotations the teenager may find useful

Some people feel that nobody will ever understand them, or make them feel safe, but actually it's just that they haven't yet found the person who will.
(Sunderland, 2010)

And like most teens she tends first to idealise and then to feel shattered or outraged when her lofty expectations are disappointed.
(Hauser et al, 2006)

He imagined laying his treasures at his mother's feet, wiping away her black moods and sullen withdrawals. Once and for all he would reclaim his heritage by restoring her world, which – he was forever being told with a thousand cues, raised eyebrows, and turned-down corners of a mouth – had collapsed because of something he had done or failed to do. (Stolorow et al, 1987)

Deep sobbing ... happens when a person senses that long-overlooked grievances have finally been heard. It is a sure sign of relief. Difficult as such open expressions of hurt usually are, they lessen pain ...
(Bar-Levav, 1988)

The very freedom to shed tears of hurt openly in the presence of someone who can be trusted with our pain has an altogether different effect. It confirms that somebody cares and that our vulnerability and hurt at least deserve a respectful hearing.
(Bar-Levav, 1988, p188)

Jealous/possessive/clingy

Objective

The objective of this exercise is for teenagers who feel very jealous and possessive in their partner relationships to gain real insight into, and understanding of, their feelings and behaviour. It is hoped that, from this more enlightened position, they will stop engaging in such desperate and often abusive interactions with their partner and learn to love in peace rather than in torment.

When teenagers are very jealous and possessive, this can result in desperate controlling behaviour known as coercive control (Stark, 2007). The following are common examples of coercive control:

- 'You must not go out in those clothes – only in these clothes.'
- 'You must have no contact with that person any more.' [out of jealousy]
- 'You must ring me or text me all the time so I know what you are doing and who you are with.'

The message, overtly spoken or non-verbally conveyed, is, 'You can only have eyes for me. Don't speak to them, don't text them, don't see them.' These teenagers often need to know what their boyfriend or girlfriend is doing all the time. This can involve insisting that their partner sees less and less of their own friends and family so they can be with them more. If these wishes are not complied with, the jealous possessive teenager can feel so desperate that they resort to verbal abuse or physical violence.

Examples

'Like when I'd be out with my friends and he'd drag me off and say he didn't want me out any longer and I'd got to go in, and it could be like half past six. I'd say, "They're my friends, I'll speak to whoever I want to," and then he'd get really mad.'

'He gets paranoid if I go out with my mates on a Saturday night, thinking I'm cheating on him, and reads my texts. Whereas I'm not allowed to know what he's up to ever, even just out of curiosity.'

'If I did see the people he didn't want you to see ... He'd physically drag me away from them.'

'They are always texting their bird wondering what they are doing all the time. Telling them not to go there, to go there. If you don't answer your phone, like "Why don't you answer your phone?," "Where were you?"'

'I'd go in about half 10 in the night and he'd stay on the phone to me until like one in the morning and he wouldn't get off the phone. I would say, "I don't want you to text me so often ..." but then he'd probably be like, "Why?" Um, could you explain why? Um, probably be awkward.'

'He'd ask me to delete all the boys' [addresses] and everything ... 'cos he didn't like me talking to other boys and everything.'

'He used to fight people that said anything to her. Yeah, even if it weren't anything bad, he would just fight them.'

(Barter *et al*, 2009)

So what's going on?

These teenagers are haunted by their unresolved past. Basically, they are what is known as 'insecurely attached' (Ainsworth *et al*, 1978). This means that during infancy and/or childhood they did not experience one or both parents as a secure base who was consistently responsive to their emotional needs. Rather they experienced that parent as sometimes being responsive and sometimes not. This sets up a reaction of panic distress in the infant or child, who feels abandoned and rejected one minute and loved and calmed the next. This is often so painful that the feelings are repressed (banished to the unconscious mind). However, in the teenage years, as Robin Anderson (former head of the Adolescent Department at The Tavistock Clinic, London) said, 'the personality cannot hold'. This means that, with all the major life and hormonal changes, there is a breakdown of the repression and all those early feelings of

panic distress and fears of abandonment come flooding back. The teenager transfers on to their teenage partner all the unresolved feelings towards their 'on-off' parent (Freud called this 'transference'). So coercive control is a form of desperate screaming for Mummy or Daddy, a panic distress, but now just focused onto their teenage partner. They are, in effect, acting like desperate toddlers who scream and scream when Mummy leaves the house because they don't yet know that she will always come back.

Most teenagers have no idea of any of this. They just know they feel desperately jealous. Ironically, the partners who stay with them and put up with all this abuse often also have abandonment issues and insecure attachments, otherwise they would do the healthy thing: say they will not be treated like this and leave.

In the discussion part of the exercise, teenagers can be helped to understand this process and gain insight into what fuels their painful jealousy and possessiveness. This section is also designed to help teenagers to understand that their behaviour is over the top. Research shows that they often don't know that. They think it is just because they care about someone a lot.

Instructions for the teenager

Do you find yourself often anxious about your relationship with your boyfriend or girlfriend? Do you find yourself texting or phoning them a great deal of the time? Are you anxious about who they are talking to and what they are doing when they are not with you? Are you worried they might be with someone else? Do you worry they might go off you, be unfaithful or leave you? If so, you are what is known as 'loving in torment'. We will explain why this might be shortly. But first, you may find it useful to think more about exactly what you feel, so that loving can be far more anxiety free in the future. Do you ever feel like any of these people in the pictures below? If you do, colour them in or tick them. If it's not any of these things, draw or write in the empty box what you feel inside when you are feeling jealous, very possessive or frightened of rejection from your partner.

I get so jealous

Can't stop texting her or phoning her

Worried about who she is with when not with me

Terrified of losing him/her

I make sure he/she does what I say

I wouldn't cope if I lost him/her

Development

Exercise:

Tick any of the feelings in the list below that you recognise as having about your partner:

- 'When you don't return my smile, it's like you've hit me.'
- 'When you look away, it's like you've gone away.'
- 'When we don't connect, it's as if you leave me in some awful desert.'
- 'When I feel he's losing interest in me, I end up doing some crazy things, like I'm possessed.'
- 'I was so afraid that she'd leave me, so I got really cross with her and controlled her to stay.'
- 'When he is with me, I often think he doesn't want to be with me.'
- 'She'll leave me one day, I won't leave her.'
- 'If he says he loves me he doesn't really mean it.'

Exercise: Loving in torment

Help the teenager to think about common origins of loving in torment and how insecure attachment can evolve. Ask them if they think any of the following happened in their childhood:

- feeling like the unfavoured sibling in the family
- feeling of having lost one's beloved parent, or lost their love to the new baby, another sibling, parent's depression or alcoholism, for example
- an on-off parent (sometimes emotionally responsive, sometimes not)
- painful separations from a parent in childhood (short term or long term)
- memories of missing their parent terribly
- being left to cry as a baby when in need of comfort (eg left to cry oneself to sleep)
- separation anxiety that was left unsoothed or not taken seriously
- being pushed away at the natural clingy stage
- a parent who left
- parents separating or divorce (75 per cent of teenagers move from secure to insecure attachment when this happens – Murray, 2007).

Discussion

An introductory word of warning

Some teenagers will be far too defended to consider childhood origins of these feelings. In this case, just use the sections below that are not about insecure attachment. Those teenagers who, for example, are locked in an idealising vision of their parents will become very defensive in the face of any suggestion that parents were at times any less than perfect. With these teenagers, it would not be advisable to go into the attachment theory below. Other teenagers who are also somewhat defensive are able to hear that the parent–infant relationship is a dance and sometimes the dance can go wrong, with the best of intentions. Sometimes this happens with the infant believing things that are not true – for example, 'Mummy loves the new baby more than me.' Teenagers often need help to know that insecure attachment is not the same as being loved. A parent can be very loving but a child still insecurely attached, particularly if the love is needy, too much or misattuning. However defended or not defended the teenager is, it is important to use words that are not about blaming parents.

Talk about how having a fear of rejection, betrayal or abandonment can make people behave in a desperate, panicky way

You might say something like this: When people have ongoing fears of rejection or abandonment, they can be driven at times to desperate behaviour. Such behaviour may include all manner of clinging, rushing away, rushing towards, slamming doors, ultimatums, threats to leave, pleading, begging, shouting, raging, extreme claims on the other person's time and, for some people, threats of or actual self-harm. The misery and self-loathing can be far-reaching. Furthermore, the fear of being left can build to such intensity that it may lead the person to paranoid acts, such as spying on their partner, going through their possessions, following them, or always texting or phoning to check what they are doing. During these times, they are desperate to re-establish a connection with their loved one, desperate to do anything that will help close the emotional gap, which can be experienced as being unbearable. What they often don't know is that they are usually reliving unbearable feelings from childhood.

Talking about coercive control as abnormal

Teenagers need help to understand that coercive control is not normal in intimate relationships and can all too easily become a form of abuse for their partner. Some teenagers think that coercive control is just about caring a lot for their partner. It is not. The partners on the receiving end of coercive control who stay and put up with being told who they can't see, what they are to wear, and endless demands to text and phone, often have their own abandonment fears. The others will just leave. This is because people hate being controlled. It is often exactly this controlling behaviour that drives the other person away, hence reinforcing the fears of abandonment. When a relationship is not working, fears of being left can lead to even more desperate behaviour, clinging and threats in an attempt to stop the partner from leaving. All in all, when people are consumed by the fear of being left, they can experience all the emotional extremes and the same frightening feeling storms of a baby or toddler.

Talk to the teenager about insecure attachment

Find a way to explain to the teenager about the common attachment origins of excessively jealous behaviour. Refer to the attachment research in the *Objective* section. Help the teenager to consider the fact that their panic distress and fundamental mistrust in their partner's loyalty or love, or fear of betrayal, is likely to be fuelled by childhood insecurities. Sometimes this was a childhood fear that the parent loved their sibling more than them. Sometimes the fear was that the parent was going to abandon them. Sometimes the parent figure was emotionally responsive and sometimes not. So when the infant reached out in some way for help with a painful emotion, when they were crying badly, they were sometimes left to deal with it on their own. From any of these origins, the infant can learn a very important lesson – that it is not safe to trust others to be there when you need them.

Explain why they may not remember it, in terms of infantile amnesia: when under the age of three, key memory systems in the brain are not yet finished. If they are able to hear this and are interested, you might say something like this:

When a child's natural instinct, to love their parent and in return to be consistently emotionally responded to, is thwarted in some way, the person may form a tragic connection in his mind between loving and rejection. Sometimes the most painful is the 'intermittent reinforcement' of a parent who blows hot and cold, who emotionally responds one minute and not the next. We know from research with other mammals that intermittent reinforcement can be the precursor to addiction. But this time it is an addiction to a person not a substance.

Quotations the teenager may find useful

For the person who fears being left, every separation, every distance is an ordeal, which is difficult for him to endure ... The slightest coldness in a farewell must mean 'good riddance' and an ever so slightly cool or moody welcome will create profound insecurity.
(Odier, 1956)

People say the past is past. This is exactly what it isn't. Painful memories, when not fully felt, thought about and worked through, live on to haunt us.
(The author)

One wonders at their blindness. Their choice [of partner] seems [mad]. There had been indications that the other was incapable of reciprocating, or loving, or accepting them in the way they desire. They had been pursuing an alluring but rejecting [partner], an exciting yet frustrating [partner]. The [person] initially may have offered conditions of hope but it fails to satisfy. It had awakened an intensity of yearning, but is essentially the elusive object of desire, seemingly there but just out of reach.
(Armstrong-Perlman, 1991)

All about me and my life

(worksheets)

My life as a film

Objective

This exercise is designed for the teenagers to reflect on their life, both the painful and the pleasurable. Often a teenager makes bad decisions as their life is dominated by impulsive actions rather than time for reflection. So here teenagers look back and review their life in terms of what or who has deeply affected who they are today, for better or worse. It is hoped that this will better inform what they want to do with their life in the future.

The exercise is also about savouring what has been really good in their life so far. As Seamus Heaney says, 'We live amongst the marvellous', but all too many teenagers don't spend time savouring 'the marvellous'. Arguably, in a world of technology and computer games, it is increasingly difficult for teenagers to enjoy an embodied, impassioned response to this beautiful planet. Instead of sitting by the side of the river, drinking in the beauty of the buttercups and feeling the sun on their skin, many teenagers are far more likely to be in their house on the internet, texting, on their PlayStation or in some internet chat room. So taking time to savour what has been really good in their life is an important thing to do.

Instructions for the teenager

It is said that many people put more time into planning Christmas than planning what to do with their life. They never sit down and consider how things have gone in the past, how things are going in the present and, based on that, what they want to do differently in the future. They don't go back and reflect on the really good times and the really bad times, and how these have influenced how they are today. So this exercise gives a space for all that so that, hopefully, you can make better decisions about your life in the future.

Imagine that your life is made into a film. On the sheet you will find three film sets:

- On the film set called 'The Amazing and Lovely', draw images (stick people will do) that speak about lovely times, lovely people, amazing things you have done or seen in your life.

- On the film set called 'The Painful and Difficult', draw or write things that speak about the painful or too difficult times in your life.

- On the film set called 'The Too Sad', draw or write things that speak about the very sad things that have happened in your life.

These fragments of your life can be randomly drawn, like a dream or collage.

Development

Ask the teenager to do a 'line down the middle' reflection. The left-hand side has the title 'Bad decisions I've taken', and the right-hand side has the title, 'Good decisions I've taken'. Again, most teenagers will never have taken the time to look at their life in this way and used it to inform how they want to do things differently in the future.

Amazing and lovely   **The painful and difficult**   **The too sad**

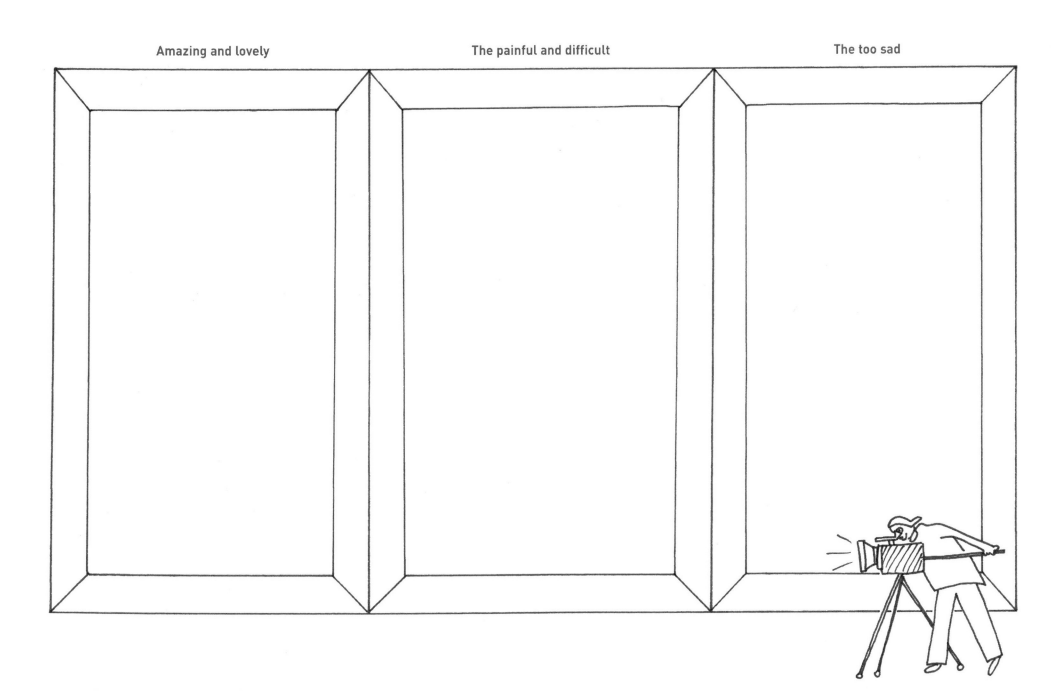

My past, present and future

Objective
So many times, teenagers who are troubled in some way have never sat down to consider their life so far. So they often suffer from having an incoherent narrative of their life. Research shows that it is essential for people to have an accurate take on all that has happened to them. Without this, myths and irrational, unfounded beliefs can be viewed as reality, often for years or even a lifetime, with all sorts of confusions arising. Tina, aged 17, still believed that 'Dad and Mum split up because I was too much'. Ben, aged 18, still believed that 'Mum left us when I was six, because I wasn't interesting enough'. One may marvel at such a distorted child view of the situation, but when such views are formed in childhood, it can be very difficult to give them up or challenge them in the teenage years. They can inform life decisions, often in very negative ways. So a key part of this exercise is to help the teenager to see far more clearly how their past is affecting their present and for you the practitioner to challenge if they have clearly been living with an irrational fantasy about events and their causation.

The exercise is also designed to offer the teenager precious time to consider their future, rather than just finding themselves in it, so to speak. 'Rehearsal of the possible' is actually spending time imagining something they want to do or be in the future. It can be very powerful, as Dina Glouberman (1989) says: 'A good way to think of it is that energy follows thought – what we do follows in the pathway or fits into the thought form created by our imagination. We need to be careful about what we imagine, for we may unknowingly become it.' Also, 'Yeats believes that, if we are able to focus completely on a thought in an imaginary vision, then this idea will realise itself in the circumstances of life ...' (McNiff, 1992, p223).

This exercise is particularly important for teenagers who feel their adulthood is already decided even before they have got there. As Billy, aged 17, said, 'We are just a family who don't do things, don't get jobs, live on the state and get drunk a lot.'

Instructions for the teenager
Look at the four sections of this window labelled, 'My past', 'My present', 'My feared future' and 'My hoped-for future'. In the window labelled 'My past', write or draw the events, people, and so on, that have really influenced how you are today. A clue to this is to think of the events and people from your past that you still often think about today. Then, in the window labelled 'My present', write or draw the events, people, and so on that have really influenced how you are today. Then, in the window marked 'My feared future', write down what you fear might be your future. Finally, in the window marked 'My hoped-for future', write down what you hope will happen in your future. What can you do to increase the probability that the latter will come true and decrease the probability that your feared future will happen?

Development
Take the teenager's desired future and put even more flesh on the bones. Ask them to do a large painting of it or a sandplay image. Alternatively, ask the teenager to talk in the first person as if their desired future is happening now. Help them by using unfinished sentences: 'Now I am ...', 'What I am feeling is ...', 'I am with ...'   Tape what the teenager says (with their permission, of course) and then play it back to them. If appropriate, ask them how they might sabotage their dream for themselves for the future and how they can stop themselves sabotaging it.

Quotations the teenager may find useful

When you reach for the stars, you may not get one, but you won't come away with a handful of mud, either.
(Leo Burnett, 2006)

To laugh often and much ... To leave the world a bit better, whether by a healthy child, a garden patch, or a redeemed social condition; To know even one life has breathed easier because you have lived. This is to have succeeded.
(Anderson Stanley 1911)

If you always do what you've always done, you'll always be what you've always been.
(Bishop TD Jakes, 1998)

Museum of Resentments

Objective

Talking about feelings can enable teenagers to take on board the emotional complexities of a situation, particularly where feelings of anger and resentment are involved. So, for example, instead of thinking, 'I hate him', a teenager can be enabled to develop far more sophisticated thought processes such as, 'I hate him, because I feel so hurt by him', and even, 'I guess he must have been really hurt by someone in his life, to call my mother names like that.'

When we help teenagers to talk about their feelings of anger and resentment, they develop curiosity about how what has happened to them in the past colours their perception of the present. Without help to speak about feelings, many teenagers will never develop the capacity. Instead, their anger and resentment moves all too quickly into blame, and perhaps into fantasies of revenge. For example, Toby, aged 13, before counselling said things like, 'I just hit him because he deserved it'. After counselling he could say, 'I think I hit him because he dissed me but I guess it was also because I was still feeling so let down by my dad moving out.'

Some key research by Hauser *et al*, (2006) found that teenagers who had committed violent crimes (often shooting or stabbing), but who then developed capacity for insight and self-awareness, went on to do well in later life. The others, who were stuck in years of anger, hate and resentment, did very badly.

Carrying around unspoken resentments for years, costs. It takes up energy; energy that could be used for far more creative pursuits. Resentments take up too much thought time and the fact that they do is indication enough that they are unprocessed. Rarely does a teenager get an arena where they can look at all the resentments in their life so that they can put down that emotional baggage and move on.

Instructions for the teenager

Think of all the resentments you feel about people in your life, past and present. They may date back a long way or may be relatively new. Draw and label each one of them on the exhibit stands in this Museum of Resentments. Then stand back and look at them. What do you feel when you see them all together in this way? Which eats away at you the most? Is there any way that you can resolve any of them? You could, for example, write the person a letter, which you may or may not send. If you are writing a letter like this, you can be as irrational or as unreasonable as you want, without needing to worry how the other person will react to what you say. In the same way, it can be valuable to write such a letter to people who are dead. Or write the resentment on a piece of paper and put it in the bin or imagine you are sending the resentment on a rocket into outer space. This is not silly but serious, as research shows that the human mind cannot distinguish between something vividly imagined and the real thing. So doing something like this can diminish the energetic charge of the resentment and its emotional hold on you and your precious thought time.

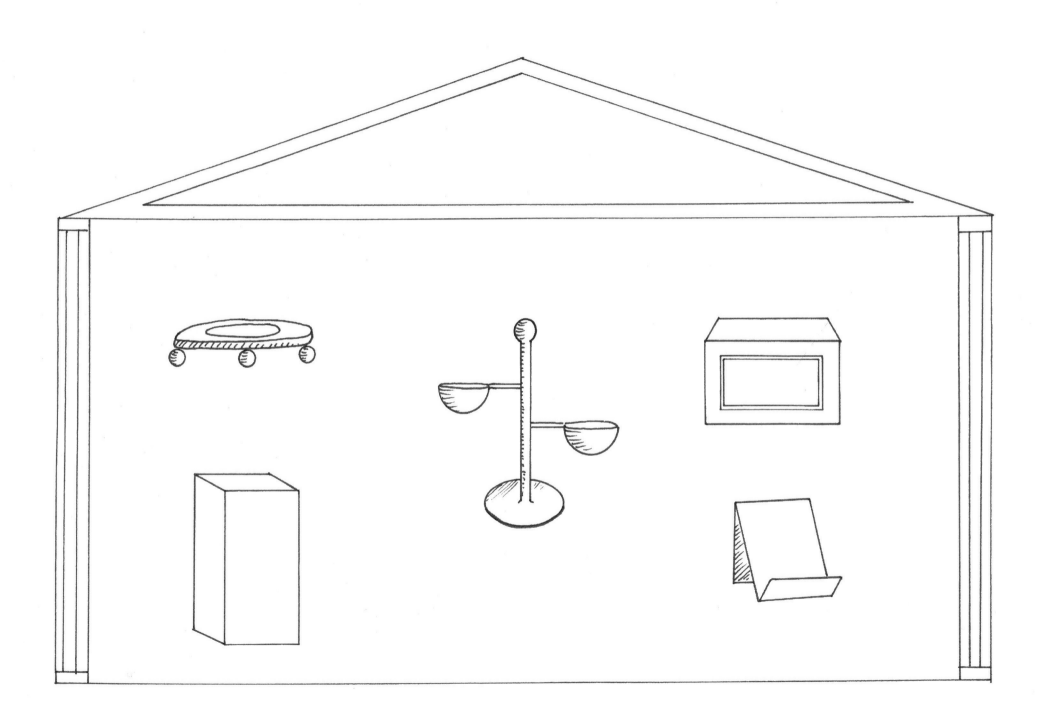

Exhibition of the worst times and the best times

Even if the listening time with the adult is only for one hour a week, 'It is something [the teenager] can carry through the rest of their week, a little torch burning inside of them that reminds them that they are not alone in the world.'
(Mears and Cooper, 2005, p48)

Objective
This exercise is to help the teenager to process important life events. It is vital that we reflect on what has happened to us. We know the cost of what happens if we don't, in terms of the emotional baggage that can so easily blight a life, and in some instances destroy it. The exercise is also about reflecting on the good times as well as the bad. It is as important to savour the good times as it is to reflect on the bad times: those moments of real connection with someone, moments of laughing and laughing, moments of beauty, moments of intense calm. Just as with the bad times, good experiences are often left not fully digested, integrated and assimilated, which means that the potential for lovely memories to nourish the teenager on an ongoing basis is diminished. Furthermore, whereas children are often good at talking about the lovely things that happen to them, energetically and passionately, teenage cynicism can crush all that.

So this exercise offers the teenager a thinking space designed to remember and properly savour what may not have been fully savoured at the time. Sharing these times with you, whose role is to listen and appreciate in a non-judgemental manner, makes the experience all the more powerful and energetically charged. Perhaps these vital experiences have never been shared or only shared in a way that was too fleeting or downplaying. The worst times tend to be those when the teenager was struggling with something very painful, shocking or overwhelming, all on their own, just as one is always alone in a nightmare. As Judd (2008) says, many children and teenagers need help with their feelings so they then feel 'more accompanied' in life.

Instructions for the teenager
Think of the most memorable good times and the most memorable bad times in your life. These are times that you will never forget. The good times may be funny, beautiful or exciting, or a deep sense of friendship with someone. The bad times may be feeling totally alone, frightened, hopeless or desperate. You find you often revisit these best times and worst times in your mind. Write or draw them on the exhibition stands in the picture. Then talk about each one of these significant times in your life in turn. What did they make you feel and how they are still affecting you today? What is it like looking at them all together? What has been the most lovely event and the most horrible event?

Discussion
Talk about how we often rush over the good times in our lives whereas we can't stop thinking about the bad times
Human beings tend to dwell on their regretted past and their feared future. They often spend far too little thought time reflecting on their good fortune, precious moments and relationships past and present. And yet the latter is a key aspect of personal development. As Clarkson (1989) says, 'The quality of contact determines whether life "passes by" or whether it is lived to the full.'

Talk about the concept of emotional wealth (Klein 1988) – that we can be poor in terms of money but very rich in terms of friendships
People, and particularly teenagers, often feel they suffer because of lack of material wealth. They can't afford those latest trainers or those designer label clothes and the latest mobile phone. It can be helpful to inform them that we feel really good on buying new things as it releases a reward chemical in the

brain called dopamine. But once that hit of dopamine in their brain wears off, which often happens pretty quickly, we can feel pretty empty again. This is compared with the far more long-lasting biochemical release of wonderful feel-good chemicals such as opioids and oxytocin, which happens when we are emotionally wealthy from really good friendships and key people in our lives.

Talk about parents who are not good at modelling spontaneity and excitement
People often need help to awaken their ability to relish and savour, to get lost in the moment, to keep all their senses open.

Talk about the concept of peak experiences
Discuss Maslow's (1971) concept of 'the peak experience', that is, unusual moments of great serenity, beauty, wonder or profound aesthetic experience; moments of profound connection with someone else.

Good and bad places I have known

Objective

As well as attachment to people, attachment to place is powerful. Some places become key parts of our life's narrative, for better or worse. We can suppress feelings about places just as we can about people. It is only when we revisit the place that we get a rush of emotion chemicals and realise how much it has meant to us. So this exercise is for teenagers to revisit those places that have been very significant in their lives, and talk about them with a listening other.

Instruction

Think of three or four places in your life that have had a major impact on you for better. Perhaps they have added to your creativity, or your sense of hope, or your dreams of what is possible. Then think of three or four places that have had a bad impact on you. They made you feel bad about yourself or are linked to feelings of loneliness, boredom, fear and so on. These can be any place – for example, a holiday place, or a particular room, or even a park bench – anywhere, however big or small. In the boxes provided, draw images and feeling words about the good and bad places. Write the age you were when you visited each place. Write the name of the place too. By the side of each place box you will find a small energy box. Draw in this the emotional energy of that particular place. For example, was it still, serene, horrible, jarring, chaotic? Then find a small figure to be you and put the figure in the place. What do you feel as you see yourself (represented by the little figure) in the place once again?

Talk to the place: 'What I feel about you is …', 'If I were to return to you, what I would like to do is …'

With the bad places you have chosen, do to them what you want – you can deface them however you like or tear them up or throw them in a bin.

With the lovely places say: 'What you have meant to me is …', 'What I miss about you is …'

Then look at them again. Which of the lovely places has touched you the most?

(In some circumstances, say with a teenager in care who has had several placements, the number of places in the picture will not be enough, so use a separate sheet for the number you need.)

Example

Tina, aged 15, drew a dark corner. It was a place in her primary school where she would hide from the bullies. She said it was great to show the counsellor this place as it had been so key in her life. The counsellor asked Tina to find a little figure to represent her child self and place it in the corner. The counsellor took another figure and stood it in the dark corner too. She said, 'I wish I had been there for you then. You were too alone and no one knew. And no one knew.'

Development

Exercise: Heaven on earth, hell on earth – have you actually been there?

Get a large piece of paper. Draw a line down the middle. On the left-hand side, write 'hell on earth'. On the right-hand side, write 'heaven on earth'. Then use words, phrases or images to describe all the events in your life that have been hell on earth for you and then the ones that have been heaven on earth. Talk about the events on both sides that have had a profound impact on you and your life, for better or worse.

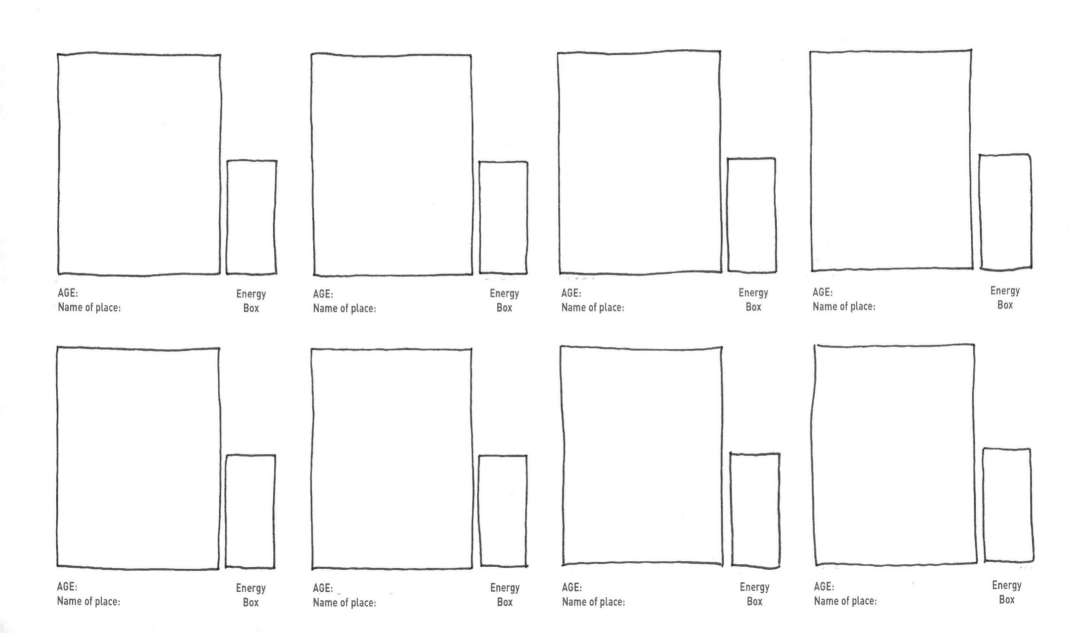

AGE:
Name of place:

Energy
Box

AGE:
Name of place:

Energy
Box

AGE:
Name of place:

Energy
Box

AGE:
Name of place:

Energy
Box

AGE:
Name of place:

Energy
Box

AGE:
Name of place:

Energy
Box

AGE:
Name of place:

Energy
Box

AGE:
Name of place:

Energy
Box

About my relationships

(worksheets)

The empowerers and the squashers

Objective

Teenagers are particularly vulnerable to suffering from low self-esteem, which can all too easily move into depression. Often, the origins of this are laid down in childhood. The teenager has experienced too much discouragement and criticism in their life and not enough praise or encouragement. The discouraging attitudes or statements can all too easily become internalised and form the basis of negative self-talk – that is, what the teenager keeps saying to themselves inside their head. Negative self-talk is so powerful that it can blight a teenager's will, determination, motivation, capacity to learn and self-esteem. It can be so damning that it is far worse than how you would ever talk to another person – for example, 'You are so stupid', 'You are useless', 'You never get anything right'. This exercise is designed to heighten the teenager's awareness of their self-talk, as the first step towards shifting to positive internal messages.

Discouragement, particularly in childhood when we are still forming a sense of self, can lead to all manner of feelings of defeat and hopelessness in the long term. When people have suffered a lot of discouragement in their lives it can also lead to what is known as 'frustration avoidance'. This means giving up very easily in the face of challenge or adversity. In fact, because discouragement is so readily taken in, it is commonly accepted among psychologists that human beings need six encouragements to counter the effects of every one discouragement.

Instructions for the teenager

A person's confidence and self-esteem can be really affected when they feel that they have not had enough encouragement in their life or not enough times when people really appreciated their opinion on things, really listened to what they had to say or really valued something they did. It is important to separate people's lack of generosity in such things from your own qualities, talents and the really lovely things about you. Look at the gallery of encouragers and discouragers in the picture. Think back to the people who have encouraged you or discouraged you in childhood and now in your teenage years. Write their names in the appropriate name boxes in the picture. Then write in the thought bubbles, by the side of these figures, the beliefs about yourself that you think each of them have left you with. For example, a particular encourager might say, 'You are creative' or 'You can make it in life'. A particular discourager might say, 'You never get anything right' or 'You won't make it'.

When you have finished your galleries, stand back and look. Which of all the people in your galleries are still influencing what you think about yourself today and also what you say to yourself inside your head? (This is known as self-talk.) It may be a person who is no longer in your life and yet they are still having a big effect on you. Colour in or mark the figures who are still having a major effect on your life, your view of yourself and life in general.

Development

Exercise: The inner critic

Explore with the teenager what it feels like to live with the inner critic that resides in their head. Ask them to make an image of their inner critic in clay. Then ask them to speak to their inner critic or do what they want to do to them. Ask them who in their life influenced the fact they have an inner critic now – for example, a teacher, a parent, a bully, a sibling. Alternatively, they may like to write their inner critic a short letter entitled, 'What it's been like living with you inside my head'. One way to deal with inner critics is to make a recording of what they say. The teenager can then have a very vivid example of their negative self-talk, and decide whether they choose to listen to it any more or just 'turn it off'.

'Thought stoppage' is an excellent cognitive behavioural therapy technique, which is very relevant here. Explain to the teenager that they can stop thinking what they are thinking if it is just negative rubbish. So if a critical voice pops up in their head, they can say out loud, 'Stop', 'Calm', or bang the table and say 'Enough'. It can also help teenagers to know that a negative or critical thought prolongs a negative feeling or mood state, so if you stop yourself thinking the negative thought you can often stop the negative feeling. We really do have the power to stop listening to an inner critic and to think of something else, or even bring to mind some lovely memory. This is a skill well worth practising. Ask the teenager to think of a few key lovely memories that they can use as a resource in this way.

Stages of Life	Empowerers	Squashers
Childhood years		
Teenage years		

Confident me – not confident me

Objective
Being with different people brings out very different aspects of ourselves. This is particularly true with teenagers who are still forming their identity – who they are and who they want to become. With some people the teenager might feel confident, warm and open. With others they can feel dull or of little worth. This exercise looks at the effect other people have on the teenager's confidence and self-esteem. It is hoped that the teenager will then feel more aware of the impact of the people in their life on the views they hold of themselves. It is also hoped that they will then be motivated to think more about who they spend their time with and relationships that are clearly not good for them.

Instructions for the teenager
Think about the people who have had a significant impact on your life, for better or worse. Who in your life has sometimes made you feel uptight, anxious, small, tight or closed? Who has made you feel the opposite: confident, open, playful, really fun to be with? Look at the picture. As you see, the figures range from closed, small and defended to open, expansive and confident. Which of the people in your life (past or present) have sometimes made you feel like one of these figures in the picture? Write the people's names under the appropriate figure. You can write more than one name under any of the figures if you like. What have you learned about yourself and/or about the people in your life (past or present)? What have you learned about who you want to spend time with?

(It may also be useful then to ask them how much they think childhood figures are still haunting them, in terms of undermining their capacity to be confident and assertive in their life today.)

Development
Exercise: Self-states
In clay, get the teenager to mould images of their different selves – the confident self, the shy self, the anxious self, the happy self, and so on. Using the unfinished sentence technique, ask them to talk to these clay images of themselves: 'What I feel about you is …', 'I like it when …', 'I don't like it when you …'.

A further development on the theme would be to ask the teenager to think about what aspects of their life they are open or closed to. For example:
- open or closed to fun
- open or closed to change
- open or closed to adventure and exploration
- open or closed to risk
- open or closed to new social experiences.

When we feel unsafe, as Bowlby (1988) said, 'We shrink from the world and do battle with it'. Ask the teenager to think about what makes them feel psychologically safe and unsafe in life. When they feel unsafe, how do they find themselves shrinking from the world or doing battle with life?

Name:	Name:	Name:	Name:	Name:
Name:	Name:	Name:	Name:	Name:

The people in my life at a party

Objective
This exercise is to enable teenagers to take a long, hard look at the people in their lives, past or present. Without such reflection time, it is all too easy to drift along in life, investing too much in draining or destructive relationships. It is also too easy to be caught in the grip of painful relational experiences from the past. These can continue negatively to influence the teenager until they are processed or worked through in the present. Focused reflection, as provided by this exercise, can be a vital first step for the teenager to improve their life with more enriching human capital.

Instructions for the teenager
Think of the people in your life, past and present, who are, or have been, very significant to you in one way or another. These are people who have markedly influenced your life for better (eg an inspiring teacher) or for worse (eg a bully). In this picture, imagine all these significant people in your life have come together at one big party. They have divided themselves into groups of like-minded people.

Think of each significant person in your life, past and present, and write their name on one of the figures in the group that is most apt for them. If someone you know falls into more than one group, because they have different sides to them, such as a dad who can be lovely one minute but very angry the next, just write their name on as many figures as you need.

When you have finished, stand back and look at what you have drawn. What does your peopled life, past and present together, look like? Do you have enough people in the positive groups? If not, what can you do to spend more time with people who are good for you and less time with people who stress you or disrespect you in some way? How much of your life have you spent with lovely, inspiring, warm people and how much of your life has been difficult because of relationships that have been painful or destructive?

Development
Exercise: Childhood figures
Find objects in the room or sandplay miniatures (see page 42 for an explanation of sandplay) to represent key people in your childhood. Place them all on a piece of paper or sandbox with an object to represent you as the child you felt you were. After you have done this, say what you have learned from your choice of objects or miniatures on the paper. You may like to rearrange them as you would have liked your childhood to be, by adding people or removing them from the paper. Is there anything you can learn from this about how you want to live your life now?

The critics

The inspirers

The drainers and takers

The encouragers

The warm
and lovely

The angry volcanoes

The grey and dull

The sad and depressed

The threatening/
dangerous

The loved and lost

The Museum of Too Alone

Like many other lonely people, Gavin has a deep sense that others do not really know who he is, that others have not really touched down to the depths of his being and witnessed the hidden world that is there.

(Mears and Cooper, 2005, p20)

Objective

The novelist Doris Lessing said that if you've known bleakness in childhood it never leaves you. That said, past experiences of intense loneliness or aloneness can be modified by talking about them with someone who is good at listening and understanding what it was like. This exercise can offer some of that essential working through.

Instructions for the teenager

Draw and/or write in the six exhibit boxes in this Museum of Too Alone the key times in your life when you felt very alone and no one was there to help you. Write the age you were at the time. Write some of the feelings you felt at the bottom of each box. If you prefer, just circle the feelings you felt from the list at the side of the page. You don't need to fill in all six exhibits, but you can add more exhibits if there are not enough here.

When you have finished, step back and look at the picture. What do you feel about what you have drawn or written? How are these too lonely times still affecting how you feel about yourself, other people or life in general? Could you have asked for help at the time? If so, what stopped you? What does this tell you about your ability to ask for help? Or did you ask for help but get no response?

Development
Exercise: Tour of the Museum of Too Alone

Photocopy the museum picture so that it is enlarged to A3 or A2. Ask the teenager to choose a figure or object to represent themselves and also ask them to choose one to be you. The teenager and you then move these chosen figures into each exhibit in turn. In this way, you are both revisiting these too-alone experiences as you would exhibits in an actual museum. You act as the first witness and, because you are there this time, it is not a re-traumatising but a re-experiencing in order to modify the experience. Ask the teenager to say or do the things they wished they had done or said at the time. You can support the process by using the unfinished sentence technique – for example, 'I felt so alone. What I needed you to know was ...'.

The teenager may experience difficulty in finding the words. If so, your figure as 'witness' can speak to the event. Holding the figure that represents you, start sentences like this: 'I am so sorry this happened to you. I can imagine how painful it must have been to have felt that ...'. You may even speak to one of the people in the teenager's life. For example, 'It was not OK that you left [teenager's name] all alone with that. You did not see his terror, his shock, his feeling overwhelmed and helpless.'

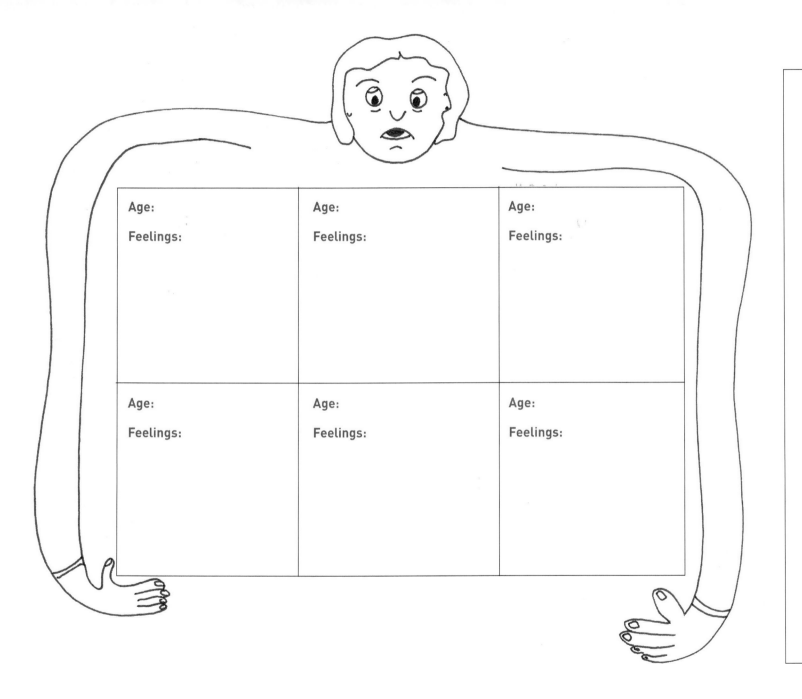

Age:

Feelings:

Age:

Feelings:

Age:

Feelings:

Age:

Feelings:

Age:

Feelings:

Age:

Feelings:

Hopeless

Despair

Heartbroken

Frightened

Terrified

Desolate

Desperate

Useless

Impotent

Wanting to burst into tears

Like your world had ended

Angry

Rage

Full of silent screams

Like giving up

Wanting to die

Not being who I could be

Objective
In our daily life we all move through different presentations of self. These are different aspects of ourselves that become more or less in the foreground depending on what is happening or who we are with. For example, being with one person might bring out a more intelligent self-state, while being with another might activate a false or inauthentic way of being in the world. Hence we might say something like, 'I hate myself when I am with X. I feel so boring and dull. I don't feel like that when I'm with anyone else.' Or, 'I love being with X. She makes me feel really good about myself.'

This exercise is to help the teenager to bring their different self-states and presentations of self more into conscious awareness. This is with the hope that the different parts of their personality can become more integrated and supported. So, for example, a more confident self-state may be able to be encouraging towards a part of the self that all too easily moves into giving up or feeling defeated. The exercise can also offer heightened awareness for the teenager of those people in their life in whose company they don't feel good about themselves.

Teenagers sometimes need informing that partner, family or friend relationships should make you feel good about yourself. You should develop emotionally and socially as a result of knowing that person. If this is not the case, something is wrong. This exercise is for teenagers who think that a key relationship in their life (personal or work) is holding them back in some way, preventing them from developing and thriving.

Instructions for the teenager
Think of the person you feel you are when you are with certain significant people in your life. Is there something about being with some of these people that brings out aspects of yourself that you particularly like or don't like? To enable you to think more clearly about this, look at the picture. Think of the key relationships in your life. Think of the ones that make you feel good about yourself and the ones that make you feel bad about yourself in some way. With the latter, maybe you are concerned that they are holding you back or affecting your ability to enjoy life and use it well. The people can be anyone – a teacher, a friend, a partner, someone in your family, someone at home or at school. Then take a look at the picture. When you think of each of your important relationships in turn, do you ever feel like one of the people in the pictures? If so, tick them or colour them in. Add the name of the person in the 'Me with ...' slot. You may also like to add a letter: Sometimes=S. Often=O. Frequently=F. Always=A.

If none of these images seems to fit what you feel about yourself when with a particular person, draw your own images in the empty boxes provided.

With the people who make you feel dull, false, submissive, and so on, how could you be different with them next time? Or is it that it is simply not good for you to be with these people?

Development
Exercise: Leap in the dark
Ask the teenager to draw a picture called 'Leap in the dark'. In the picture, ask them to draw themselves leaping away from the relationship in which they are not thriving, and landing in a new imaginary land. In this imaginary land, the teenager finds themselves surrounded by people (fictitious or real), who are encouraging, inspiring and extremely supportive. Ask the teenager to draw these people (stick figures will do) and then give each person a speech bubble. What are they saying? What would the teenager want to do if they were to have

an imaginary day out with these people and could go anywhere? Using the picture they have drawn as a starting point, discuss with the teenager what support they need to dare to taste life anew, to take a risk, to live a larger life, to stop depriving themselves by investing time in relationships that they feel are holding them back.

Exercise: The different 'mes'
In a sandtray (see page 42 for an explanation of sandplay), find figures to represent all the different 'yous' that you present to the world. Then get the figures representing your stronger, confident self-states to talk to the weaker ones, in order to think about how you could be more compassionate to the weaker more vulnerable parts of yourself instead of intolerant or critical.

Me with...	Me with...	Me with...	Me with...	Me with...
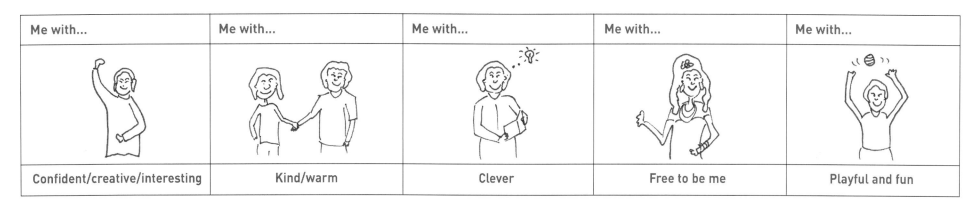				
Confident/creative/interesting	Kind/warm	Clever	Free to be me	Playful and fun

Me with...	Me with...	Me with...	Me with...	Me with...
Submissive/no backbone	Voiceless or can't find my words	Closed, guarded, private	Prickly	Dull

Me with...	Me with...			
False	Unimportant/a nobody			

Power over and power with

Objective
All too often in teenage relationships with parents and peers, there can be some form of abuse of power, albeit at times very subtle. This is not surprising as, for centuries, children have been disciplined at home and at school in ways that have involved some form of frightening 'power over' to make sure that they become compliant and obedient. So, in a way, many of us have had an early training in submission/dominance modes of interaction. In the UK, around a third of boys and a quarter of girls admit to having bullied other children.

> A quarter of adults who were bullied as children say they went on to suffer harmful long-term emotional effects.
>
> Around a third of boys and a quarter of girls admit they have bullied other children.
>
> A third of bully victims, aged 10 to 14, do not tell anyone about their problem. The figure rises with older children.
>
> One in five 11 to 19 year-olds experiences bullying or threats via email, internet chatrooms or text message.
>
> (NSPCC, 2011)

Where 'power with' has not been modelled enough or well enough at home, it is all too easy for teenagers to find themselves playing victim or persecutor roles in their important relationships. 'Power over' or dominant interactions can be found in nagging, controlling, criticising, put-downs, verbal or physical abuse. 'Power under' is where someone takes on the submissive position, giving up any personal authority, healthy protest and will, leading to feelings of impotence, low self-esteem and, often, unspoken rage. (The latter is often unconscious until the abusive relationship is reflected on with the help and psychoeducation of an empathic adult.)

This exercise aims to help teenagers to become more aware of submission/dominance patterns in their relationships as a key first step to shifting to more healthy modes of interaction.

Instructions for the teenager
Look at the drawings of relationship scenes with 'power over' and 'power with'. Starting with the 'power over' section, write 'me' next to the figures that represent you in some of the key relationships in your life, past or present. Try to be as honest with yourself as you can. Draw more scenes in the empty circles if you need them. Now stand back and look at what you have drawn. What have you learned? Are you more often the dominant one in the relationship, the submissive one, or a mixture of both? Or have you played different roles in different relationships? Now turn to the 'power with' drawings and tick or colour in any of these that you have enjoyed in your life. They don't have to be relationships that are always like this but relationships where for a lot of the time there was a sense of 'you and me together'.

If in your relationships, past and present, you have been in too many 'power over' or 'power under' interactions, think about what you can do to change things. If you feel you don't want to change things, are you addicted to the buzz of power? If not, how can you be with people and/or choose people to ensure that for far more of the time you enjoy 'power with' interactions? If you repeatedly find yourself being submissive or dominant in your relationships, think about what you may unconsciously be playing out from painful relationships in your past.

Development
Exercise: Power replays
Ask the teenager to think about their childhood in terms of
submission/dominance modes of relating. Ask them to think about home and
school. Using sandplay miniatures, drawing or clay, ask the teenager to depict
relationships in their childhood or the present when they were in a submissive
position and an adult in their life (eg a teacher, parent or relative) was adopting
a 'power over' way of relating (*see* page 42 for an explanation of sandplay). Ask
the teenager to write what they would want to say to that person in their life
who abused power in this way. Finally, ask them to consider how, without being
aware, they might be replaying 'power over' ways of relating now, either as
victim or persecutor.

You might also like to explain to the teenager the psychoanalytic term
'identification with the aggressor'. This means that, even despite our best
intentions, we can treat someone else in exactly the same negative ways that
we have been treated. In other words, people bully as they have been bullied,
control as they have been controlled. It is often only as a result of working
through our feelings about the original 'persecutors', and our feelings of
shame, fear and humiliation, that we can stop doing this.

After they've gone

Objective

We all need help to work through feelings after significant loss. There are no exceptions. Sadly, people – teenagers in particular – who feel they can manage without help all too often turn to the alternative 'help' of self-medication – for example, alcohol, over-eating, drugs or self-harm. When teenagers have suffered a loss, such as their parents splitting up, losing a friend because they have moved to a new school, or someone in their life dying, it is vital that they work through their pain and loss in order not to suffer from depression, anxiety or problems with anger, now or in later life. It is also important to know about the neuroscience of grief. Grieving children and teenagers often get into trouble at school because uncomforted grief changes brain chemistry, activating high levels of acetycholine. This can trigger feelings of anger and hostility.

This exercise provides the teenager with a language for grief, describing some of the most common and natural feelings resulting from loss. Finding the right words in this way can be a vital first step for teenagers to begin their mourning process.

Instructions for the teenager

A painful loss can hurt hugely. It is vital, as part of the healing process, to find someone to talk to who really understands your pain. If you don't, and just decide instead to try to cut off from what you are feeling or just bottle up your feelings, research shows that this can badly affect physical and emotional health and blight future happiness. Some teenagers use drugs and alcohol to deal with their grief but this choice often leads to them spoiling their life and life chances.

Look at the picture. Think of people who have left your life in some way – temporarily, permanently or for long periods of time. They are people who you really miss because you don't see them as much as you used to. Which of the images speak most clearly about your hurt, pain, anger and resentment? Tick any of the images that convey what life feels like after these people have gone. If none of the images are right for you, draw your own in the empty boxes provided.

Development

Exercise: What wise people have said about loss

Offer the following quotations to the teenager. Explain that most of the statements were written by famous authors or poets, all of whom had suffered the loss of a loved one. Discuss which quotations the teenager can relate to and why.

Her absence is like the sky, spread over everything.
(CS Lewis, 1966)

Comforter, where, where is your comforting?
(Gerard Manley Hopkins, 2009)

Water, water everywhere
Nor any drop to drink.
(Coleridge, 2010)

I'd walk down and I'd stare at the house for ages ... I'd keep saying it in my head – 'He's dead, he's dead, he's dead'. But it didn't mean anything.
(Rosemary Dinnage, 1990)

What helps in breaking up is a reminder that there isn't much to do except to grieve and hurt.
(Susie Orbach, 1994)

Exercise: The very missed person in your mind

The teenager is asked to draw or write the lovely things they most appreciated and enjoyed about this person who is now no longer in their life or who they see far less frequently than before (eg the separated parent).

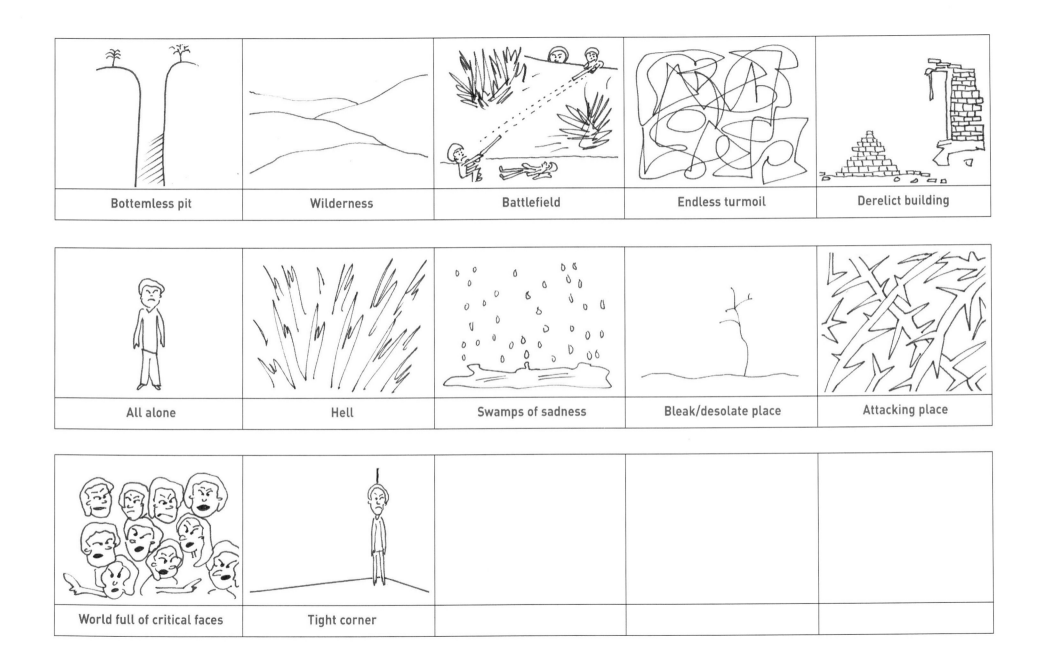

Ouch, that hurts!

Objective

If a teenager gets hurt, say by a parent walking out on the family or a girlfriend or boyfriend ditching them, it is all too easy for them to harden their hearts and/or cut off from their distress and pain. Brain scans have shown that human beings are capable of dramatic ways of cutting off from emotional pain. This is known as dissociation. In brain scans of dissociation, the pain centres and parts of the brain that register emotional meaning and threat are simply not activated. The visual centres are still activated. In other words, 'I see something painful but I don't feel it' (Lanius *et al*, 2003). There is, however, a price for cutting off from emotional pain:

- Cutting off from emotional pain often means cutting off from that of others and hence a major compromise of the capacity for compassion and concern.
- 'The body often keeps the score' (Van der Kolk, 1994), with all manner of troubling negative bodily symptoms and illnesses.
- As Freud said, feelings pushed down into the unconscious 'simply proliferate in the dark' (1915). The result can be very debilitating neurotic symptoms.

This exercise is therefore designed to support the teenager in staying open to the pain of feeling hurt, so that they can start to work it through to the point where it is modified. It is hoped that the containing function of the images will help the teenager to feel safe enough to do this. Some teenagers will need help in knowing that what they are feeling is hurt. Many will have wrongly labelled their painful arousal as hate, rage or other 'easier' feelings.

Instructions for the teenager

When someone walks out on you, or calls you or someone you care about names, or doesn't appreciate something really good about you, or ditches you, or puts you down, you might feel really angry. But that is not the only thing you will feel. The other human response to all this is to feel hurt. When someone has been hurt, the pain centres in the brain light up (Zubieta *et al*, 2003; Singer

et al, 2004, 2006). It is because emotional hurt is so painful that some people try to cut off from their feelings. However, if this is adopted as a defence it can come with an expensive price tag. The cost often entails some kind of ill-health, depression, anxiety or problems with anger at some point in life, and becoming less compassionate towards others' emotional pain.

In the Museum of Hurts look at each exhibit in turn. Think of times or events in your life when you have felt hurt. Choose an exhibit stand appropriate for your various hurtful experiences. For example, choose the 'ouch' stand for a little hurt and one of the others for a major hurt. Think of a title or phrase to describe the event and write this by the exhibit. What was the worst thing about it? What would you want to say to the person who hurt you, if they were standing in the room right now? What do you want the person who hurt you to understand? Try saying it to them now as if they were in the room.

- 'What I want you to know is ...'
- 'I am so hurt that you ...'
- 'I feel anger/hate because you ...'.

Development

Ask the teenager to focus on particular hurts in the Museum. Which are the most emotionally charged? Ask them to use clay to make a sculpture of the hurt, or ask them to do a sandplay about it, or to play it out in music (*see* page 42 for an explanation of sandplay). It may help to use all these languages of expression, as each offers a different perspective and different form of working through. Voice your empathy for their hurt.

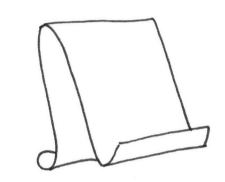

Event:

Event:

Event:

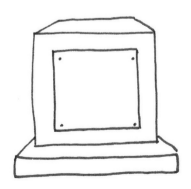

Event:

Event:

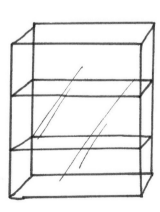

Event:

'It's their stuff not mine'

Objective

This exercise is about the intergenerational transmission of misery. When a parent has suffered considerable emotional pain, loss or trauma and doesn't get help to work through these feelings, their children can be deeply affected. Despite their very best efforts and intentions, the parent can pass on aspects of their own misery to their children. This can happen from generation to generation. It only takes one person to break the cycle, by getting some form of counselling or therapy through which the pain can be addressed and successfully modified.

Some teenagers need help to become more aware of the possibility that they may be negatively impacted by a parent's emotional baggage. This awareness is not intended to blame in any way but rather to give the teenager more options in terms of what to do and how to be in their relationship with that parent.

Some teenagers may not have made the connection between their own unhappiness and their parent's persistent negative moods and dysregulated emotional states. Once they have that awareness, then they often feel far more empowered to think about appropriate action and to end the sense of helplessness that is very common in such circumstances. Furthermore, they often feel far better about themselves when they separate what is 'theirs' and what belongs to their parents.

Instructions for the teenager

It is very common for children and teenagers to be negatively affected by their parents' 'emotional baggage', meaning their parents' unworked-through feelings about their own childhood or painful losses or traumatic experiences in their lives. These so often trigger repeated depressed, angry or anxious emotional states in the parent. Even if they are lovely and fine for lots of the time, their repeated negative emotional states are still likely to be weighing you down in some way.

The first step to altering things is to think about what is really going on and how much you think you might be being affected. So start by filling the suitcase entitled 'Your parents' emotional baggage'. Fill it with all the anxieties, fears, worries and painful life experiences you think your parents are carrying around with them – for example, 'Dad's father left when he was four', 'Mum lost her first baby', 'Dad was badly bullied by his older brothers', 'Mum has a hang-up about germs', 'Both parents fear taking risks'. It is fine to put both parents in the one suitcase. There are some other words in the side panel to jog your memory.

Then look at what you have written. Consider which aspects of your parents' emotional baggage you've ended up carrying in your own life (meaning being affected by it). Write what these are on the suitcase entitled 'Your emotional baggage'. Look at what you have written and/or drawn. Now turn to the figure who has broken free from the suitcase and is flying high. Write on the kite the aspects of you that have not been affected by your parents' emotional baggage – for example, your ability to take risks, your sense of calm, your courage, your not worrying about money, your generosity. Congratulate yourself on this. Finally, think how you could put down the baggage that you are carrying because of your parents' baggage. What would you need to be able to have a conversation about this with your parents or, even further, try to persuade them to go and get some professional help with their problems?

Development
Positive intergenerational transmission

Ask the teenager to consider positive 'intergenerational transmission'. In other words, ask them to draw or write down the good things that have been passed down to them from their parents – for example, particular family traits or qualities.

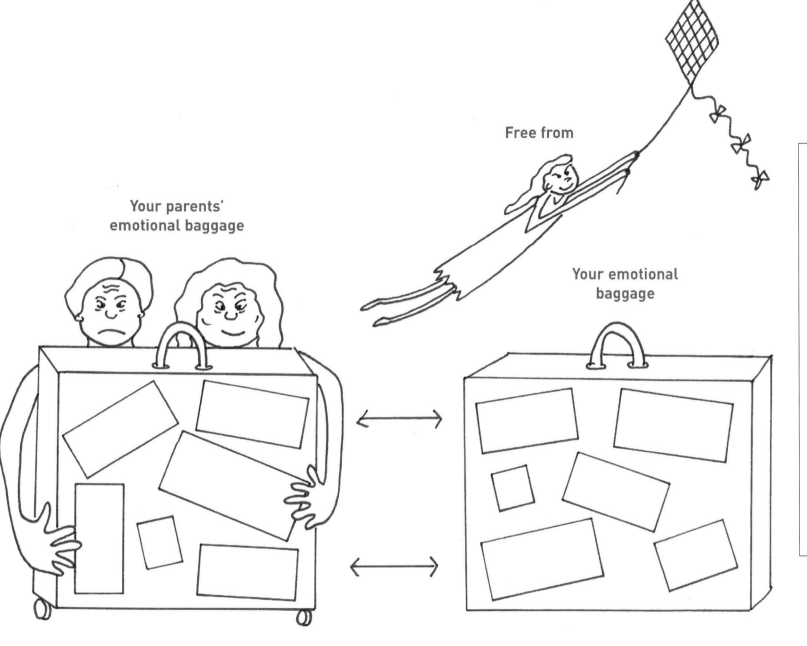

Free from

Your parents' emotional baggage

Your emotional baggage

Parental despair

Parental bleakness

Parental bitterness

Parental low-self esteem

Parental anger

Parent's closed beliefs of what is right and proper

Parent's closed attitude to money/sex/power/success

Parent's predujices

Parental need for you to be perfect

The shamers

Objective

Shame is a very powerful and painful emotion. It is experienced as an assault on the self. Guilt is arguably far easier to deal with as it is about something you have done rather than your very person. Shaming events can result in long-term negative core beliefs about the self as worthless, rubbish, unimportant or intrinsically bad. Furthermore, when you have been shamed, there is always shame-rage underneath, even if a person is unaware that it is there. This is extreme and intense, a direct response to the acute sense of assault from the shamer on one's very person. This exercise aims to enable the teenager to appreciate that they do not have to remain passive in their response to someone shaming them. It is also hoped that they will feel empowered to access their healthy anger and protest. As Bar-Levav (1998) says, 'Anger helps us reassert our sense of power and maintain our dignity and self-respect.'

Instructions for the teenager

Shaming events, particularly in childhood, are very powerful. They can leave you fearful, particularly about new experiences, new challenges and new people, in case you get shamed again. If you have never really told anyone about the people who have shamed you and worked through your feelings about it, you can be in danger of carrying emotional baggage into your adult years. This baggage is often in the form of anxiety, feelings of defeat and hopelessness and, in particular, social avoidance or social phobias. One way to prevent baggage is to go back and think about that experience, talk about it with someone and then find your anger about it. So, think of times in your life when someone has shamed or humiliated or told you off in a frightening way. Did you feel like any of the people in the pictures? If so, tick the particular picture and name the shamer. If what you felt is not on the pictures here, draw your own images in the empty boxes provided. Now turn to the list of words by the side of the page. Circle any words in the list that you felt when the person shamed you. Finally, take a large piece of paper. Draw your protest, rage or anger at being treated in this way. How do you feel now you've done this?

Development
Exercise: From shaming to finding your 'no'

This exercise is about the teenager taking their power back when they have been shamed as a child. It is about using clay to express angry feelings towards the shamer. The exercise works because both vividly imagined activity and the real thing activate some of the same neural pathways in the brain. It is also possible safely to express the intensity of shame rage by using clay or another art material. This can prevent the feelings being played out destructively in other relationships (displacing on to other people feelings that actually belong to the original shamer). It also means that feelings do not have to be turned inwards against the self.

Some people worry that the teenager will go and enact the revenge for real once it has been 'rehearsed' through the art image. But most teenagers understand the difference between symbolic play and what is acceptable in the outside world. Teenagers who need it should be given a clear explanation of the boundaries of the experience. That said, if you are in any doubt as to the teenager's ability to understand the distinction between symbolic play and reality, don't do the exercise.

Instructions: When people say negative things about you when you are a child, or you get the sense they are thinking negative things about you, it can be powerful. This is because in childhood your sense of self is still forming. So you can be in danger of thinking you are what they think you are. From the list below, tick any of the things you believe to be true about yourself that you think might have been influenced by shaming times in your childhood.

A tiny speck	Shrivelled	Wanting to be invisible	Frozen	Walled off
.	✡			
Name:	Name:	Name:	Name:	Name:

Wanting to hide	A person without a voice	Crushed	A nothing	A nobody
			✕	
Name:	Name:	Name:	Name:	Name:

Rubbish	Scum	Worthless	Terrified	Very, very alone
Name:	Name:	Name:	Name:	Name:

Name:	Name:	Name:	Name:	Name:

The aspect of you that felt blighted. Please tick:

Your self-esteem

Your spontaneity

Your confidence

Your courage

Your assertiveness

Your life force

Your ability to say no

Your drive

Your will

Your ability to be real

Your hopes and dreams

Your creativity

Your healthy anger

Your ability to protest

Psychological messages and core beliefs about yourself, originating from shaming or squashing experiences in childhood
I am: A loser Flawed A sinner A burden Rubbish Insignificant Ordinary Boring A reject No good at anything Not likeable Odd Different Worthless

If there are other things you believe yourself to be that are not on this list, write your own. Now, by each of the words, write down the name of the person in your life who has made you think about yourself in this way.

Then make an image of each shamer, controller or bully in clay or playdough. Now squash the clay or hit it or bang it anyway you like so the shamer is truly squashed. As you do it, say something like, 'How dare you treat me like this, you xxxx.' How do you feel now you have done this – at last taken your power back from these people who abused their power when you were just a little boy or girl?

Relationship going nowhere? (parent or partner)

Objective

It can be difficult for teenagers who are embarking on partner relationships for the first time in their life to know what a good relationship is and what a bad or dead one is. Without a backdrop of life experience it can be hard to know. It can also be difficult to know what a good parent–teenager relationship is. After all, many teenagers only have their own model. We always think that our parent–child relationship is normal, often until we have actually left home and/or see other models.

It can also be difficult for teenagers to know when to stay and try to make something work and when to leave because the relationship is not in any way enabling them to thrive. It can be difficult for adults to know whether a relationship is comfortable but ultimately life limiting. It can be doubly difficult for teenagers to know this. The same dilemmas can occur when an older teenager is thinking about whether to stay with their parents for a bit and live at home or leave to live their own independent life.

This exercise helps the teenager to address the quality of an important relationship in their life (partner or parent) and determine whether they have sold out to comfort and familiarity at the price of really developing and thriving.

Instructions for the teenager

Are you in what seems like a good relationship with a parent or partner and yet you often find yourself feeling that something is wrong, missing or not quite right? Do you sometimes feel that there must be more to a relationship than this? Do you feel somehow trapped or tied down with an urge to break free? Look at the picture. Think of your relationship with your partner or parent. Does your relationship make you feel like any of the figures in the pictures? If so, tick them. Then imagine yourself breaking free by moving on or, if it's with a parent, becoming more separate or more independent. In the balloons, write what your worst fears and best hopes would be if you did actually do this. What have you learned about your feelings and your relationship from this exercise?

Development

Remove the rock from your shoe rather than learn to limp comfortably.
(Paul and Collins, 1992)

If the exercise has clarified for the teenager that they feel trapped or imprisoned in their relationship (partner or parent) and the negatives indisputably outweigh the positives, help them to consider their resistance to breaking free. The following questions can help:
- What are the pros and cons of breaking free?
- What support do you need to break free?
- What is your investment in staying when you feel trapped?
- What do you imagine would happen if you left or changed things?
- What is the worst possible thing that could happen if you left?
- What is the best possible thing that could happen if you left?
- What do you imagine would happen if you stayed in this relationship for its comfort and familiarity?

Quotations the teenager may find useful

These quotations may also support the teenager in their consideration of creative action in their relationship life:

When you are facing the gates of hell you have your back to the gates of heaven.
(Anon)

When my house burnt down, I could see the rising sun.
(Chinese proverb)

The future belongs to those who believe in the beauty of their dreams.
(Roosevelt 2001)

A fly caught in a spider's web	A bird with its wings clipped	A fish struggling on a hook	A caged bird	Between a rock and a hard place
Living in a cul-de-sac	Under someone's thumb	Living in a dead end	A no-man's land	A barren landcape
Tied to someone's apron strings	Being smothered	Standing at barred windows	Being trapped inside someone else's life	Being trapped financially

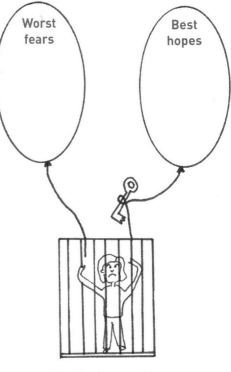

Breaking free

Worst fears

Best hopes

You feel trapped or imprisoned

Loving someone who isn't good at loving

Objective
This exercise addresses the fact that coercive control and emotional and physical abuse in teenager partner relationships is very common. Here are some of the shocking statistics:

One in four teenage girls have been hit by a boyfriend (one in nine report severe physical abuse).

Seventy-two per cent of girls and 51 per cent of boys reported some form of emotional partner violence.

Girls aged 13 were as likely to report physical violence in their intimate relationships as those aged 16.

Fifty-nine per cent of girls and 50 per cent of boys reported instigating emotional abuse.

Thirty-one per cent of girls and 16 per cent of boys reported some form of sexual partner violence.

About half of the boys interviewed said that the main reason they were in the relationship was for sex and in some cases it was the only reason.

(Barter et al, 2009)

Research also shows that the more teenagers have witnessed domestic violence at home as children or, more generally, submission/dominance relationships, the more likely they are to put up with coercive control in their partner relationships. The majority of girls who experienced abuse remained in the relationships for a considerable time. Generally, as the relationship progressed so did the violence and the fear. Most had experienced abusive relationships in childhood (Bergman, 1992; Barter et al, 2009)

Examples
'He bit me on the face, it was horrible, really disgusting. Because when I was trying to show my point of view, he doesn't appreciate it.'

'I caught her snogging another boy. So I slapped her and beat him up ... I had to ... I think I was right to do it.'

'He tells me I'm fat all the time, even though I'm size 10. He tells me I'm nothing without him and he's doing me a favour by being with me and he could do better ... He gets paranoid if I go out with my mates on a Saturday night, thinking I'm cheating on him and reads my texts. Whereas, I'm not allowed to know what he's up to ever, even just out of curiosity.'

'When I'd be out with my friends he'd drag me off and say he didn't want me out any longer and I'd got to go in, and it could be like half past six. I'd say, "They're my friends I'll speak to whoever I want to", and then he'd get really mad.'

'If I did see the people he didn't want you to see ... he'd physically drag me away from them.'

'I said I didn't want to go any further but they persistently asked and asked and if they don't get their own way they put on like a strop. Like [my boyfriend] storms out and then you feel like well "yeah OK then whatever makes you happy" sort of thing.'

(Barter et al, 2009)

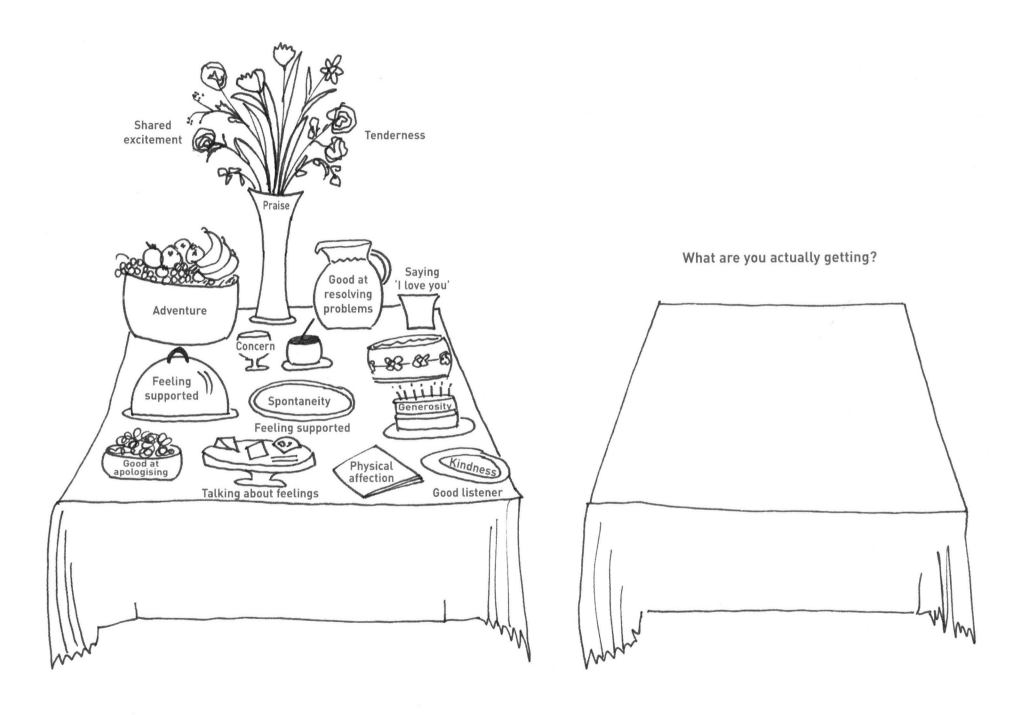

Shared
excitement

Tenderness

Praise

Adventure

Good at
resolving
problems

Saying
'I love you'

Concern

Feeling
supported

Spontaneity

Generosity

Feeling supported

Good at
apologising

Physical
affection

Kindness

Talking about feelings

Good listener

What are you actually getting?

Many teenagers who love someone who isn't good at loving fall into the same trap. They try so hard to awaken the love in the other by all manner of self-sacrifice, over-generous acts, compliance and over-tolerance. As illustrated above, they put up with all manner of abuse and coercive control just to keep the relationship. Sadly, this often results in them putting their own development on hold, as they enter into a life of emotional deprivation and attacks on their confidence and self-esteem. Furthermore, in a desperate attempt to please, they may stifle those aspects of themselves that the other person criticises and attacks – for example, their passion, drives, dreams, ambitions. All this tends to bring more and more misery and disappointment over time. And all the time they stay in this abusive relationship they are missing out on thriving by being in relationships that, for the most part, are warm, appreciative and emotionally nourishing.

So the exercise is designed to heighten the teenager's awareness of bad-deal relationships, the long-term psychological costs they are paying in terms of abuse and neglect, and what they are missing out on by letting the relationship continue.

It is also hoped that the teenager is enabled to differentiate between their own lovability and the other person's incapacity to love.

Instructions for the teenager

On the table laid out with a feast, colour in all the things you are getting from your relationship. Now turn to the bare table next to it. On this table, draw or write what you are actually getting overall – the bad things as well as the good things. Are you loving someone who isn't good at loving? If you think you are, can you relate to the quotation below?

When they speak about their relationship, one wonders at their blindness. Their choice [of partner] seems [crazy]. There had been indications that the other was incapable of ... loving, or accepting them in the way they desire. They had been pursuing an alluring but rejecting other, an exciting yet frustrating other. The [teenager] initially may have offered conditions of hope but it fails to satisfy. It has awakened an intensity of yearning, but is essentially the elusive object of desire, seemingly there but just out of reach.
(Armstrong-Perlman, 1991)

Development
Exercise: Power replays

Instructions: Ask the teenager to look at their possible 'early training' (childhood) in 'power over/power under' modes of relating. Using sandplay miniatures, drawing or clay, ask the teenager to depict relationships in their childhood when they were in a submissive position and an adult in their life (eg a teacher, parent or relative) was adopting a 'power over' way of relating. Ask the teenager to write what they would want to say to that person in their life who abused power in this way. Finally, ask them to look at how, without being aware, they might be replaying 'power over/power under' ways of relating now in their partner relationship. It is often only as a result of working through feelings about the original 'bullies' and the shame, fear and humiliation that resulted, that the teenager can realise that they really don't want to carry on repeating this in their partner relationships now.

Discussion

Discuss the following poem with the teenager in terms of possible personal relevance.

Seeing Rarities as Pearls

When you didn't bring me flowers,
Or kisses with my peaches
Or offerings of time 'just for us',
I thought there was nothing wrong with it,
I thought that's all you got.

When I waited for weeks to earn that one smile,
And after five years
I'd only collected half a page of compliments
(Which I'd tried to spread out, to make it look more)
I thought there was nothing wrong with it,
I thought that's all you got.

When you gave me some little ground on which to walk,
Said, 'I'm too tired to listen to you'
And blended me into your day-to-day,
I thought there was nothing wrong with it,
I thought that's all you got.

When I arranged meals and outings and birthday surprises,
And you didn't,
When I bathed you and held you and thought-and-felt-about-you,
And YOU thought-and-felt-about-you,
I thought there was nothing wrong with it,
I thought that's all you got.

Until one day
Someone brought me pearls with the birdsong
Every morning.

(The author)

Talk about why some teenagers are vulnerable in terms of staying in abusive relationships as opposed to leaving them

You could say something like this: When teenagers have not felt really loved and valued in childhood, or when sometimes relationships at home have been about 'power over/power under', they can be particularly vulnerable to putting up with abuse in partner relationships. The hook to make them stay is 'seeing rarities as pearls'. This means that if their partner shows them love and affection some of the time or even just a bit of the time, they often stay. It's as if they mistake crumbs for a full meal, and see rarities as pearls. This means they often stay in emotionally impoverished relationships and put up with all sorts of unkindness or cruelty that other teenagers, who have known more warmth and kindness in their childhood, wouldn't dream of putting up with. The awful thing is that sometimes teenagers put up with so much abuse and neglect in their partner relationships [share the statistics above if you like] and then they get a text saying something like, 'You are so dumped'. In other words, if the partner is cruel in the relationship they are unlikely to be any different in the way they end it.

As this teenager posted on the internet:
'I loved him with all my heart but he just took away every drop of hope I had, he crushed my heart. Don't trust a boy with your life coz he will just abuse that.'
(thisisabuse.direct.gov.uk 2011)

www.direct.gov.uk/en/YoungPeople/HealthAndRelationships/FamilyAnd Relationships/DG_10032439

All about my relationship with my parents

(worksheets)

The unsaid things

Objective
This exercise is for teenagers who feel stuck in their relationship with a parent or other important person in their life. Over time, they have built up all sorts of resentments, which have not been voiced effectively or at all. But the teenager is not happy with the status quo. In fact, the stuck relationship may mean they feel miserable for too much of the time. Also, perhaps they remember so many good times when they got on well with this parent (or other important person in their life) and things felt mutually really good. So there is a real feeling of loss too. This exercise can be used as the first step to try to tackle things. After this, the teenager may appreciate the offer of a facilitated meeting between them and their parent. Often such a conversation, which maybe takes no more than an hour, can actually heal months or years of relationship pain.

Instructions for the teenager
Think of your relationship with your parent or another important person in your life: friend or partner. Think particularly about the bits that don't feel good to you. Look at the little notes in the picture. Choose one or more and write them to that person. Don't let your rational, logical brain take over and say something like, 'But I could never really say that to them'. It is an exercise of let's pretend. You may never actually send the notes. There are some blank notes for you to fill in as you please. You can also use the notes to write to someone who has died. Write things you would have liked to have said to them.

How do you feel now you've written the notes? Is there a note that stands out as being of particular importance to you? Are you stopping your relationship with this person from improving by not finding a good way to say these things in reality? Is the effect of leaving some of these things unsaid adding to your stress and feelings of unhappiness? Or do you think you are right in thinking that the person for whom you feel these things is too emotionally fragile, defended or locked in anger to really be able to hear these things and benefit from them? Or would it be just too hurtful? There is a reality with some people in some circumstances of 'hitting people with honesty'.

Development
Exercise: Finding your voice in the face of fear
This development will support the teenager who believes that saying one of these things in reality would improve one of their relationships and yet they feel too frightened to say it. Ask them to draw what they fear would happen if they said it. Then ask them what sort of support they would need to be able to find their voice. It may be appropriate to offer to facilitate the parent–teenager conversation yourself. If appropriate, ask the teenager to talk about times in their life when they did find their voice, when what they had to say was both heard and respected. What did it feel like? Ask them to find a mental image to anchor that instance of assertiveness and courage firmly in their mind.

Discussion
Discuss any possible resentment the teenager has about parents not being telepathic: 'They should know what I need or feel without me having to tell them'. It can help teenagers to know that this irrationality is very common in close relationships and is often a throwback to infancy, when the parents' role was indeed to intuit the needs of their infant.

Discuss the problem in relationships when more and more resentments about unmet needs and hurt feelings are stored up and not voiced. In a type of therapy called transactional analysis, this is known as 'stamp collecting'. Once lots of stamps are collected, these are commonly then 'cashed in' by one of the people in the relationship leaving or doing something that really hurts the other person in another way.

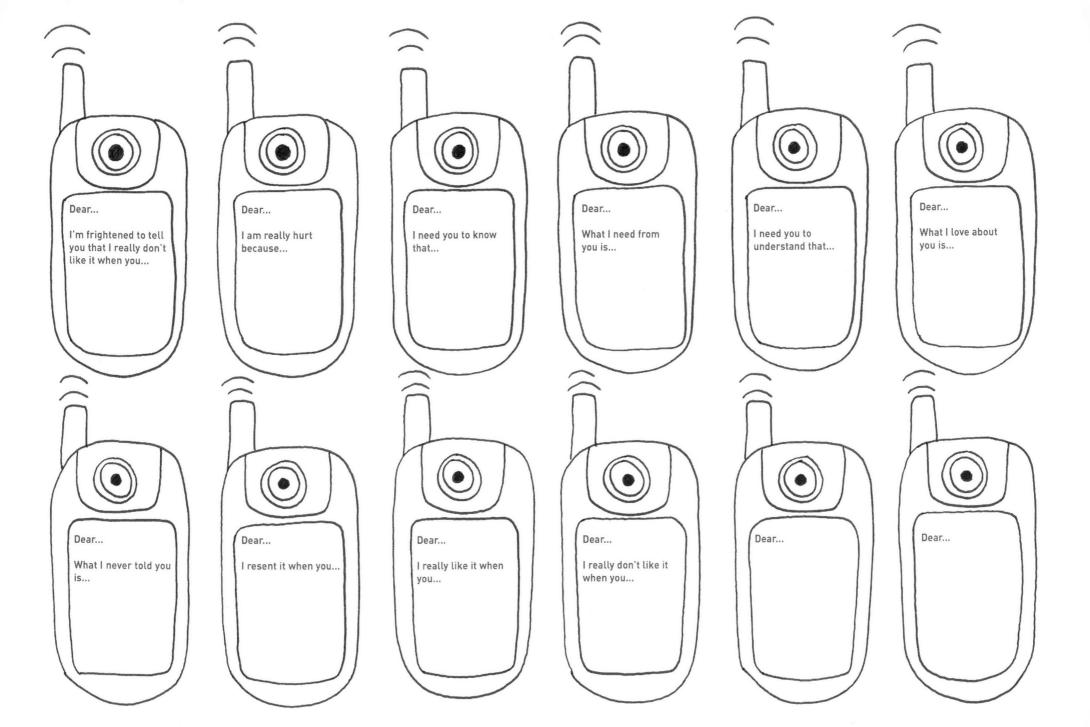

Mum and me/Dad and me

Objective
This exercise is for a teenager and their parent (mum or dad) who are both motivated to improve their relationship. It is designed to ease communication and to facilitate a deeper and more authentic level of connection between the two. The teenager can draw their answer rather than speak it if they prefer, or draw some answers and voice others.

Instructions for the teenager
Say to the two people: I'm going to say to you both some unfinished sentences. I will ask A (teenager) to finish the sentences first. OK A, you can say your answer, or do a super-quick drawing for your answer, or a combination of both. If you don't want to finish one of the sentences you can just say 'pass'. B (parent) should just listen to what A says without speaking. You can't respond or interrupt in any way. You just have to listen. At the end of the list I will give B some unfinished sentences to help you to respond to what A has said. Then we will begin again, this time with B finishing the sentences.

Here are A's sentences:
- I like it when you ...
- I don't like it when you ...
- I love it when you ...
- I like it when together we ...
- I wish together we could ...
- I want you to know that ...
- I wish you knew that ...
- It feels like you don't understand that ...
- I am frightened of you when you ... (Don't give this sentence to a parent to answer, as it can burden and worry the teenager.)
- I feel angry with you when ...
- I feel good when you ...

- I feel like rubbish when you ...
- I feel sad when you ...
- I feel sad that we never seem to do ... any more.
- If I had three wishes for you they would be ...
- If I had three wishes for me they would be ...
- If I had three wishes for us they would be ...
- One of my worst times with you was ...
- One of my best times with you was ... (Good to finish on a positive note.)

B's chance to respond:
- I was surprised when you said ...
- I didn't know that you felt ...
- I was sorry to hear that ...
- I feel hurt that ...
- Thank you for letting me know that ...
- I am delighted to hear that you ...
- I agree with you when you said that ...
- I am really thinking about what you said about ...

Important note
Only offer this session to a parent and teenager if you know the parent will provide the teenager with a good relational experience overall, and not burden them with their own worries, anxieties or a barrage of unspoken resentments, anger, lectures on behaviour, and so on. You may speak to the parent before the session to ensure they know what is expected of them, and to establish the necessary boundaries.

As practitioner, it will be important for you to comment on the 'big feelings' in the session after both teenager and parent have finished the exercise, being most careful not to take sides. It may also be appropriate, after you have done this, to ask both people if you have failed to comment on something that was very important to either of them. It is also good to ask them before the end of the session if they want to say anything to each other, draw anything for each other or do anything with each other as a way of finishing. People often do amazing things at the eleventh hour. But don't ask this question if doing so would open up more pain that there isn't time to work through. Keep using the unfinished sentence structure right to the end of the session if you feel the two people need a structure to keep them interacting with each other positively, not negatively.

Development
Exercise: When Mum's/Dad's feelings get too big

The following exercise can be particularly helpful if you are working with teenagers who are coping with a parent's raw feelings of depression, fear or anger, which are spilling out in the family home. But only do this if you feel the parent can hear what the teenager is saying without feeling threatened and lashing out in self-protective anger. Ask the teenager to do a 'super-quick drawing answer' for each of these unfinished sentences (unless of course they prefer just to speak their answers, but this can be more scary).

Dad/Mum:
- When you get sad I feel ...
- When you get angry I feel ...
- When you get scared I feel ...
- I feel worried when you ...
- I feel angry when ...
- I love it when together we ...

The parent is requested simply to listen to the whole list of sentences. They are not to interrupt or say anything. When the teenager has finished all the sentences, in their response, ask the parent to use the safe structure of the unfinished sentences in the 'chance to respond' section of the main exercise. Don't reverse this by asking the parent to finish the sentences as the teenager could feel burdened even further by parental feelings.

Best times and worst times of us

Objective
This exercise is designed for a parent and teenager who are motivated to work together and listen to each other in order to improve the quality of their relationship. Where this is the case, it can be really helpful to stand back and think about their positive and negative ways of relating. It also offers an opportunity for both parties to reflect on what is working well in their relationship and what is not working well. By considering things in this way it is hoped that the two of them can put more energy into shared activities and ways of relating that are good for them and avoid the things that may be harming their relationship.

Instructions for the teenager
Give the parent and teenager a very large piece of paper each (A1 size is ideal). Tell them that they will be working on their own for the first part of the exercise. Ask them each to draw a line down the middle of their piece of paper. On the left-hand side of the paper as them to write, 'Best times with you', and on the right-hand side of the paper ask them to write, 'Worst times with you'. Give them just 10 minutes (time structure adds to the safety of the exercise) to do drawings and/or write words for both sides of the picture. When they have finished, ask both parent and teenager in turn to talk about or show what they have written or drawn. Ask the teenager to go first. The parent must remain silent to ensure the highest quality listening. After they have listened, however, the parent can ask any questions they need just for clarification. Then ask the parent to start a sentence, 'So what I understand you saying is ...'. The teenager can correct them where they are wrong. The parent can also finish the following sentences:
- What surprised me in what you said/drew was ...
- What hurt me in what you said/drew was ...
- What surprised me in what you said/drew was ...
- What moved me in what you said/drew was ...
- What pleased me in what you said/drew was ...

The teenager must just listen. The practitioner once again summarises, 'So [parent's name] what I heard you saying was ...'. The exercise is then reversed with the parent showing the teenager their drawings.

You may then want to ask both parent and teenager the following:
- Having looked at both your sets of images, what have you learned about your relationship?
- What are the similarities and the differences in terms of what you have drawn/made?
- Is there anything you would like to change in your relationship, do more of or do less of as, a result of what you have done here?

Then ask both people how they could share more best times and what they can do to prevent a repetition of worst times.

Development
Communicating through colour cards
When working with a parent and teenager it can be useful to support a teenager who is not able to speak about their feelings well with a different system of communication. Show the teenager how they can use colour cards. For example, instead of moving into challenging behaviour or withdrawing into their bedroom from a place of hurt, anger or 'she just doesn't get it', they simply slip a card into their mum's hand. When they hand her a yellow card it means, 'I am hurt', a blue card means, 'Can we talk?', and a purple card means, 'I need you to listen to what I am feeling right now'.

Bibliography

Ackard DM, Neumark-Sztainer D, Story M & Perry C (2006) 'Parent–Child Connectedness and Behavioral and Emotional Health Among Adolescents', *Am J Preventative Med*, 30 (1), pp59-66.

Ainsworth M, Blehar M, Waters E & Wall S (1978) *Patterns of Attachment*, Erlbaum, Hillsdale, NJ.

Allen J & Fonagy P (2006) *The Handbook of Mentalization-Based Treatment*, Wiley-Blackwell, London.

Alvarez, A (1971) *The Savage God: A Study of Suicide*, Penguin, Harmondsworth.

Alvarez A (1992) *Live Company: Psychoanalytic Psychotherapy with Autistic, Borderline, Deprived and Abused Children*, Routledge, London.

Anderson R (2006) Public lecture 'Troubled Teenagers', The Centre for Child Mental Health, London.

Angelou, M (1994) 'Million Man March Poem' in *The Complete Collected Poems of Maya Angelou*, Random House, London.

Armstrong-Perlman EM (1991) 'The Allure of the Bad Object', *Free Associations*, 2 (3) 23, pp343–356.

Armstrong-Perlman EM (1995) 'Psychosis: The Sacrifice That Fails?', Ellwood J (ed) *Psychosis: Understanding and Treatment*, Jessica Kingsley, London.

Balint E (1993) *Before I Was I: Psychoanalysis and the Imagination*, Free Association Books, London.

Bannister A (2003) *Creative Therapies with Traumatized Children*, Jessica Kingsley, London.

Barnardo's (2011) online, www.barnardos.org.uk/what_we_do/our_projects/young_carers/young_carers_real_stories/

Bar-Levav R (1988) *Thinking in the Shadow of Feelings*, Simon and Schuster, New York.

Barnes J (1980) *Metroland*, Robin Clark, London.

Barrows PS (ed) (2003) *Key Papers from the Journal of Child Psychotherapy*, Brunner-Routledge, London.

Barter C (2009) *Safeguarding Young People from Exploitation and Violence in Teenage 'Dating' Relationships*, University of Bristol, Big Lottery Fund and NSPCC.

Barter C, McCarry M, Berridge D & Evans K (2009) *Partner Exploitation and Violence in Teenage Intimate Relationships*, NSPPC, London.

Batmandghelidji, C (2008) Public lecture 'Working with Challenging Teenagers', The Centre for Child Mental Health, London.

Benjet C, Thompson RJ & Gotlib IH (2010) '5-HTTLPR Moderates the Effect of Relational Peer Victimization on Depressive Symptoms in Adolescent Girls', *J Child Psychol Psychiatry*, 51 (2), pp173–9.

Benson H (2006) 'The Conflation of Marriage and Cohabitation in Government Statistics – A Denial of Difference Rendered Untenable by an Analysis of Outcomes', Bristol Community Family Trust, Bristol.

Bergman L (1992) 'Dating Violence Among High School Students', *Social Work*, 31 (1), pp21–27.

Berne E (1961) *Transactional Analysis in Psychotherapy*, Grove Press Inc, New York.

Bessie Anderson Stanley (1911) 'What is Success?' Mitchell J (ed), *Heart Throbs, Volume Two In Prose and Verse, Dear to the American People*, Chapple, Boston Mass.

Blume ES (1990) *Secret Survivors: Uncovering Incest and its Aftereffects in Women*, John Wiley, Chichester/New York.

Booth A, Johnson DR, Granger DA, Crouter AC & McHale S (2003) 'Testosterone and Child and Adolescent Adjustment: The Moderating Role of Parent-Child Relationships', *Developmental Psychology*, 39 (1), pp85–98.

Bowlby J (1978) *Attachment and Loss: Volume 3 – Loss, Sadness and Depression*, Penguin, Harmondsworth.

Bowlby J (1979) *The Making and Breaking of Affectional Bonds*, Tavistock, London.

Bowlby J (1988) *A Secure Base: Clinical Applications of Attachment Theory*, Routledge, London.

Brisch KH (2009) *Teenagers and Attachment*, Worth Publishing, London.

British Medical Association (2006) *Child and Adolescent Mental Health – A Guide for Healthcare Professionals*, British Medical Association, London.

Brown G (1999) *Energy of Life*, Harper Collins, London.

Brown University (2002) *The Brown University Child and Adolescent Behavior Letter*, Vol 18, No 4, April 2002.

Burnett L (2006) cited in Doveston M & Keenaghan M, 'Improving Classroom Dynamics to Support Students' Learning and Social Inclusion: A Collaborative Approach', *Support for Learning: British Journal of Learning Support, 21 (1)*, pp5–11.

Busch AL & Lieberman AF (2010) 'Mothers' Adult Attachment Interview Ratings Predict Preschool Children's IQ Following Domestic Violence Exposure', *Attachment & Human Development*, 12 (6), pp505–27.

Cabinet Office (2004) *Alcohol Harm Reduction Strategy for England*, Prime Minister's Strategy Unit, London.

Cardinal M (1993) *The Words to Say It: An Autobiographical Novel*, Women's Press, London.

Carroll L (1856) Letter of 21 May in Green RL (ed) (1953) *The Diaries of Lewis Carroll, Volume 1*, Cassell, London.

Cassidy J (ed) (2008) *Handbook of Attachment*, Guilford Press, London.

Centre for Social Justice (2007) *Breakthrough Britain*, Centre for Social Justice, London.

Centre for Social Justice (2008) *Couldn't Care Less: A Policy Report from the Children in Care Working Group*, Centre for Social Justice, London. |

Centre for Social Justice (2011) *Mental Health: Poverty, Ethnicity and Family Breakdown*, Centre for Social Justice, London.

Clarkson P (1989) *Gestalt Counselling in Action*, Routledge, London.

Claxton G (2008) *What's the Point of School? Rediscovering the Heart of Education*, Oneworld Publications, Oxford.

Cline F & Fay J (2006) *Parenting Teens with Love and Logic*, NavPress Publishing, Colorado Springs, CO.

Coleridge ST (2010) *The Rime of the Ancient Mariner*, Arcturus Publishing Ltd, London.

Cooper P & Tiknaz Y (2007) *Nurture Groups in School and at Home: Connecting with Children with Social, Emotional and Behavioural Difficulties*, Jessica Kingsley Publishers, London.

Cottrell B (2003) 'Parent Abuse: The Abuse of Parents by Their Teenage Children', Overview Paper, National Clearinghouse on Family Violence, Public Health Agency of Canada.

Cozolino LJ (2002) *The Neuroscience of Psychotherapy: Building and Rebuilding the Human Remain*, WW Norton and Co, London.

Cozolino LJ (2006) *The Neuroscience of Human Relationships, Attachment and the Developing Social Brain*, WW Norton and Co, London.

Damasio AR (2000) *The Feeling of What Happens*, Heinemann, London.

Damasio AR (2000) 'Subcortical and Cortical Brain Activity During the Feeling of Self-Generated Emotions', *Nature Neuroscience*, 3 (10), pp1049–56.

Darwin C (1965) *The Expression of the Emotions in Man and Animals*, University of Chicago Press, Chicago. (Original work published 1872)

Davidov M & Grusec JE (2006) 'Untangling the Links of Parental Responsiveness to Distress and Warmth to Child Outcomes', *Child Development*, 77 (1), pp44–58.

Deblinger E & Runyon MK (2005) 'Understanding and Treating Feelings of Shame in Children Who Have Experienced Maltreatment', *Child Maltreatment*, 10 (4), pp364–76.

Department for Education and Employment (1999) *National Healthy Schools Standard: Guidance*, DfEE, Nottingham.

Department for Education and Skills (2003) *Every Child Matters*, DfES, London.

Department for Education and Skills (2005a) *Developing Children's Social, Emotional and Behavioural Skills: A Whole-School Approach*, DfES, London.

Department for Education and Skills (2005b) *Primary National Strategy for School Improvement: Social and Emotional Aspects of Learning for Primary Schools (SEAL)*, DfES, London.

Department of Health (2004) *The Child Health Promotion Programme: Pregnancy and the First Five Years of Life*, DoH, London.

Department of Health (2006) *Drug Use, Smoking and Drinking Among Young People in England in 2005: Headline Figures*, TSO, London.

Depression Alliance (2011) online, www.depressionalliance.org

Depressionperception.com 'Depression: Facts and Statistics', online, www.depressionperception.com/depression/depression_facts_and_statistics.asp

Dickinson E (1999) *The Poems of Emily Dickinson*, Franklin RW (ed), Harvard University Press, Cambridge, MA.

Dietrich A (2004) 'Neurocognitive Mechanisms Underlying the Experience of Flow', *Consciousness and Cognition*, 13 (4), pp746–61.

Dinnage R (1990) *The Ruffian on the Stair: Reflections on Death*, Viking, London.

Directgov 'Abusive Relationships', online, www.direct.gov.uk/en/YoungPeople/HealthAndRelationships/FamilyAndRelationships/DG_10032439

Dube SR, Felitti VJ, Dong M, Giles WH & Anda RF (2003) 'The Impact of Adverse Childhood Experiences on Health Problems: Evidence from Four Birth Cohorts Dating Back to 1900', *Preventive Medicine*, 37 (3), pp268–77.

Edgar JL, Lowe JC, Paul ES & Nicol CJ (2011) 'Avian Maternal Response to Chick Distress', *Proc Biol Sci*, 278 (1721), pp3129–34.

Eisenberger NI, Lieberman MD & Williams KD (2003) 'Does Rejection Hurt? An fMRI Study of Social Exclusion', *Science*, 302 (5643), pp290–2.

Esslin M (1982) *Theatre of the Absurd*, Pelican, Harmondsworth. (Original work published 1961)

Faber A & Mazlish E (2006) *How to Talk So Teens Will Listen and Listen So Teens Will Talk*, Piccadilly Press, London.

Fairbairn WRD (1940) 'Schizoid Factors in the Personality', *Psychoanalytic Studies of the Personality* (1952) pp3–27, Tavistock/Routledge, London.

Fanthorpe UA (2005) *Collected Poems 1978-2003*, Peterloo Poets, London.

Feinstein L (2000) *The Relative Economic Importance of Academic, Psychological and Behavioural Attributes Developed in Childhood*, Centre for Economic Performance, London.

Feinstein S (2007) *Parenting the Teenage Brain: Understanding a Work in Progress*, Rowman & Littlefield Education, Landham, MD.

Feldman R (2010) 'The Relational Basis of Adolescent Adjustment: Trajectories of Mother-Child Interactive Behaviors from Infancy to Adolescence Shape Adolescents' Adaptation', *Attach Hum Dev*, 12 (1-2), pp173–92.

Field T, Diego M, Hernandz-Reif M, Schanberg S & Kuhn C (2002) 'Relative Right Versus Left Frontal EEG in Neonates', *Developmental Psychobiology*, 41 (2), pp147–155.

Fonagy P & Target M (1997) 'Attachment and Reflective Function: Their Role in Self-Organisation', *Development and Psychopathology*, 9 (4), pp679–700.

Fosha D (2000) *The Transforming Power of Affect*, Basic Books, New York.

Fox M (1983) *Original Blessing: A Primer in Creation Spirituality*, Bear and Co, Santa Fé, NM.

Fredrickson BL (2004) 'The Broaden-and-Build Theory of Positive Emotions', *Phil Trans R Soc Lond B*, 359, pp1447–51.

Freud S (1909) 'Analysis of a Phobia in a Five-Year-Old Boy', Strachey J (ed), *The Standard Edition of the Complete Psychological Works of Sigmund Freud*, Hogarth, London, 1953–73, Vol 10, pp3–149.

Freud S (1914) 'On Narcissism', *The Standard Edition of the Complete Psychological Works of Sigmund Freud*, Hogarth, London, 1914–1916, *Volume 14*.

Freud S (1915) 'Repression' pp139–157 in *On Metapsychology: The Theory of Psychoanalysis*, Vol 11 of The Penguin Freud Library, Richards A & Strachey J (eds) (1991) Penguin, Harmondsworth.

Galinsky E (2000) *Ask the Children: The Breakthrough Study That Reveals How to Succeed at Work and Parenting*, Harper Collins, New York.

Gámez-Guadix M, Straus MA, Carrobles JA, Muñoz-Rivas MJ & Almendros C (2010) 'Corporal Punishment and Long-Term Behavior Problems: The Moderating Role of Positive Parenting and Psychological Aggression', *Psicothema*, 22 (4), pp529–36.

Garasky S, Stewart SD, Gundersen C, Lohman BJ & Eisenmann JC (2009) 'Family Stressors and Child Obesity', *Soc Sci Res*, 38 (4), pp755–66.

Geddes H (2005) *Attachment in the Classroom*, Worth Reading, London.

Gibran K (1991) *The Prophet*, Pan, London.

Giedd J (2002) *The Teen Brain,* Medicine for the Public lecture series, Research Channel.

Giedd JN, Blumenthal J, Jeffries NO, Castellanos FX, Liu H, Zijdenbos A, Paus T, Evans AC & Rapoport JL (1999) 'Brain Development During Childhood and Adolescence: A Longitudinal MRI Study', *Nature Neuroscience*, 2 (10), pp861–3.

Giedd JN, Stockman M, Weddle C, Liverpool M, Alexander-Bloch A, Wallace GL, Lee NR, Lalonde F & Lenroot RK (2010) 'Anatomic Magnetic Resonance Imaging of the Developing Child and Adolescent Brain and Effects of Genetic Variation', *Neuropsychol Rev*, 20 (4), pp349–61.

Glouberman D (1989) *Life Choices and Life Changes Through Imagework: The Art of Developing Personal Vision*, Unwin Hyman, London.

Gordon J & Grant G (1997) *How We Feel: Insight into the Emotional World of Teenagers*, Jessica Kingsley Publishers, London.

Gottman J (1998) *Raising an Emotionally Intelligent Child*, Prentice Hall, New York.

Gottman J (2007) *The Seven Principles for Making Marriage Work*, Orion, London.

Greenberg JR & Mitchell SA (1983) *Object Relations in Psychoanalytic Theory*, Harvard University Press, London/Cambridge, MA.

Guntrip H (1969) *Schizoid Phenomena, Object-Relations and the Self*, Hogarth, London.

Gussow M (1994) *Conversations with Pinter*, Nick Hern Books, London.

Hall P (2007) *Help Your Children Cope with Your Divorce*, Vermillion, London.

Hariri AR, Bookheimer SY & Mazziotta JC (2000) 'Modulating Emotional Responses: Effects of a Neocortical Network on the Limbic System', *Neuroreport*, 1 (17), pp43–48.

Harrison L & Harrington R (2001) *Adolescents' Bereavement Experiences*, Joseph Rowntree Foundation, London.

Hattersley LA, Shrewsbury VA, King LA, Howlett SA, Hardy LL & Baur LA (2009) 'Adolescent-Parent Interactions and Attitudes Around Screen Time and Sugary Drink Consumption: A Qualitative Study', *Int J Behav Nutr Phys Act*, 2009, 6:61.

Hauser ST, Allen JP & Golden E (2006) *Out of the Woods: Tales of Resilient Teens*, Harvard University Press, London/Cambridge, MA.

Hillman J (2006) Public lecture 'Creativity and Soul', The Centre for Child Mental Health, London.

HM Government (2011) *No Health Without Mental Health: A Cross-Government Mental Health Outcomes Strategy for People of All Ages.*

Hoffman M (1984) 'Empathy, Its Limitations and Its Role in a Comprehensive Moral Theory', Gerwirtz J & Kutines W (eds), *Morality, Moral Development, and Moral Behaviour*, Wiley, New York.

Home Office (2010) *Expect Respect: A Toolkit for Addressing Teenage Relationship*, online, http://thisisabuse.direct.gov.uk

Horney K (1970) *Neurosis and Human Growth: The Struggle Toward Self-Realization*, Norton, New York. (Original work published 1950)

Horney K (1977) *The Neurotic Personality of Our Time*, Routledge, London. (Original work published 1937)

Hughes D (2001) Public lecture 'Attachment Difficulties in Troubled Children', The Centre for Child Mental Health, London.

Hughes D (2004a) 'An Attachment-Based Treatment of Maltreated Children and Young People', *Attachment and Human Development*, 6, pp263–278.

Hughes D (2004b) 'Connecting with Troubled Children', Working with Attachment Disordered Children conference, Centre for Child Mental Health, London.

Hughes D (2007) *Attachment: Focused Family Therapy*, WW Norton and Co, New York.

Hunter M (2001) *Psychotherapy with Young People in Care: Lost and Found*, Routledge, London.

Institute for Public Policy Research (IPPR) (2006a) *Britain's Teenagers' Social Skills Gap Widens*, IPPR, London.

Institute for Public Policy Research (IPPR) (2006b) *Freedom's Orphans: Raising Youth in a Changing World*, IPPR, London.

Jakes TD (1998) in von Oech R, *A Whack on the Side of the Head*, Warner Books, New York.

Jaser SS, Fear JM, Reeslund KL, Champion JE, Reising MM & Compas BE (2008) 'Maternal Sadness and Adolescents' Responses to Stress in Offspring of Mothers With and Without a History of Depression', *Adolesc Psychol*, 37 (4), pp736–46.

Jeffers S (1992) *Dare to Connect*, Piatkus, London.

Jenner S (1999) *The Parent-Child Game*, Bloomsbury, London.

Jeffers S (2007) *Feel the Fear and Do it Anyway*, Vermillion, London.

Johnson S (2006) *Attachment Processes in Couple and Family Therapy*, Guilford Press, London.

Johnson SB, Blum RW & Giedd JN (2009) 'Adolescent Maturity and the Brain: The Promise and Pitfalls of Neuroscience Research in Adolescent Health Policy', *J Adolesc Health*, 45 (3), pp216–21.

Johnson WL, Giordano PC, Manning WD & Longmore MA (2010) 'Parent-Child Relations and Offending During Young Adulthood', *J Youth Adolesc*, 40 (7), pp786–99.

Judd D (2008) Helping Children Speak about Feelings Conference, Centre for Child Mental Health, November 1.

Kafka F (1981) *Stories 1904–1924*, Underwood JA (tr), Futura, London.

Katz A, Buchanan A & Bream V (2001) *Bullying in Britain: Testimonies from Teenagers*, Young Voice, East Molesey.

Kiernan K (1997) *The Legacy of Parental Divorce: Social Economic and Family Experiences of Childhood*, Joseph Rowntree Association, London.

Kipling R (1987) *The Man Who Would Be King and Other Stories*, Oxford University Press, Oxford.

Klein M (1988) *Envy and Gratitude and Other Works 1946-1963*, Virago, London.

Kohut H & Wolf ES (1978) 'The Disorders of the Self and Their Treatment', *International Journal of Psycho-Analysis*, 59, pp413–424.

Kuntsche E, Pickett W, Overpeck M, Craig W, Boyce W & de Matos MG (2006) 'Television Viewing and Forms of Bullying Among Adolescents from Eight Countries', *J Adolesc Health*, 39 (6) pp908–15.

Lanius RA, Hopper J & Menon R (2003) 'Individual Differences in a Husband and Wife Who Developed PTSD After a Motor Vehicle Accident: A Functional MR1 Case Study', *American Journal of Psychiatry*, 160 (4), pp667–669.

Lawrence DH (1972) *Selected Poetry*, 2nd edn, Sagar K (ed), Penguin, Harmondsworth.

Levine P (2006) *Trauma Through a Child's Eyes: Awakening Healing*, North Atlantic Books, New York.

Lewandowski AS & Palermo TM (2009) 'Parent-Teen Interactions as Predictors of Depressive Symptoms in Adolescents with Headache', *J Clin Psychol Med Settings*, 16 (4), pp331–8.

Lewis CS (1966) *A Grief Observed*, Faber and Faber, London. (Original work published 1961)

Lindhiem O, Bernard K & Dozier M (2011) 'Maternal Sensitivity: Within-Person Variability and the Utility of Multiple Assessments', *Child Maltreat*, 16 (1) pp41–50.

Lowenfeld M (1991) *Play in Childhood*, MacKeith Press, London.

Loydell RM (1992) *Between Dark Dreams*, Acumen, Brixham.

LSN Institute for Education (2009) *Tackling the NEETs Problem. Supporting Local Authorities in Reducing Young People Not in Employment, Education and Training*, online, www.lsnlearning.org.uk

Manley Hopkins G (2009) *Gerald Manley Hopkins: The Major Works*, Oxford University Press, Oxford.

Marr N & Field T (2001) *Bullycide: Death at Playtime*, Success Unlimited, London.

Maslow AH (1971) *The Farther Reaches of Human Nature*, Viking Penguin, New York.

Maudsley H (1918) *Religion and Realities*, John Bale, Sons & Danielsson, London.

McCambridge J, McAlaney J & Rowe R (2011) 'Adult Consequences of Late Adolescent Alcohol Consumption: A Systematic Review of Cohort Studies', *PLoS Med*, 8 (2)

McCormick CM & Mathews IZ (2007) 'HPA Function in Adolescence: Role of Sex Hormones in its Regulation and the Enduring Consequences of Exposure to Stressors', *Pharmacology, Biochemistry, and Behavior*, 86 (2), pp220–33.

McGough R (1986) *Melting Into the Foreground*, Penguin, Harmondsworth.

McGough R (1990) *Summer With Monika*, Penguin, Harmondsworth. (Original work published 1967)

McGough R (1992) *Defying Gravity*, Penguin, Harmondsworth.

McNiff S (1992) *Art as Medicine*, Piatkus, London.

Mears D & Cooper M (2005) *Working at Relational Depth in Counselling and Psychotherapy*, Sage, London.

Medicinenet.com (2011) online, www.medicinenet.com/teen_depression/article.htm

Miga EM, Hare A, Allen JP & Manning N (2010) 'The Relation of Insecure Attachment States of Mind and Romantic Attachment Styles to Adolescent Aggression in Romantic Relationships', *Attach Hum Dev*, 12 (5), pp463–81.

Mitchell J (1997) *Wilde* screenplay, Sony Pictures Classics.

Mollon P (1993) *The Fragile Self: The Structure of Narcissistic Disturbance*, Whurr, London.

Morgan N (2007) *Blame My Brain*, Walker Books Ltd, London.

Murray J (2001) 'TV Violence and Brainmapping in Children', *Psychiatric Times*, XVIII (10).

Murray L (1997) *Subhuman Redneck Poems*, Carcanet, Manchester.

Murray L (2007) Presentation to the Early Years Commission, The Centre for Social Justice, London.

Murray L (2008) Presentation for Early Years Commission Centre for Social Justice, Whitehall, London.

Murray L, Arteche A, Fearon P, Halligan S, Goodyer I & Cooper P (2011) 'Maternal Postnatal Depression and the Development of Depression in Offspring Up to 16 Years of Age', *J Am Acad Child Adolesc Psychiatry*, 50 (5), pp460–70.

National Association of Crime Reduction (NACRO) (2012) 'Offender Health', online, www.nacro.org.uk/policy/offender-health/

National Child Development Study (1970) Economic and Social Data Service (ESDS) http://www.esds.ac.uk/longitudinal/access/ncds/l33004.asp

National Health Service (2006) Chief Executive's Report to the NHS Department of Health, June 2006.

National Health Service Information Centre (2008) *Statistics on Alcohol: England 2008*.

National Institute for Health and Clinical Excellence (NICE) (2005) *Depression in Children and Young People*, The British Psychological Society and the Royal College of Psychiatrists, Leicester/London.

National Society for the Prevention of Cruelty to Children (NSPCC) (2011) research and studies, NSPCC, London.

Nietzsche F (1911) *Human All Too Human*, George Allen & Unwin Ltd, London.

Odier C (1956) *Anxiety and Magical Thinking*, International Universities Press, New York.

Orbach S (1994) *What's Really Going On Here?*, Virago, London.

Padel R (1995) *Whom Gods Destroy: Elements of Greek and Tragic Madness*, Princeton University Press, Princeton, NJ.

Panksepp J (1998) *Affective Neuroscience: The Foundations of Human and Animal Emotions*, Oxford University Press, Oxford.

Parentline Scotland (2010) quoted in scotsman.com, 'One in Ten Calls to Helpline from Parents Abused by Violent Teens' online, news-scotsman.com, 24 January 2010.

Paul SC & Collins GM (1992) *Inneractions: Visions to Bring your Inner and Outer worlds into Harmony*, Harper, SanFrancisco.

Peale, NV (1994) *You Can if you Think You Can*, Vermillion, London.

Petrash J (2003) *Understanding Waldorf Education: Teaching from the Inside Out*, Gryphon House, Beltsville, MD.

Peltonen K, Ellonen N, Larsen HB & Helweg-Larsen K (2010) 'Parental Violence and Adolescent Mental Health', *Eur Child Adolesc Psychiatry*, 19 (11), pp813–22.

Pikó B & Balázs MA (2010) 'Control or Involvement? Relationship Between Parenting Style and Adolescent Depression', *J Am Acad Psychoanal Dyn Psychiatry*, 38 (3), pp503–31.

Polster E (1987) *Every Person's Life is Worth a Novel*, WW Norton and Co, New York.

Polster E & Polster M (1973) *Gestalt Therapy Integrated*, Brunner/Mazel, New York.

Porchia A (2003) *Voices*, Copper Canyon Press, Washington.

Reid S (1990) 'The Importance of Beauty in the Psychoanalytic Experience', *Journal of Child Psychotherapy*, 16 (1), pp29–52.

Resnick R (1993) Personal communication during couples therapy training at the Metanoia Trust, London.

Ribbens McCarthy B (2005) *The Impact of Bereavement and Loss on Young People*, Joseph Rowntree Foundation, New York.

Rich A (1963) *Snapshots of a Daughter-in-Law: Poems, 1954-1962*, Harper & Row, New York.

Rivers I & Noret N (2008) 'Well-being Among Same-Sex and Opposite-Sex Attracted Youth at School', *School Psychology Review*, 37 (2), pp174–187.

Robinson P, Davidson L & Debrot M (2004) 'Parent Abuse on the Rise', *American Association of Behavioral Social Science Online Journal*, online, http://aabss.org/Perspectives2004/AABSS_58-67.pdf

Rodgers B & Pryor J (1998) *Divorce and Separation: The Outcomes for Children*, Joseph Rowntree Foundation, London.

Roosevelt E (2001) '*It Seems to Me: Selected Letters of Eleanor Roosevelt*', Schlup L and Whisenhunt D (eds), The University Press of Kentucky.

Rosso IM, Young AD, Femia LA & Yurgelun-Todd DA (2004) 'Cognitive and Emotional Components of Frontal Lobe Functioning in Childhood and Adolescence', *Annals of the New York Academy of Sciences*, 1021, pp355–62.

Rowan J (1983) *The Reality Game: A Guide to Humanistic Counselling and Psychotherapy*, Routledge, London.

Rowan J (1986) *Ordinary Ecstasy: Humanistic Psychology in Action*, Routledge and Kegan Paul, London.

Rowe D (1988) *The Successful Self*, Fontana, London.

Saluja et al (2004) 'Prevalence of and Risk Factors for Depressive Symptoms Among Young Adolescents', *Arch Pediatr Adolesc Med*, 158 (8), pp760–5.

Sapolsky R (2004) *Why Zebras Don't Get Ulcers*, Saint Martin's Press Inc, New York.

Sassoon S (1996) cited in *Traumatic Stress: The Effects of Overwhelming Experience on Mind, Body and Society*, van der Kolk BA, McFarlane AC, Weiseth L (eds), Guilford Press, New York.

Schmahmann JD & Caplan D (2006) 'Cognition, Emotion and the Cerebellum', *Brain*, 129 (2), pp290–2.

Schore A (1997) 'Early Organisation of the Non-Linear Right Brain and Development of a Predisposition to Psychiatric Disorders', *Development and Psychopathology*, 9, pp595–631.

Schwartz OS, Dudgeon P, Sheeber LB, Yap MB, Simmons JG & Allen NB (2011) 'Parental Behaviors During Family Interactions Predict Changes in Depression and Anxiety Symptoms During Adolescence', *J Abnorm Child Psychol*, 2011, Jul 26.

Segal J (1985) *Phantasy in Everyday Life: A Psychoanalytical Approach to Understanding Ourselves*, Penguin, Harmondsworth.

Sentse M & Laird RD (2010) 'Parent-Child Relationships and Dyadic Friendship Experiences as Predictors of Behavior Problems in Early Adolescence', *J Clin Child Adolesc Psychol*, 39 (6), pp873–84.

Sher L (2006) 'Functional Magnetic Resonance Imaging in Studies of Neurocognitive Effects of Alcohol Use on Adolescents and Young Adults', *International Journal of Adolescent Medicine and Health*, 18 (1), pp3–7.

Siegel DJ (1999) *The Developing Mind*, Guilford Press, New York.

Sigfusdottir ID, Asgeirsdottir BB, Sigurdsson JF & Gudjonsson GH (2011) 'Physical Activity Buffers the Effects of Family Conflict on Depressed Mood: A Study on Adolescent Girls and Boys', *J Adolesc*, 2011, Feb 17.

Singer T, Seymour B, O'Doherty J, Kaube H, Dolan RJ & Frith CD (2004) 'Empathy For Pain Involves the Affective But Not Sensory Components of Pain', *Science*, 303 (5661), pp1157–62.

Singer T, Seymour B, O'Doherty JP, Stephan KE, Dolan RJ & Frith CD (2006) 'Empathic Neural Responses Are Modulated By the Perceived Fairness of Others', *Nature*, 439 (7075), pp466–9.

Sisk CL & Zehr JL (2005) 'Pubertal Hormones Organize the Adolescent Brain and Behavior', *Frontiers in Neuroendocrinology*, 26 (3-4), pp163–74.

Slemming K, Sørensen MJ, Thomsen PH, Obel C, Henriksen TB & Linnet KM (2010) 'The Association Between Preschool Behavioural Problems and Internalizing Difficulties at Age 10-12 Years', *Eur Child Adolesc Psychiatry*, 19 (10), pp787–95.

Smith PK, Mahdavi J, Carvalho M, Fisher S, Russell S & Tippett N (2008) 'Cyberbullying: Its Nature and Impact in Secondary School Pupils', *Journal of Child Psychology and Psychiatry*, 49, pp376–385.

Sowell ER, Thompson PM, Holmes CJ, Jernigan TL & Toga AW (1999) 'In Vivo Evidence For Post-Adolescent Brain Maturation in Frontal and Striatal Regions', *Nature Neuroscience*, 2 (10), pp859–861.

Sroufe A, Egeland B, Carlson E & Collins A (2005) *The Development of the Person: The Minnesota Study of Risk and Adaptation from Birth to Adulthood*, Guilford Press, New York.

Steele M, Steele H & Johansson M (2002) 'Maternal Predictors of Children's Social Cognition: An Attachment Perspective', *Journal of Child Psychology and Psychiatry, and Allied Disciplines*, 43 (7), pp861–72.

Stephenson K (2008) 'Parent Abuse Is Domestic Violence: Behavioural Adolescents Victimize Parents at an Alarming Rate', online, www.suite101.com/content/parent-abuse-is-domestic-violence-a67177

Stoddard SA, McMorris BJ & Sieving RE (2010) 'Do Social Connections and Hope Matter in Predicting Early Adolescent Violence?', *Am J Community Psychol*, 48 (3-4), pp247–56.

Stolorow RD, Brandchaft B & Atwood GE (1987) 'Affects and Selfobjects', *Psychoanalytic Treatment: An Intersubjective Approach*, Analytic Press, New Jersey/London.

Stortelder F & Ploegmakers-Burg M (2010) 'Adolescence and the Reorganization of Infant Development: A Neuro-psychoanalytic Model', *Psychiatr Hung*, 25 (6), pp538–544.

Strauch B (2004) *Why Are They So Weird?: What's Really Going On In a Teenager's Brain*, Bloomsbury, London.

Sunderland M (2006) *What Every Parent Needs to Know*, Dorling Kindersley, London.

Sunderland M (2009) *Smasher*, Hinton House Publishers Ltd, Buckingham.

Sunderland M (2010) Public lecture 'Therapeutic Conversations with Children and Teenagers', Centre for Child Mental Health, London.

Sweeting H, West P, Young R & Der G (2010) 'Can We Explain Increases In Young People's Psychological Distress Over Time?', *Soc Sci Med*, 71 (10), pp1819–30.

Taylor G (1997) *Disorders of Affect Regulation: Alexithymia in Medical and Psychiatric Illness*, Cambridge University Press, Cambridge.

Teicher MH, Andersen SL, Polcari A, Anderson CM, Navalta CP & Kim DM (2003) 'The Neurobiological Consequences of Early Stress and Childhood Maltreatment', *Neuroscience and Biobehavioral Reviews*, 27 (1-2), pp33–44.

Teicher MH, Samson JA, Polcari A & McGreenery CE (2006) 'Sticks, Stones, and Hurtful Words: Relative Effects of Various Forms of Childhood Maltreatment', *The American Journal of Psychiatry*, 163 (6), pp993–1000.

Teicher MH, Samson JA, Sheu YS, Polcari A & McGreenery CE (2010) Hurtful Words: Association of Exposure to Peer Verbal Abuse with Elevated Psychiatric Symptom Scores and Corpus Callosum Abnormalities', *Am J Psychiatry*, 167 (12), pp1464–71.

The Children Act 2004 (2004) HMSO, London.

Trachtenberg P (1988) *The Casanova Complex: Compulsive Lovers and Their Women*, Poseidon, New York.

Troy M & Sroufe LA (1987) 'Victimisation Among Preschoolers: Role of Attachment Relationship History', *J Am Acad Child Adolesc Psychiatry*, 26, pp166–172.

Unicef (2007) *An Overview of Child Well-Being in Rich Countries: A Comprehensive Assessment of the Lives and Well-Being of Children and Adolescents in the Economically Advanced Nations*, United Nations Children's Fund.

Van der Kolk BA (1989) 'The Compulsion to Repeat the Trauma: Re-enactment, Revictimization, and Masochism', *Psychiatric Clinics of North America*, 12, pp389–411.

Van der Kolk BA (1994) 'The Body Keeps the Score: Memory and the Evolving Psychobiology of Posttraumatic Stress', *Harv Rev Psychiatry*, 1 (5), pp253–65.

Van der Kolk BA (2002) 'Beyond the Talking Cure', Shapiro F (ed), *EMDR and the New Paradigm*, APA, New York.

Van der Kolk BA (2003) 'The Neurobiology of Childhood Trauma and Abuse', *Child and Adolescent Psychiatric Clinics of North America*, 12, pp293–317.

Van der Kolk BA (2006) 'Clinical Implications of Neuroscience Research in PTSD', *Annals of the New York Academy of Sciences*, 1071, pp277–93.

Van der Kolk BA (2009) Public lecture on child trauma, The Centre for Child Mental Health, London.

Van der Kolk BA, Mcfarlane CA & Weisaeth L (eds) (1996) *Traumatic Stress*, Guilford Press, New York.

Van der Kolk BA & Saporta J (1991) 'The Biological Response to Psychic Trauma: Mechanisms and Treatment of Intrusion and Numbing', *Anxiety Research*, 4, pp199–212.

Wachtel PL (2008) *Relational Theory and the Practice of Psychotherapy*, Guilford Press, New York.

Wade T & Pevalin D (2004) Martial Transitions and Mental Health, *Journal of Health and Social Behaviour*, June (Vol.45).

Waitley D (1985) *Seeds of Greatness: The Ten Best-Kept Secrets of Total Success*, Cedar, London.

Watzlawick P (1983) *The Situation Is Hopeless, But Not Serious*, WW Norton and Co, London/New York.

Weisskirch RS (2011) 'No Crossed Wires: Cell Phone Communication in Parent-Adolescent Relationships', *Cyberpsychol Behav Soc Netw*, 2011, Jan 4.

Weissman MM & Klerman GL (1992) 'The Changing Rate of Major Depression: Cross-National Comparisons', *Journal of the American Medical Association*, 268 (21), pp3098–3105.

White A (1979) *Beyond The Glass*, Virago, London. (Original work published 1954)

Wickes FG (1988) *The Inner World of Childhood: A Study in Analytical Psychology*, 3rd edn, Sigo Press, Boston, MA. (Original work published 1927)

Wilde O (1949) *De Profundis*, Methuen, London.

Willemen AM, Goossens FA, Koot HM & Schuengel C (2008) 'Physiological Reactivity to Stress and Parental Support: Comparison of Clinical and Non-Clinical Adolescents', *Clin Psychol Psychother*, 15 (5), pp340–51.

Williamson M (1992) *A Return To Love*, Random House, New York.

Winnicott DW (1971) *Playing and Reality*, Penguin/Basic, Harmondsworth/New York.

Winstons Wish (2011) online, www.winstonswish.org.uk/

World Health Organization (2011) 'What is Depression?', online, www.who.int/mental_health/management/depression/definition/en/

Xiuqin H, Huimin Z, Mengchen L, Jinan W, Ying Z & Ran T (2010) 'Mental Health, Personality, and Parental Rearing Styles of Adolescents with Internet Addiction Disorder', *Cyberpsychol Behav Soc Netw*, 13 (4), pp401–6.

Yalom ID (1980) *Existential Psychotherapy*, Basic Books, New York.

Yoo SS, Gujar N, Hu P, Jolesz FA & Walker MP (2007) 'The Human Emotional Brain Without Sleep: A Prefrontal Amygdala Disconnect', *Current Biology*, 17 (20).

Yurgelun-Todd DA & Killgore WD (2006) 'Fear-Related Activity in the Prefrontal Cortex Increases with Age During Adolescence: A Preliminary fMRI Study', *Neuroscience Letters*, 406 (3), pp194–9.

Zimmermann P, Mohr C & Spangler G (2009) 'Genetic and Attachment Influences on Adolescents' Regulation of Autonomy and Aggressiveness', *J Child Psychol Psychiatry*, 50 (11), pp1339–47.

Zubieta JK, Ketter TA, Bueller JA, Xu Y, Kilbourn MR, Young EA & Koeppe RA (2003) 'Regulation of Human Affective Responses by Anterior Cingulate and Limbic and m-Opioid Neurotransmission', *General Psychiatry*, 60 (11), pp1057–1172.